D0734584

# UNCANNY VALLEY

# Also by Lawrence Weschler

## Political Reportage

*The Passion of Poland*

*A Miracle, A Universe: Settling Accounts with Torturers*

*Calamities of Exile: Three Nonfiction Novellas*

## Passions and Wonders

*Seeing is Forgetting the Name of the Thing One Sees:
Thirty Years of Conversations with the Artist Robert Irwin*

*Shapinsky's Karma, Boggs's Bills and Other True-Life Tales*

*Mr Wilson's Cabinet of Wonder*

*A Wanderer in the Perfect City: Selected Passion Pieces*

*Boggs: A Comedy of Values*

*Robert Irwin Getty Garden*

*Vermeer in Bosnia: A Reader*

*Everything that Rises: A Book of Convergences*

*True to Life:
Twenty-five Years of Conversations with the Artist David Hockney*

## Recent Art Monographs

*Deborah Butterfield*

*Tara Donovan*

*Liza Lou*

*The Richard and Mary Gray Collection: Seven Centuries of Art*

*Mark Dion: The Marvelous Museum*

*The Art Guys: Forever Yours*

*Michael Light: L.A. Day/L.A. Night*

# UNCANNY VALLEY
## and Other
## Adventures in
## the Narrative

LAWRENCE WESCHLER

COUNTERPOINT
BERKELEY

## Uncanny Valley
and Other Adventures in the Narrative

Library of Congress Cataloging-in-Publication Data is available.
ISBN 978-1-58243-757-6

Cover and interior design by Domini Dragoone
Cover art: detail from Mark Tansey, *Derrida Queries de Man* (1990)
Printed in the United States of America

COUNTERPOINT
1919 Fifth Street
Berkeley, CA 94710
www.counterpointpress.com
Distributed by Publishers Group West
10 9 8 7 6 5 4 3 2 1

FOR OLIVER

*and in memory of*
TOM EISNER
(1929-2011)

*Living wonders*
*Brimming friends*

# Contents

# Uncanny Valley:
## ON THE DIGITAL ANIMATION OF THE FACE
### (2002)

F aces hit walls all the time in the movies, but this was different: The Wall these filmmakers kept running up against, or so I was being told, was the Face itself. Digital animators, that is, in their quest to perfect ever more believable computerized simulations of a human being, a credible cyberactor moving through time and space. Bodies—walking, standing, running, slouching, brawling—turns out, I was being assured, that these are all quite doable, no longer that big a deal. Hands—grasping, signaling, stroking, idling at rest—granted, they're a bit more of a challenge, but not all that much more, and at least conceptually within reach. But a believable human face—a credible face in motion, and what's more, *emoting*—damn, but that was proving tough. A hard nut. A daunting massif. And some were beginning to ask themselves whether this particular Wall was even theoretically scalable.

Which didn't seem all that surprising to me (and let me admit right here at the outset that I'm a rank outsider; I don't even know how I got called onto this story). Naturally, I surmised, they can't do faces because, as everybody knows, faces (as opposed, say, to arms, or thighs, or abdomens) are the Seat of the Soul, and souls simply aren't quantifiable; they don't resolve themselves into so many bits—no matter how many.

On the flight out to San Francisco, in whose environs I

was going to be spending the next few days ambling among the cyberscenti, taking the Massif's measure, as it were, I once again recalled the formulations of one of my favorite touchstone philosophers, the late-medieval number-mystic Nicholas of Cusa (1401–64).[1] Faced with the claims of the ever more positivist Scholastics of his own time, Cusa likened true knowledge of God and the Infinite to a circle, within which was slotted a regular compounding n-sided polygon: a triangle, say, and then a square, a pentagon, a hexagon, and so forth. Keep adding sides—a hundred, a thousand, a million—and true, Nicolas conceded, it seems like you'd be getting closer and closer to the encompassing circle. But in fact, he went on to point out, you'd be getting further and further away, because a million-sided polygon, for example, has precisely that: a million angles, a million sides. Whereas a circle has no angles and only one "side." And, bracketing the God question (for a moment, anyway), it seemed to me that the Face-stalkers had set themselves a similarly impossible challenge, because a million-bitted face, no matter how seemingly close, was destined to fall infinitely (albeit infinitesimally) short of the simple, seamless whole that is any actual face (and any actually human way of perceiving that face).

TELL YOU ONE THING, though: Those guys (and most of them, incidentally, *are* guys) sure are having themselves a helluva good time.

Take Henrik Wann Jensen, for example, over at Stanford—my first stop. Guy spends his days and late nights thinking about milk. "Dinosaurs are easy," he assures me; "milk is hard."

A research associate in the Computer Graphics Lab in the university's (figures) William Gates Hall (to which he is late for our appointment because, as he explains, there was a mysterious power outage at his apartment complex, which prevented him from getting his car past the electronically controlled gates of his garage, so that he'd had to bike over instead—all of which seems oddly freighted with metaphorical significance of some sort), the young Dane focuses his interest on translucency, luminosity, the soft sheen of the real: milk, marble, human skin. To glow or not to glow: That is the challenge.

Light hits a surface and bounces off, Jensen explains to me, himself vaulting over to his blackboard to sketch out a billiardlike bankshot, and if the surface is sufficiently opaque and reflective—metal, say, or plastic, or an antlike exoskeleton—the formulae and algorithms are all pretty straightforward and they don't require all that much computer power to flesh out. Which is one reason the early breakthroughs in realistic computer animation involved plastic toys or shiny insects (or leathery dinosaurs). But photons of light behave differently upon contact with flesh and marble—and milk: They don't just ricochet off the surface; they penetrate, scattering about inside there in confounding quantum fashion and then emerging at entirely different places and at altogether different angles than the standard Newtonian billiard model might have predicted. Use the standard formulae, and skin will end up looking like plastic, marble like concrete, and a glass of milk like a column of chalk.

Jensen boots up his computer and powers up a set of exemplary illustrations, his life's work. "For instance," he says, "this is a glass of digital milk, illuminated by an orbiting light source, using the standard Newtonian algorithms"—and indeed, the stuff looks distinctly unpalatable: not even liquid. "But instead if you use the photon-mapping technique we've been developing, granted it will take your computer a whole lot more time to churn out the calculations, but you'll end up with something more like this." Like something straight out of an ad, that is. Got Milk, indeed.

"Note the meniscus." Jensen, the proud father, points to the infinitesimal upslope along the milk surface's rim as it meets the circumference of the glass, an effect of surface tension. "Most modelers forget about the meniscus, and as a result, something just doesn't look right." This, I will find, is a typical sort of comment among the cyberscenti—marvel both at the tiniest of details and at the human capacity (nay, *propensity!*) for *noticing* those tiniest of details.

The meniscus, naturally, turns out to have all sorts of light-scattering characteristics distinct from the rest of the milk, and all of that needs to be taken into account—counted and gauged and painstakingly crunched. And milk matters, not simply as an exercise. It turns out, according to Jensen, that skim milk evinces exactly the same light-scattering characteristics and color (a slight bluish-gray) as the whites of a person's eyes.

And the sort of formulae that help infuse milk with luminosity turn out to do the same for marble and skin, as Jensen now showed me across a series of other rotating examples on his computer screen: the digital rendition of a bust of Diana, goddess of the moon (and hence, in a sense, of reflectivity itself), and then a close-up of a human nose (an enthralling deep red blushing deep inside the nostril's deep black). Dispense with such subtle details (and their attendant calculations), Jensen explains, and you end up getting some of the less than satisfactory effects you encounter, say, in the recent feature film version of *Final Fantasy.*

Time and again over the next several days, my interlocutors would bring up the case of *Final Fantasy,* far and away the most ambitious (and expensive) attempt so far to render realistic cyberhumans moving through digital space—and something of a commercial fiasco. Few wanted to criticize their fellow artists' efforts outright (and they all marveled at certain particular effects and jaw-dropping breakthroughs), but the film kept getting invoked as a mere instance along the way, and as such, an indication of just how much more territory remained to be crossed.

"It's interesting," Jensen now commented, "that one of the more convincingly rendered characters in that film is the black man, which isn't surprising, black skin being more conventionally reflective than white—that guy, and then as well the old man, the chief scientist. The *Final Fantasy* people make a big deal out of the wrinkledness and blotchiness of his face as being the explanation

for its heightened sense of reality, but actually I think something else is at work. Because older actors and actresses in America always go to great lengths to disguise their age with heavily caked-on makeup, which is highly reflective and hence less prone to light-scattering. We're *used* to old people on the screen looking like that, which is why the relative lack of light-scattering in the old scientist's face doesn't bother us."

Of course, the way light hits the face, no matter how complex and time-consuming the requisite programming needs (and Jensen, incidentally has been moving to simplify matters in that regard with a new computational model, that of "diffusion approximation," which he has taken to deploying on his most all-consuming rendering challenge yet, the peachfuzz on a woman's cheek), is as nothing compared to the subtlety and complexity of the way light radiates out from the inside of that face—the light, that is, of consciousness.

"Her face lit up as he entered the room": Model that!


THAT EVENING, IN PREPARATION for the next day's interviews at Industrial Light & Magic and DreamWorks, I found myself sampling an especially luminous essay of Jean-Paul Sartre's on the face ("Only the lips moved," he writes at one point, "but the whole face smiled"—which actually, as it turns out, isn't exactly right; a lot of other things move besides the lips, if only infinitesimally so, but it is still highly suggestive of the fugitive quality of the challenge at hand). Sartre himself also invokes a marble bust in his exploration of a human face, but this time so as to heighten the contrast between the two. A marble bust, he suggests, exists in "universal time," which is to say, the time "of instants set end to end, of the metronome, of the hourglass, of fixed immobility." Such a bust floats in "a perpetual present." But the face "creates its own time within universal time . . . Against [that] stagnant background, the time of living bodies stands out because it is oriented . . . In the midst of these stalactites hanging in the present, the face, alert and inquisitive, is always ahead of the look I direct toward it . . . A bit of the future has now entered the room: a mist of futurity surrounds the face: its future." The face, Sartre goes on to insist, "is not merely the upper part of the body . . . It is corporeal yet different from belly or thigh: what it has in addition is its voracity; it is pierced with greedy holes." The greediest, the most ravenous of those holes, of course, being the eyes. For "now the two spheres are turning in their orbits: now the eyes are becoming a look," and in so doing changing the very nature of the thing they are looking at—say, that chair over there—a change that is in turn reciprocal. "If I watch his eyes, I see that they are not fastened in his head, serene like agate marbles. They are being created at each moment by what they look at."

Sartre goes on to conclude that "If we call transcendence the ability of the mind to pass beyond itself and all other things as well, to escape from itself that it may lose itself elsewhere; then to be a visible transcendence is the meaning of a face."[2]

"Being a visible transcendence" is Sartre's way of saying (and at the same time, granted, emphatically *not* saying), having or expressing or being *a soul*. And try animating that! And in so trying, realize, of course, that the very origin of the verb "to animate" is the Latin word for soul, the *anima*, such that to animate is "to ensoul," and it is one of the core paradoxes of the challenge these guys are facing that it turns out to be relatively easy to animate a line, the line sketch of a mouse, a digital plastic toy, a puffball monster doll, or a cyberant—and much much more difficult to approximate, let alone actually achieve, a synthetically ensouled, realistically rendered human face.

"BUT WE DON'T HAVE to," the guys over at Industrial Light & Magic were telling me the next morning when I brought up Sartre, Cusa—the whole caboodle. "Our job isn't to simulate an actual human face with 100 percent fidelity. Our job is merely to fool the audience. Once you believe it, we're done."

Not as if *that* is proving all that easy. There are hundreds, thousands of tiny details to be gotten just right, and one of the ironies of the work is that success is gauged precisely to the extent that they all go unnoticed. As another of the fellows at ILM commented to me, "We fail when the audience notices *anything*." Ed Hooks, an actor and acting coach who lately has taken to coaching animators, marveled at their contradictory challenge, as seen from the other side (the receiving end) of the process, noting how "you're telling people, 'Be amazed, but don't notice.'"

In a phone interview, Hooks, who's now based in Chicago, went on to contrast the actor's process with the animator's: "When I'm coaching an actor and he asks me, 'Should I raise my eyebrow here?' my reply is likely to be, 'I dunno. Don't think about your eyebrow. Think about the emotion you're trying to convey, and the eyebrow will take care of itself.' But with an animator, it's the exact opposite. You're building from the outside in. Bits don't experience emotions, and emotions get conveyed exclusively through such things as a raised eyebrow, which in turn has to be precisely calibrated. Raised, okay, but by how much? And what happens to the chin when the eyebrow gets raised? To the ear? To the other ear? and so forth." Each of these details first has to be noticed by the animator even before it can be captured and programmed. And these guys have become champion noticers.

Here are some of the things I found out across a couple days in the animation trenches: Anger is signaled by a heavy brow, but a heavy brow can likewise signal mere intentness—the difference is in the upper eye muscle. An eyeblink is more than the top lid slicing downward; at the same time the lower lid gets pulled up and in, toward the nose bridge. Eye pupils converge toward the nose as they gaze into the distance. From a distance, one gauges where someone else is looking by a combination of the shape of the eye (i.e., the way the surrounding muscles are pressing in on it) and the disposition of its white. One gauges how that person is *feeling* the same way. Close up, the really tough things to get right with the eyes are the semilunar fold and the caruncula, which is to say the overlapping tissues surrounding that little pink nub pressed right up against the nosebridge: They move along with the pupil, as for that matter does the entire upper lid. Get those wrong and all you've got is a robotic approximation. Not all the skin on the face has the same texture and elasticity—everything depends on the underlying bone, muscle, fat, and integument, not to mention the skin itself—hence facial skin doesn't pull and crinkle the same way all over, and each patch therefore requires different algorithms. The physics of saliva sloshing around in the mouth turn out to be identical with those of the tempest-tossed sea in *The Perfect Storm*, and you can use the one to model the other (or, anyway, the folks at ILM did). The folks over at Dream-Works went to huge lengths to get the uvula inside Shrek's capacious mouth thrumming and vibrating just right, even though (predictably) it ended up being entirely obscured in black shadow. When a mouth opens, it doesn't just open like a garage door; rather, owing to the stickiness of caked saliva, there's a sort of unzipping effect toward both corners. The way you can tell a true smile from a faked or forced one is that in the one the upper eyefold lowers slightly (*every time!*), and it doesn't in the other:

This cannot be faked. The face is the one place on the body where muscles don't necessarily attach to bone: Often muscles fold one atop the other, one into the other, a fact that presented an enormous challenge to the early anatomical dissectors, who found themselves mangling whole systems the moment they sliced through the skin (and also helps explain why, for current animators, legs and arms are so much easier compared to faces). More-recent research through scrupulous video observations—live dissections, as it were—has yielded, according to the most prominent practitioner of the art, Paul Ekman, a facial action coding system featuring forty-six numbered muscles capable of producing over five thousand different expressions. To really get the face right, you have to model it in conjunction with the whole body; otherwise, you can get a weird effect where the body seems to be saying one thing and the head another. The same splay of muscles will communicate different emotions depending on the color of the skin.

And that's not even to mention hair. Don't get me (or them) started on hair. Hair is a whole other essay.

The point, though, is that these guys have noticed a hell of a lot already, and they're noticing more every day. (Theirs already *is* a million-sided inscribed polygon.)


THE PROCESS MOVES FROM modeling to animation. "The modeler builds the car," is how *Final Fantasy*'s Roy Sato, at Square animation in Hawaii, put it to me over the phone. "The animator drives it." It's the modelers who compile the archive of noticed effects (and sets of effects), delivering them in the form of a vast inventory of potential commands (recast in terms of each fresh character) to the animator, who in turn works directly under the director. "Make Shrek angrier in this scene," commands the director, and the animator in turn does so by tweaking a set of controls previously laid in by the modeler. And now make Princess Fiona blush!

These days there are two principal methods for laying in those possibilities: key frame and facial capture. The first hearkens back to the earliest traditions of animation, which is to say moving from one drawn expression to the next across a series of in-between frames, twenty-four per second. Only, with computers, there's a lot less hands-on drawing—or, rather, the modeler tends to draw with a mouse and a keypad—and the computer itself performs a lot of the in-between.

At the PDI/DreamWorks shop in East Palo Alto, for example, Lucia Modesto, a veteran of both *Antz* and *Shrek*, offered me a jaw-dropping demonstration of the cyberpossibilities around, say, Shrek's face. The PDI facial system, originally developed thirteen years ago by in-house guru Dick Walsh, is muscle- and anatomy-based (the desks in the surrounding cubicles are strewn with anatomy-for-artists text-

books, heavily bookmarked and annotated). Which is to say that even in the case of a manifestly invented face like Shrek's, the underlying bone and muscle structures are first painstakingly laid in. To demonstrate this point, Modesto showed me two different furrowed-brow effects on the 3-D rotatable cybermodel of Shrek's head splayed across her computer screen—one of which took account of the bone ridge underneath the brow, and the other of which failed to. "The second is obviously wrong," she noted. "It fails to take account of his skull, which of course stays in place as the muscle and skin slide over it. He has a skull in there," she stated emphatically, before pausing. "I mean, not really," she acknowledged sheepishly. "Actually, it's just numbers."

Along the left side of Modesto's screen ran a scroll of activating commands—over five hundred of them, ranged according to facial part. "Right brow," for instance: Raised, Mad, Sad . . .

Fifteen possible commands, all told, for the right brow alone, commands that incidentally activated not just the brow itself but the other parts of the face that such a gesture would in turn activate as well. There was a library of twenty-five phonemes. So that it was possible to get Shrek's head to mouth out "Stop that!" while simultaneously raising its left brow angrily, turning sideways, and flaring its nostrils. Click, click, click, and voila! Nostril flare too much? No problem: click, lose the nostril flare. Want to see how Princess Fiona's face would look doing exactly the same thing? Simple. Click, click—and there she is: "Stop that!"

Over at ILM, Modesto's counterpart, Geoff Campbell, was spending his days studying video takes of his own eyes, slotted into windows in the corner of his monitor. (He was the one slaving away at the caruncula problem.) His head is shaved entirely bald (no hair to worry about!), and he can do the same sort of thing as Modesto with his characters (*Star Wars* Yoda types, for example). Only, he has the various effects graphed out across a flowchart. The nose flare starts here, rises here, falls away here, while atop it the left eyebrow starts to squint here and returns to idle over here. Want to accentuate one or the other? Just tweak the attendant slope with your mouse, and there you have it.

In a certain sense, this sort of animation hearkens back as well to the traditions of marionette-puppetry: Pull a string, and the arm goes up; pull another, and the hand turns in. Only here you're marionetting dozens of facial muscles, one atop the next. More strings—more commands—are getting added with each new generation of characters (and in animation, a generation is simply a matter of a few years), and it's easy to see how down the line things could get hopelessly tangled. (Wittgenstein once suggested that philosophy unties knots in our thinking, hence its results will be simple, but philosophizing has to be as complicated as the knots it unties.[3] Trouble is, these body-philosophers are getting more and more, rather than less and less, tied up.) At a certain point, Modesto acknowledged, it could get way too hard to animate in this fashion; there could be way too many controls for anyone to be able to drive the characters. And all of this, remember, to approximate the sorts of things our own faces do automatically, without giving matters a second thought.

One is reminded of the old story about the Hollywood lighting director, out on the Palisade, watching the sun setting over the ocean—the incredible succession of tones and colors and blushes cast across clouds and palms and breaking waves, till finally darkness swallows it all up. "Amazing," the lighting director sighs, at length, "the effects That Guy can get with just one unit."

And it's something of that same temper that in turn animates the second approach to facial depiction: facial capture. Facial capture is a relatively recent elaboration of the more familiar motion capture systems that have already been being used for years now to model body movement. In the latter, ping-pong-sized sensors of various sorts get attached at the key joints and junctions along the limbs and bodies of live actors as they act out the various gestures that their animated counterparts will be expected to make. On the video monitors, these sensors register as moving dots across a grid, which in turn get connected by the appropriate rays, which then serve as guidelines for the digital draftsman.

And it's pretty much the same with facial capture, as Seth Rosenthal and Steve Sullivan proceeded to show me at their own shop in a neighboring shed at ILM's San Rafael facility. Only instead of ping-pong sensors, they work in black dots. "We're the pox guys," Rosenthal averred. "Yeah, a pox on all the actors!" Sullivan concurred enthusiastically. And indeed their method consisted in exactingly spangling the faces of their stand-in actors with painted black dots of varying sizes, at precisely established nodal points. As those actors in turn played out their various assigned scenes, the dots on their faces registered on Rosenthal and Sullivan's screens as moving white dots against a black backdrop, dots that in turn could be joined by lines to form the basis for moving mesh-masks of truly uncanny immediacy. The more dots you add, of course, the subtler the effects you can capture. Or, anyway, up to a point.

For this, too, began to beg a question. One is reminded of the Borges story about the Land of the Cartographers, where things got to a stage where the map of the province took up an entire city, and the map of the country an entire province. Within a generation of that, the map of the country was taking up the entire country and corresponding to the country at every point. (Within a few generations of *that*, however, according to Borges, the people of that empire at last started coming to their senses, realizing that such a map was useless and presently "abandoning it to the inclemencies of the sun and the winters. In the deserts of the West, certain tattered fragments of the Map are still to be found, sheltering Animals and Beggars; in the whole country," Borges concludes, "nothing else remains of the Disciplines of Geography.")[4] And the question hovering just beyond the edge of this whole phenomenal exercise—at least as regards the replication of increasingly lifelike and realistic human faces and characters—is *why bother at all?*

Why not just use actors?

Surprisingly, this was a sentiment I encountered a good deal among my animation contacts. "We ask ourselves that question every day," one of the guys over at ILM acknowledged, laughing. "Fortunately, it's not our job to answer it." Juan Buhler, a senior animator at DreamWorks, concurred, noting that "There are already too many real humans on this planet, and some of them are great actors." Lucia Modesto, among others, likened the whole quest to something of a macho Everest challenge—you do it because it's there, but there's really no good reason. "Animation ought to be about what you can't get in reality," she insisted. While agreeing with that general sentiment, however, Buhler went on to note that while the final achievement of a completely believable digital human might be a pointless and even absurd goal, the myriad discoveries along the way (for example, he'd been collaborating with Jensen on the luminosity-of-skin algorithms) made the whole adventure worthwhile.

THERE WERE ALREADY IN fact a few plausible uses for the technology—tactical piecemeal deployments, perhaps, as opposed to longer-term strategic ones. President Clinton's synthetically altered star-turn in *Contact*, for example. Or the way in which the team at Sony had been able to insert entirely digital head-to-toe synthetic kids into the Quidditch scenes in *Harry Potter* (scenes that would have been deemed too dangerous for actual kids to attempt, or else, in which, after the fact, the director had found the delivered performances of some of his stunt doubles somehow wanting). Nifty commercial and music video effects . . .

Longer term, one could imagine the delights of creating nonexistent actors from scratch (not that anybody was going to save any money doing so, not for a long time anyway), or, say, changing the ethnicities of actors who do exist, or even more. Alvy Ray Smith, the now-retired founder of Pixar and one of the most thoughtful visionaries of the bunch, noted how "in a sense, an actor today is like an animator stuck in his own body. This technology might someday enable a Robert De Niro, for example, to drive somebody else's notional body, to spectacular effect." (Smith avers as to how *Being John Malkovich* is his favorite recent film: He's a bit obsessed with it.)

Such visions, however, beg a further question, and in some senses the very question with which we began: Is such an ambition even conceptually envisionable? Will anyone ever be able to digitally replicate a human soul?

"Ah," Alvy Ray Smith retorted by phone from his Seattle home when I broached the Cusan analogy with him, "now you're getting into the question of consciousness itself, which is one of the really great questions. I for one think we are explainable, and

I am unwilling to invoke God or some other vitalistic force to get there. It's a matter of religion with me." (At the core of Smith's belief system, that is, was a refusal to suspend his faith in the lack of necessity of having recourse to such notions as God or the soul.) "Now," he continued, "whether we can get there—'there,' in this case, meaning the creation of an entirely convincing, feature length live-action film made up of entirely digital actors—I don't know." He paused. "We may yet encounter a sort of Godel's incompleteness theorem along the way."[5]

The great Japanese engineer and roboticist Masahiro Mori (author, among other things, of *The Buddha in the Robot*) may already have hit upon the form such a Godelian roadblock could take in this quest for an entirely convincing digital human (and specifically a convincing human face) with his notion of the Uncanny Valley.[6]

While contemplating the coming evolution of robots, he pointed out the way we can quite readily empathize with a robot that's, say, 20 percent humanlike, and even more so with a robot that's 50 percent humanlike, and even more than that with a robot that's 90 percent humanlike—indeed, you can plot out a rising slope of anthropomorphizing empathy. (From Mickey Mouse through Shrek, say.) But only up to a point. Somewhere beyond 95 percent, Mori hypothesizes, there's a sudden precipitous drop-off into, as he puts it, the Uncanny Valley. When a replicant's almost completely human, the slightest variance, the 1 percent that's not quite right, suddenly looms up enormously, rendering the entire effect somehow creepy and monstrously alien (no longer, that is, an incredibly lifelike machine but rather a human being with something inexplicably wrong—part of Mori's point being how incredibly finely attuned we humans are at perceiving those infinitesimally disquieting failings).

Andy Jones, one of the principal figures behind *Final Fantasy*, makes a similar point, arguing that while a completely convincing replication of human beings had never been his team's goal (such that the widespread criticism of the film's "failings" in that regard is to a certain extent unfair), still, he, too, had noticed how "it can get eerie. As you push further and further, it begins to get grotesque. You start to feel like you're puppeteering a corpse." (Modesto similarly pointed out how her team had had to pull back a little on Princess Fiona: She'd been beginning to look too real, and the effect was getting distinctly unpleasant.)

Can that Valley be traversed? Note that even Mori portrays it as a *valley*, rising sharply back up on the other side as it approaches 100 percent similitude.

Myself, I started out on this story convinced that it couldn't be (it's a matter of religion with me, too). And yet . . . And yet . . .

For one thing, there are forces at work burrowing, as it were, from the other side. At one point in our conversation, I half-jokingly suggested to Rosenthal and Sullivan over at ILM that if they ever did get around to replicating an actual human actor, most likely that actor would be someone whose visage had already started taking on opaque and exoskeletal characteristics, which is to say someone like Cher or Michael Jackson. "Precisely," they crowed as one. "Botox is our friend!" Botox, that is, the injected biochemical agent that removes age wrinkles by incidentally killing off the underlying expressive muscles. In all seriousness, they suggested, one likely deployment of their technology in the years ahead might be for extending the acting careers of people like Cher by artificially injecting into their performances expressions of which their faces were no longer physically capable.

Occasionally, in these conversations, I would trot out my prediction that one of these days, maybe five years off, we'd be treated to the buzz-spectacle of two huge studios racing to complete their competing digitized megaprojects for summer release. One of them would be following a Pygmalion theme (a cybernaut falling desperately in love with his creation), the other a dead-president plot (a cabal attempting to disguise the fact of the president's brain-death for its own nefarious purposes). "And exactly how would that be different from what we've in fact got?" quipped one animator, regarding the latter. "In any case, we can do either of those already today," Butler at DreamWorks pointed out to me. "Just hire an actor."

And indeed such seems to be the solution Andrew Niccol (*The Truman Show*'s screenwriter) has hit upon for his first directing credit, the soon-to-be released *S1m0ne* (get it?), based on his own screenplay, in which the Al Pacino character, a down-and-out film director, tries to pass off an entirely digital actress as the real thing—to comic and presently cascadingly calamitous effect. Naturally, the technology wasn't good enough yet to contrive an actual cyberlead, but it was good enough to take the real actress standing in for Simone and make her look more convincingly robotic! "We're simulating a simulation" is how the real-life director, Niccol, chose to characterize the situation for me.

Alvy Ray Smith, for his part, continues to feel the prospect of an actual cyberlead is at least conceivable. "But not in five years," he told me. "It took us twenty years after we founded what would become Pixar in 1974 to even get to the point where we could make a convincing full-length animation featuring plastic toys. More recently, *Toy Story 2* was consuming seven hours of computer time per frame, and that's twenty-four frames per second of screen time. By my estimation, the sort of computer power needed to crunch the numbers necessary for rendering completely convincing humans is something like two thousand times what we have today. By a simple application of Moore's law, we're not going to be there for another twenty years. And even then, we'll only be able to get there using human actors, with all their idiosyncratic mannerisms and specificities, as our models."

OF ALL THE THINGS I witnessed during my reporting of this story, the one that most truly shook my faith in the Cusan impossibility of fabricating synthetic souls ex nihilo was an eight-second short the guys at ILM put together a few years back, the evocation of the plight of a cybercreature named "Hugo."

Hugo is an entirely synthetic creation—a phantasm of light and algorithm. A troll-like figure with Spockian ears, heightened cheekbones, and a sunken chin, he gazes off to the side of the camera, stammering, "Me? What do you mean I'm not real? Oh, I see, this is a joke, right? You must be talking about the other one." At which point he gulps nervously and gives a forced smile.

As do we. I, anyway, bought it completely. Part of the enchantment effect had to do with the voice (and voices, all my interlocutors agreed, are essential to the magic, both distracting us from transient imperfections and carrying us along). But mainly it had to do with the story. Turn off the sound, and one immediately noticed the too-stiff ears, the way the eyes move when Hugo blinks, the overly rubbery consistency of the skin around the lips, and the lack of detail inside the mouth (the inner lips, tongue, and teeth not having been tracked in the motion capture upon

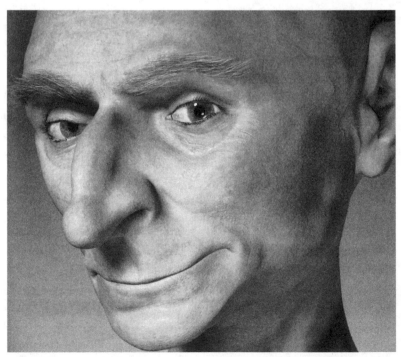

which the creature was based). But with the sound on, we were immediately transported into the story. The narrative. A convincing and absorbing narrative had been precisely what was lacking in *Final Fantasy* (whenever that film bogged down in clunky exposition, your mind had an opportunity to wander over to all the ways in which the rendering was falling short—in fact, it couldn't help but do so). The sense of narrative—our tendency to experience everything as narrative—being at the very core, ironically, of our ensouled and incarnate natures.

For example, there's the story about the two Oxford dons out on the Commons, lost in disputation about the implications of Zeno's paradox. You know, the one about the arrow that gets halfway to its target, and then halfway across the remainder of the distance, and then halfway across the remaining remainder, and so forth, such that it can never actually reach its goal. (Not entirely surprisingly, it turns out that one of ILM's proprietary programming softwares is in fact called "Zeno.") So anyway, these two

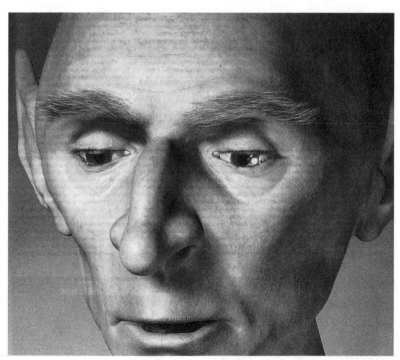

dons—one of them is a mathematician, and the other one is an engineer—they're arguing over the implications of Zeno's paradox, and just then a beautiful woman goes sauntering by, and the mathematician, lost in the complexities of Zeno's paradox, despairs of ever being able to attain her. But the engineer knows he can get close enough for all practical purposes.

Close Enough for All Practical Purposes.

We long to lose ourselves in stories—*that's who we are*. Well-crafted stories transport us, allow us to soar. One day perhaps, things being close enough for all practical purposes, to soar right over the Uncanny Valley, to traverse the Cusan Divide?

I don't know. Could be.

# Four Easy Pieces

## I.
## ON COMING FACE-TO-FACE WITH MYSELF

E ach of the presenters at the Chicago Humanities Festival is assigned a host, and mine that year was the exceptionally graceful and gracious art dealer Richard Gray, who, following my little talk, invited me over to his apartment—not surprisingly an exceptionally graceful and gracious apartment perched overlooking a gentle bend of Lake Shore Drive, with beyond its arcing traffic, the gleaming expanse of the lake—mainly so that he could show me his collection of old master drawings, which were completely enthralling: old old masters and newer old masters and even a few contemporary pieces, with, coming around one corner: me.

Which is to say, a black and brown ink sketch of *mein* very *selbst* that David Hockney had undertaken a few years earlier when I'd happened to be visiting him at his London digs. Gray beamed

triumphantly at my shock of recognition—and indeed, I was completely gobsmacked—but it took me a while (indeed a few days)
to work out the exact content of my consternation. For it wasn't
the only portrait Hockney had ever made of me: Over the twenty
years that I've been writing about him in magazines and catalogs
and books, he has had occasion now and again, here and there, to
capture my likeness. Though nowhere near as often as with several of his other regular subjects, who he's portrayed hundreds of
times: A huge swath of his production consists of a record of the
gradual aging of that tight-knit community of friends and family—
his mother, Celia, Gregory, Mo, Ian, and all the other lovingly rendered likenesses one keeps coming upon at museums and galleries
and in books. I'm at best a bit player in their intimate confederacy,
and, though with the rest of them, I suppose it goes with the territory, it honestly never even occurred to me that any of those drawings of me might ever end up gracing some relative stranger's walls.
Who could possibly want such a picture?

Not that it bothered me exactly (it's not that I felt exploited
or betrayed or anything like that). I didn't begrudge Hockney the
right to spread his drawings about in any manner he saw fit (he'd
always made sure to give me a high-quality photo or laser print
of any of the pictures he'd made of me). I just felt strange. And it
was the precise nature of that strangeness that I kept trying to nail
down in the days that followed.

It wasn't that I felt embarrassed to have my visage up there on
the wall, laid bare before the potentially withering evaluations of
any of the complete strangers who might have had occasion to pay
a call on my gracious host (what did I care what they thought?)—
though I did feel embarrassed. No, it occurred to me a few days
later that what was embarrassing me (and I grant you that this is
completely nonsensical magical thinking) was the way that I would
be eavesdropping on them, that there I'd inevitably be, looking out
on the quotidian doings of people whose lives I had no business
observing. My host and his wife in their Skivvies!

I had no idea how such a perverse notion could have entered my head. Except that, on second thought, I did. I knew precisely where I'd gotten it from.

Several years earlier I had been doing a profile of Breyten Breytenbach, the great Afrikaner poet and painter who'd served almost eight years as a political prisoner in apartheid jails, during which time his captors had fiendishly forbidden him to paint (fully understanding how for him an empty canvas would have constituted an open field of freedom, a freedom they were intent on denying him). And even though that inability to paint had bedeviled him every day of his incarceration, he subsequently found that upon his release, the one place he could hardly bring himself to revisit was his painting studio. For several weeks he circled it skittishly. "I was afraid," he told me as  we now sat in that very studio, "because I hadn't painted for seven and a half years, and with painting, like music, you worry that it's something that if you don't practice it, a lot of it goes—a lot of the technical ability. I was really scared in front of that first canvas."

I asked him, at the time, if he still had the painting with which he'd finally started up once again, and he said, oh yes; he rummaged around in the back and pulled it out. It was dated February 1, 1983, and the image, quite competently rendered actually, in dull grays and browns and blues, consisted of a wall, a mirror, and his own face in the mirror, all bruised and pummeled and haggard, with the eyes closed. I asked him why he'd painted himself with his eyes closed, and he replied, "It was all too tender still; I couldn't look at myself yet." (I've often thought about that answer in the years since, and it has seemed ever more astonishing: He couldn't look at himself, so he painted a picture of himself with his eyes closed. Who or what in such a situation is looking at who or what? And who are we, where are we, gazing over the shoulder of that regard?)

Funny, at any rate, the way ideas like that insinuate themselves, transmogrify, and pop up, years later, unbidden: resplendent and bizarre.

## II.
## TORQUED BRUEGHEL

I was going to have to be catching an early afternoon flight out of town so I'd had to pull a few strings to get in to see Richard Serra's *Torqued Ellipses* show before the usual 11:00 AM opening time at the Temporary Contemporary, Frank Gehry's converted warehouse exhibition annex to L.A.'s Museum of Contemporary Art.

Perhaps you've seen pictures of those remarkable monumental pieces. You may have even experienced one or two of them here or there on your own travels. How to describe them, though, to those who haven't? Well, imagine a vast ellipsis—the size, say, of half a basketball court—traced onto the ground. Now, imagine gradually levitating that elliptical shape into the air and slowly rotating it such that by the time you've got the thing hovering twenty feet above the ground you've negotiated something like a ninety-degree rotation from its original position. Now, imagine casting the shape across which that form has floated in two-inch-thick Cor-Ten steel. Slice a narrow vertical passage into the form, such that a person could circumnavigate the whole thing on either the inside or the outside of the wall. And now leave the thing out to rust to a gloriously garish orange-brown. While you're at it, surround its magnificent hulking presence with an even vaster ellipsis, one that you

rotate as well, only this time counterclockwise, providing a narrow vertical passageway on the other side, such that a visitor entering the maze might experience an initially tapered pathway widening as he or she went along, while the opening above, initially quite wide and expansive, would itself taper precipitously the deeper in one went, and then vice versa, until, suddenly, one was delivered into the heart of the labyrinth, that original half-basketball-court-sized elliptical agora, its walls pitching vertiginously from side to side. Way cool.

And now imagine Serra's having performed a half dozen variations on that theme and scattering them all about Gehry's vast open hangar space, the lurch and swell and soar and buckle of all that drunken steel.

And then imagine having the place entirely to yourself, as I did for a good half hour, ambling drop-jawed and woozy from one such variation to the next.

A quarter to eleven now, though, and almost time to leave, but just as I was getting set to go, I noticed that a big yellow school bus had just pulled up to the hangar's glass-walled entrance. Its door sprung open and out poured (how to describe *this*?) a teeming Brueghelian throng. A classful of variously misshapen, fate-mangled, brain-damaged, and sight-stunted teenagers, stumbling and gawking and tumbling gleefully into the cavernous hall, one holding on to the next, each of them having been provided with a musical instrument of some sort—a tambourine or a harmonica or a Jew's harp or some bongo drums or a cowbell or a whistle—all of them clanging and banging and whooping away, wending their slow, blind progress by means of sound alone: a sheer cacophonous bliss. They'd break off into little strings of marvel, a few heading down one passageway, another few down another, each experiencing the widenings and tightenings of the surrounding space through the tips of their outstretched fingers and the barometric shifts in the echoing pitches of their instruments alone. The looks on their faces! One boy peeled away, made his way into the heart of one of the mazes, sat himself wedged against the leaning wall, and began keening metronomically, forward and then vertical and then *past* vertical—a big, broad grin across his face as the back of his skull finally reached the wall with a gently gonging tap: headbanger heaven.

And me, I meandered unnoticed from one group to the next. I remember thinking how I really should get all this down on paper, and then, how no, no writing could possibly capture it (and I still don't think I have). I wished instead that I'd had a video camera: It would have made a great movie: only, a silent one, so that viewers might have been vouched the exact opposite experience of those enthralled kids.

Mainly, though, I wished that Serra could have been there to see it.

III.
# MOTES IN THE LIGHT
(2004)

One balmy evening late last summer, my friend John and I drove over to the St. Ann's Warehouse performance space, slotted snug under the Brooklyn Bridge overpass on the Brooklyn side of the East River waterfront, to see a screening of Bill Morrison's *Decasia* the way it was meant to be seen. Which is to say with Michael Gordon's astonishing symphonic score being performed live by an orchestra ranged on scaffolds, one row of instrumentalists atop the next, behind three translucent screens that had in turn been arrayed in a sort of triangle, the audience seated on the floor inside, watching as three separate versions of the film were being projected onto the three screens in slightly staggered fashion—their intersecting cones of light expanding through the smoky air above us—while a conductor energetically directed the proceedings from her precarious perch on a sort of gangplank thrust out above it all. Morrison has fashioned his film entirely out of snippets of severely distressed and heartrendingly decomposed nitrate film stock: decades-old mouldering footage of geishas and desertscapes, waves breaking and clouds racing, dervishes whirling and boxers training, children playing and cells dividing—a mottled pullulating mass (the frenzy of moths at twilight). And with Gordon's smearily decomposing score lashing the images along, and the players arrayed behind the sweltering screens progressively stripping out of their clothes—the violinists down to their bras, the hairy-chested tuba player wrapped Laocoönlike in his instrument, the percussionists spraying sweat off their gleaming torsos—the whole thing packed an incredible wallop.[1]

So anyway, afterward, you can imagine the spent exhilaration with which we left the theater and broached the warm night air, and the sense of baffled slippage with which we now spied another cone of light, this one spreading straight up vertically, high into the sky, from some mysterious source behind and beyond the dilapidated storage buildings between us and the river. We ambled down the block toward the waterfront to get a better view, and suddenly the entire downtown sweep of Manhattan opened before us, with two beams of light shooting out from its painfully stunted skyline. At which point, ah yes, we remembered, this was September 10, the eve of the anniversary of the disaster.

We joined a small throng gathered there on the waterfront, taking it all in, those two clean beams of light defiantly splitting the night sky. Several individuals were busy taking pictures (and several of them, improbably, were using flashes). It took a while for our eyes to adjust, but then things really began to get strange.

Because within the expanding cones of light, tiny specks of light seemed to be floating, suspended, like the spangle in an upturned snowglobe—flecks, though, of what? Confetti? Ashes? *Souls?* At first the swirl of motes seemed random and limited to the base of the light cones, maybe the first hundred feet above the upturned searchlights. It was hard to tell exactly from all those miles away. But the more we gazed, the more somehow *volitional* their movements came to seem—float, slide, wobble, but then dart and dash. Near collisions narrowly averted, sudden surges straight up. What could they possibly be? Birds? The scale was all wrong, confoundingly so, and there were thousands of them, tens of thousands, and the closer we looked, the higher they seemed to rise, hundreds of yards, all the way up, seemingly miles.

John and I decided to hop into his car, a convertible, to go investigate. We lowered the roof and negotiated the cloverleaf onto the bridge, the same bridge across which all those stunned and shell-shocked crowds had trod, in the opposite direction, that skybright morning just short of three years ago . . . (Oh, and by the way, can I just interject here, that Christo's curtain gates in Central Park this past winter were okay, I suppose, but they had nothing on the thrillingly majestic cavalcade of flexing lines you can experience any day or night of the year on the traverse across the Brooklyn Bridge?) Anyway, the brilliant motes, carnivaling about in the lightbeams beyond the bridge cables, seemed no more decipherable the closer we came. Surely they had to be alive, but how could they be soaring like that so high into the sky, and were they huge or tiny or what? Traffic began to bunch up, and it took a good hour on the other side of the bridge to wend our way the last mile toward the bank of searchlights; we had our necks craned the entire while, the solution to the mote puzzle no more apparent. Eventually we parked and trod the last few blocks toward ground zero. Whereupon, rounding the corner, into that veritable blast of white light, we finally managed to figure it all out.

The motes were *moths*. Hundreds of thousands, millions of moths, rising thousands of feet into the air. Surely, it seemed, every single moth on the Eastern Seaboard had come to pay their respects that gleaming anniversary night.


IV.
# THE JUDD ANT

So the other afternoon I happened to find myself walking the length of the late Donald Judd's enigmatically posed (if strangely imposing) processional of giant concrete dice, spread out a full (and precise) kilometer across an otherwise empty wildgrass expanse along the periphery of his marvelous Chinati Foundation in Marfa, Texas. I say "dice," though of course the (exactly) sixty-four boxy concrete structures are not exactly mammoth dice: Rather, at least dimensionally, think of a pair of dice cubes glued cheek-by-jowl one beside the next and then hollowed out, either lengthwise (five meters long by two and a half high and two and a half meters deep, exactly) or through the narrow core (two and a half meters by two and a half and five meters deep); some of them completely hollow so you can see clean through, others stoppered either at the front or the back (like packing crates, alternately

wide or deep, lying on their side); the whole lot of them gathered
into (at first) seemingly random clusters, three long see-through
boxes in a starlike splay here, and then three wide stoppered boxes
one behind the next, and then . . . groups of three or five or six
spread one beyond the next (till you have traversed precisely fifteen
such groupings) as you tramp the kilometer's length of the wide
wildgrass field.

Open, closed; wide, narrow; three, six, five; radial, side by
side, one behind the other: the didactic character of the experience
("Hmm, that's true, you can try it that way, and then this other, and
if you add one more you can do it this way, and now hollow them
out the other way, and now stopper the hollows") gradually giving way to an experience more lyrical, or perhaps poetical (certain
effects seeming to repeat themselves like deep tidal refrains, just
beyond the reach of conscious apperception) before the whole mad
enterprise begins to throb as deeply existential (the sheer absurdity
of the effort involved in lugging these huge concrete slabs out onto
this godforsaken field, the defiant assertion of value involved, the
primordial insistence on a brute human trace across this otherwise
barren high desert expanse).

Not bad, not bad, I found myself thrumming as I now doubled back, returning the length of the rutted path, reprising the

fifteen groupings in reverse, ambling toward the Foundation's headquarters compound way up ahead, humming along (didactical poetical existential), my gaze now drifting absentmindedly to the ground before me (churned tire-ruts and dried mud puddles and tufts of dried grass), when—I swear to God—I happened to notice a little ant dragging an improbably long stalk of dried blond wildgrass. And I mean a stalk a good five or six times its own body length. Pulling and pulling on the damn thing, and now laying it down and traipsing back along its length so as to be able instead to push it forward, much of the time (swear to God) tilting the stalk a good forty-five degrees into the air, laying it down again, nudging it leftward, going around to the other side, nudging it right, returning to the back to lift it skyward and to shove it forward once again. And so on. And on. Relentlessly.

By this time I was completely absorbed. Minutes passed—the ant, the straw, their rutted course—till finally the ant dragged the thing under and presently around a tuft of wildgrass, lay the straw down, pulled back momentarily (seemingly) to appraise the situation, and now began nudging it ever so slightly this way and that, lining it up perfectly (as I now suddenly perceived, astounded) with another length of dry straw, which in turn perfectly abutted another length still, the three lengths of identical blond straw now perfectly aligning—nudge, push, nudge, nudge, pull—into one long length. Whereupon, apparently satisfied, the accomplished ant simply wandered off into the gathering evening light.

As, at length, did I, wondering, Had Judd first got it from the ant, or the ant from the Judds, or was it that Judd had conditioned me even to be able to notice the ant, or was the ant simply God (or, at very least, God's high priest), *or what?*

# Three
# Improbable
# Yarns

## MR. WILSON IN BELGRADE

It can get downright weird. You're going to have to bear with me
on this one: There are all sorts of false starts, seeming feints,
and side-tributaries in the telling of this story, but trust me, by the
end it all comes together, sort of.

So, like I say, I was home, minding my own business, rifling
through my latest email, this was about two years ago, when—not
so very unusually—I spotted yet another missive from Serbia. Ever
since having covered the aftermath of the Balkan wars for the *New
Yorker*, I'd been subjected to a steady if intermittent stream of hate
mail bearing the telltale ".yu" coda in the sender's e-return-address.
"You obviously must not be able to get enough of the taste of the
blood of Serbian infants with your morning cereal." You know:
that sort of thing. Anyway, here was yet another one, emanating
from some e.place like rabbit@enet.yu or some such. And for a few
days I didn't even bother to open it: Who needs such images rat-
tling around in his head?

Anyway, eventually I did open it, and—surprise!—this
wasn't that kind of message at all. On the contrary, it was from
a fellow named Rasa Sekulovic, who introduced himself as an

experienced literary translator (English into Serbian), veteran for example of texts by Salman Rushdie, and what he was inquiring about was whether or not I'd allow him to translate my book on the Museum of Jurassic Technology in Los Angeles, *Mr. Wilson's Cabinet of Wonder*, into Serbian and then see to its publication in Belgrade.

Now, as it happens, that book has received a bunch of translations: a work of magic-realist nonfiction, as it were, it's far and away my most translated book, showing up in Italy, Germany, France, and even Japan, usually finding a home in the catalogs of the respective publishers of Borges and García Márquez and Umberto Eco. Japan, of course, was strange (and even stranger the busloads of Japanese tourists who now began pulling up at the doors of the Museum in Culver City)—*but Serbia?* What on earth were people in Serbia going to make of my odd little text? Still, I figured what the hell, and by reply missive, I extended my somewhat dubious permission—don't even bother worrying about the royalties.


SO ANYWAY, HOLD ALL that in the back of your mind for a moment, as I pick up the narrative somewhere seemingly altogether different—and in fact, a couple years before that.

I happened to be visiting David Wilson's little museum one day. It occurs to me that I ought to say something here about the Museum of Jurassic Technology, for the benefit of those who haven't ever read the book, or maybe even for some of those who have, because the place really does exist. Several of the book's reviewers, at the time of its publication in 1995, indicated that they'd thought I was making the whole place up and had even gone so far as to call Information in L.A. to confirm its reality (though why they imagined that, had I been making the place up from scratch, I wouldn't have had the wit to place a listing for my fictional creation with Directory Assistance in L.A., I'll never know). (Which reminds me about the single coolest review the book ever got, which wasn't even published in any journal, but instead took the form of this guy who went to visit the Museum one day about six months after the book's publication: He spent about two hours puttering around the Jurassic's labyrinthine backhalls before reemerging at the front desk, where he hesitantly asked the fellow seated there, "Excuse me, but are you either David Wilson or Lawrence Weschler?" Informed by the sitter in question that he was indeed David Wilson, the visitor leaned in confidentially before triumphantly declaring, sotto voce, "Come on, tell me the truth, does that guy Weschler really exist?")

Where was I? Oh, yeah, the Museum of Jurassic Technology in Culver City, halfway between downtown L.A. and Venice Beach, a place that really does exist (go ahead: Call Information; you'll see), a deceptively diminutive little storefront operation that specializes in the breathtakingly lovely and loving display of some of the most astoundingly incredible material you'll ever encounter—incredible because, as it happens, some of it may not be entirely true. Or not. You can't be sure. There's this sense of slippage: horned humans, pronged ants, mice on toast, microminiature *painted* renditions of Snow White and all seven of her dwarfs strung out along the shaft of a needle, the medicinal uses of urine—an entire hall given over to an exhibition on the career of Geoffrey Sonnabend, an American neuropsychiatrist who, during the 1930s, in despair over the collapse of his researches into memory pathways in carp, suffered a complete nervous breakdown and was shipped off by his mother to a spa near Iguazu Falls, in the Mesopotamian region of Latin America, which is where, one night, he happened to attend a recital of German lieder by Madelena Delani, the famed Romanian chanteuse, most famous perhaps for the fact that she suffered from Korsakov's syndrome, a condition that had ravaged all her long- and short-term memory with the exception of the memory of music itself, a condition that imparted a "uniquely plaintive air" (*New York Times*) to her haunted and haunting singing; after which he

(Sonnabend) spent a shatteringly insomniac night across which he came up with an entirely new theory of memory, a theory it would take him the whole next decade to elaborate into the three-volume masterwork in which he argued that memory itself is essentially an illusion that we all throw in front of ourselves to disguise from ourselves the fact that we've in fact forgotten everything, a theory that has in the meantime proved particularly intriguing owing to the fact that no sooner had it finally been put to paper than its author himself seemed to fall into complete oblivion, that is until his recent resurrection there in the halls of the Jurassic itself.

You know, that sort of thing.

SO, ANYWAY, WILSON AND I were sitting there one day whiling away the time at the front desk when the mailman delivered a mysterious little package covered over with myriad colorful stamps from Italy. Inside, without any accompanying letter, was a beautifully produced little hardcover book, just published by Rizzoli, *Un Cosi bel Posto*, by one Fabrizio Rondolino, a narrative that apparently (neither of us could actually read Italian) purported to relate the true life love story of Geoffrey Sonnabend and Madelena Delani. Though as mystified as I was, Wilson hardly seemed the least bit upset by this sudden appropriation of his creation. On the contrary, he seemed entirely pleased by this confirmation of the palpable reality of these individuals whose existence heretofore had seemed entirely confined to the halls of his emporium.

Later that evening, I myself was dumbfounded to recall an incident that had taken place about nine months earlier, around the time of my own book's publication. Shortly before that date, I'd been approached by the radio producer David Isay to see whether Wilson and I would be willing to collaborate with him on a half-hour audio version of my little narrative—completely rereported for radio, to be broadcast on NPR's "All Things Considered." We'd agreed, and there had ensued several days' worth of surreptitious taping at the museum, eventually yielding over forty hours of overheard conversations among and with visitors to the Jurassic, which, following another several months' editing, had eventually yielded the finished documentary.[1]

And what I suddenly remembered that evening was how the documentary had included a passage where I intoned on how people came from all over the world to visit the Museum's many exhibits, as, for example, in this instance—and here the sound of a doorbell bubbled up from behind my narration, followed by that of a young man with a foreign accent launching into a series of queries—"this fellow here who'd come all the way from Rome, Italy, to pursue his researches on the career of Geoffrey Sonnabend, an American neuropsychiatrist who, back in the thirties" . . . and so forth. Listeners were then invited to eavesdrop as the fellow indicated to Wilson how much trouble he'd been having tracking down Sonnabend's three volumes ("Yeah," Wilson said, "those books are quite hard to find"), whereupon he asked Wilson whether he himself happened to have the books there at the Museum, and Wilson sighed that no, as it happened, he didn't ("They're really *really* hard to find," he assured the young man), at which point the young man shrugged audibly and proceeded on into the Museum's backhalls.

A few days later, when I got back to New York, I called up Isay and went over, and we foraged around for the original tape of that overheard conversation, and indeed, fiddling with the dials, sharpening the sound, we were able to make out the fellow's self-introduction: "Hello, my name is Fabrizio Rondolino and I've come here from Rome, Italy, and I'm especially interested in . . ." and so forth. Incredibly, of all the days we could have chosen to tape there at the museum, we'd managed to pick the one on which occurred the sole ever meeting between David Wilson and Fabrizio Rondolino—and the amazing thing, listening once more to the whole conversation, was how neither of them had broken irony the entire time. They'd both gone on as if theirs were the most commonsensical sort of conversation to be having.

BUT THAT'S NOT THE story I wanted to tell you. Because the thing is—and now I have to come back to my Belgrade Rabbit friend (and as I say, this was a few years later)—Rasa now did indeed begin translating my Mr. Wilson book; he was sending me updates every few days until about three weeks into the process, when he sent me a fairly breathless piece of email: "You'll never believe what just happened," he wrote. "I didn't ever mention this to you before but my girlfriend is also a translator, in her case of Italian into Serbian, and she happened to be reading the part of your book I've translated up to this point and she almost had a heart attack, because, you see, she came upon the stuff about Geoffrey Sonnabend, and as it happens, she's been commissioned by the same publisher here in Belgrade to translate a book by an Italian writer which claims to be a narrative about the love story of Sonnabend and Delani."

Now, this was in the fall of 1998, and in the weeks thereafter the Belgrade publishers got in touch with all of us and we began planning to converge on Belgrade—Wilson, Rondolino, and me—for a great reunion on the occasion of the simultaneous Serbian publication of both books that upcoming March. And we would have gone, too, except that just then, in response to Milosevic's escalating rampages in Kosovo, NATO started its air blitz, and the whole thing had to be called off (the event, not the books' publication—I've got my copy right here: *Kabinet cuda gospodina Vilsona* by Lorens Vesler).

And here's the really weird part. It turns out that Rondolino . . . (Actually, I should mention that in the meantime I was able to get a report on the book from some friends who read Italian, and they say it's actually quite marvelous, recounting as it does the story of a pair of lovers who seduce each other one evening and the next morning the woman has completely forgotten that they ever met and they have to seduce each other all over again that night, and so on and so forth, night after night thereafter—kind of a cross between Valentine's Day and *Groundhog Day*, I suppose.) Anyway, it turns out that Rondolino's day job, from which he'd only just resigned, had been as the press spokesman for the Italian prime minister, in which capacity he'd been having to justify the stationing of NATO planes at Italian bases, from whence they'd been heading off to rain bombs down on Belgrade.

As I say: weird, weird, wondrous world. Go figure.

*POSTSCRIPT:*

AND WHILE YOU'RE AT it, figure this. That piece was published in the Book Review of the *Los Angeles Times* on February 4, 2001. Almost exactly three years later, I happened to be visiting the MJT and plastered across the billboard directly across the street was an ad heralding the Valentine's Day 2004 release of the latest Adam Sandler–Drew Barrymore vehicle, a film entitled *50 First Dates.* The pair were portrayed on a beach blanket by the sea, Sandler gamely plucking a ukulele, gazing puppy-wistfully on a wide-eyed, completely bewildered Barrymore. "Imagine," the ad's legend invited us, "Imagine having to win over the girl of your dreams every friggin' day." Frig, indeed: Who could possibly imagine that?

## II.
# THE POEM ON THE TRAIN
### A LETTER TO THE EDITOR OF *THE THREEPENNY REVIEW* (1995)

So I'm leafing through your wonderful Winter 1995 issue on the 5:42 out of Grand Central, the Jewish jokes issue as I've come to think of it, I've just finished Alan Shapiro's marvelously moving and funny memoir, and now I'm browsing about, as I often do with 3PR on my first day's immersion, and my eyes glide across a long poem—I haven't even noticed the title or the author, and my eyes fall on the word "Flemings," and—steeped in Shapiro-consciousness—this reminds me of a great Jewish joke, and my eyes spy the word "Walloons" and then drift down to "Belgian" and "Rabinowitz," and this not only reminds me of the joke (for, of course, it *is* the joke) but it reminds me of the occasion when I first heard it, in a living room in Cape Town in South Africa during the recent election campaign, when Albie Sachs, the great ANC lawyer and hero who'd survived a car bombing (in exile in Maputo, as late as 1988), losing an arm but somehow salvaging both his life and his uncanny sense of humor and optimism, was trying to convince a roomful of hesitant old Jews to vote for the ANC, at which point the man next to me leaned over to whisper the joke to me—and my eyes drift a bit higher up in the poem, and I see the capitalized abbreviation "ANC," and this is really starting to get weird, and a bit higher still I see how the poet introduces this whole story with the phrase, "There's one a journalist told me," and now my eyes bolt to the bottom of the page—Robert Pinsky!—and of course it was me, it was I, it was the author of this note, who told Pinsky that joke in the first place, just a few months earlier, at a party in New York in honor of Czeslaw Milosz and Robert Hass, who'd just been giving a reading (Pinsky had introduced Hass and of course his splendidly moving poem, "Impossible to Tell," is dedicated to him), and here I was, on the 5:42 out of Grand Central, the whole thing coming back at me, a double, triple, quadruple echo— uncanny! And it's wonderfully moving how that joke obviously resonated for Pinsky that evening, thinking of his dead friend (the reverberations he in turn brought to my telling of it).

ANYWAY, FOR ME THE truly marvelous thing about the joke the eve-ning *I* first heard it was *just who* whispered it in my ear, as Albie Sachs stood up there exhorting his dubious old Jewish listeners to vote ANC (even though the ANC had often supported the PLO) because that way hope would return to the country and in its wake so, once again, would their children—"Your children will come home from their homeless exiles in Chicago and California, come home to you and us and to where they belong" (not a dry eye in the house). At which point my neighbor Adam Michnik, of all people, the great Solidarity theorist and long-time Polish oppositionist, veteran of years and years in Polish communist prisons and now the editor of the country's foremost daily, *Gazeta Wyborcza*, who was in Cape Town attending a conference on the theme of forgiveness and settling accounts with the prior regime—it was Adam Michnik, the Jew who refused to leave Poland (as the vast majority of those few Jews still remaining in the country did at the time) in the wake of the anti-Semitic purges of 1968 largely instigated in response to his own student radicalism—it was Adam who leaned over and whispered to me, regarding Albie Sachs, that he was "the Belgian Army Joke Come to Life." Michnik has this incredible stammering stutter, which he's learned to play like a Stradivarius (as masterfully, it occurs to me, as Sachs deploys that extravagantly voluble armless sleeve of *his*), and he was stuttering as he whispered it to me—I was listening to Albie Sachs waxing wry and expansive in one ear, Adam Michnik whispering sly and all stuttery in the other—the one about the Belgian army, how it's coming completely apart at the seams, the Walloons and the Flemish are at each other's throats, and finally the general comes down to the barracks; everybody freezes to attention; he orders the Walloons to one side of the hangar, the Flemish to the other; and finally there's just this one private standing there, shivering, in the middle—"And what are *you?*" demands the general. "A Belgian, sir!" replies the mortified private. "And what's your name?" "Rabinowitz!"

And so what I end up wondering is are these jokes themselves in fact perhaps the only truly living things on this small planet, and we humans merely the stories they tell themselves between-tides as they flit so merrily about, all of mankind being merely the medium in which they get to play out their own eternally self-renewing and mischievous liveliness?[1]

III.

# POPOCATEPETL

## (MY GRANDFATHER'S GEOGRAPHICAL AND MY MEDICAL FUGUE)

## (2001)

> *The giant seethes and belches whilst*
> *down below the anchorfolk stammer and flail.*

P opocatepetl.

It's been eighty years since the last major eruption of that powerfully looming volcano, forty miles north of Mexico City, and perhaps a lifetime since any of the gentle anchorfolk were required to pronounce its name.

Popocatepetl (POH-puh-KAT-uh-peht-l).

Stammering, flailing, they try to wend their way about the word's impossible convolutions, as if attempting to tie a cherry stem into a knot inside their mouths, using only their tongues—to cite the metaphor deployed recently by a novelist who was describing the obverse challenge of some old Southern California Chicano trying to overmaster a commonplace English locution.

Popocatepetl (POH-poh-kuh-TEH-peht-l).

As it happens, I was having no such problem: Popocatepetl. Popocatepetl. Popocatepetl. See? I can say it hundreds of times without the slightest hitch.

But that's only because of my grandfather.

My grandfather, Ernst Toch, was a prominent composer in 1920s Berlin at the time he invented the then entirely new musical idiom of pieces for spoken chorus. Weimar Rap, as it were.

Nobody had ever tried such a thing before. The most famous of these confections of Toch's was his *Fuge aus der Geographie*, the *Geographical Fugue*, in which he arrayed the names of cities, countries, and other such landmarks in strict fugal counterpoint, exactingly casting them among separate a cappella soprano, alto, tenor, and bass sections, to stirring and quite telling effect: *Ratibor! Und der Fluss Mis-sis-sip-pi und der Stadt Ho-no-lu-lu und der See Ti-ti-ca-ca . . .*

And presently:

*Der Po-po-ca-te-pe-tl liegt nicht in Ka-na-da, sondern in Me-xi-ko, Me-xi-ko, Me-xi-ko.*

And so forth (*Ka-na-da Ma-la-ga Ri-mi-ni Brin-di-si*). From its first performance, in June 1930 (a few years, as it happens, after Popocatepetl's last major eruptions), at the Fest der neuen Musik in Berlin—its phrases repeating and expanding, looping in and out of one another in a strictly cadenced delirium—the three-minute piece proved an immediate sensation, indeed becoming one of Toch's most performed pieces, though Toch himself considered it little more than a trifling diversion.

The years passed, Hitler rose to power, and Toch fled, presently surfacing in Southern California, where he took to composing for Hollywood, and himself now began trying to overmaster the daunting sinuosities of the English language (like trying to tie a cherry stem into a knot using only his tongue).

A few months after his arrival, in 1935, there came a knocking at the door of his rented Pacific Palisades home, and he opened it to find a diffident young man inquiring, "Excuse me, sir, but are you Dr. Ernst Toch?" Confirming, with some difficulty, that such was indeed the case, the young man pressed on, "*The* Ernst Toch, composer of the *Geographical Fugue?*" Yes, yes, my grandfather assured the young fellow, but seriously it was just a joke. No, no, the boy insisted, that Fugue was a major piece, one of the most significant of recent years—no, no, my grandfather interrupted, trust me, it was just a joke. On the contrary—and so forth, their little talk proceeded, until at length the kid was able to extract Toch's permission to see to the work's translation and promulgation in America, for starters by way of his friend Henry Cowell's seminal periodical, *New Music*. The young man at the door was John Cage, recent graduate of Los Angeles High School.

Cage was as good as his word: The piece was translated (a pretty straightforward operation with the exception of the replacement of the German "Ratibor" with its rolling R-sound, so pivotally crucial at the Fugue's stirring crescendo, with an English approximate: "Trrrrrrrrrinidad!"), and it did indeed go on to receive a wide exposure. Indeed, though Toch, for his own part, went on to considerable success (three Academy Award nominations, a Pulitzer Prize for his *Third Symphony*) and continued prolific to the end of his life (seven symphonies, an opera, countless quartets and quintets and trios and pieces for piano solo), the *Geographical Fugue* remains probably the piece for which he's best known (I keep running into people who encountered it in high school and college chorus classes). For his own part, Toch eventually got quite good at English, and even managed a reprise of the spoken chorus idiom some years later with an elaborate parody of American cocktail party chatter recast in strict three-fourths time, his 1960 "Valse." (*My how super-dooper—Hold your tongue, you strapper—Let's behave, not like children, but grown-ups—She is right—She is right.*)

Toch died in 1964, and a good twenty years later, when I happened to be profiling the indefatigably spry nonagenarian musical lexicographer Nicolas Slonimsky for the *New Yorker*, I myself had occasion to knock on the door of Slonimsky's dear friend John Cage. No mean gleam himself, Cage proved immensely sweet and cordial, and when I mentioned that I was the grandson of the composer Ernst Toch, his face brightened even further. "Ah, Toch," he said, "Toch—was he onto some amazing stuff, what with those pieces for spoken chorus and some of those other experimental works. Why'd he then have to go and squander it all on all those damn string quartets?" He was smiling sweetly as he said it, the look of a benign sage who would have saved them all if he could.

Anyway, somewhere in there I'd become the improbable executor of my grandfather's estate—improbable in that I'm pretty hapless, musically speaking. I do what I can. And at one point, this must have been over twenty-five years ago, I found myself producing a sampler LP of the Old Man's music, including a rendition of that *Geographical Fugue*. As everybody else may already know but I sure didn't at the time, recording a piece of music hardly consists of simply herding the musicians into a room and laying down a sequence of takes until you get the piece just right. That—and, even so, we're talking about twenty, thirty, fifty takes—turns out to be just the beginning. Then you have to take the tape (and in this predigital instance, we were still talking about spool upon spool of the unwieldy acetate stuff) into the studio, and day after day, night after night, you and the engineers pore over the tapes, snipping a syllable here, an ambient pause there, an intook breath, an exhaled exclamation, razor-cutting and Scotch-splicing the most nearly immaculate possible performance into existence out of thin, or rather thick, thick air.

So don't talk to me about Popocatepetl. Believe me, I know from Popocatepetl. Sometimes, still, to this day, I dream Popocatepetl.

And hearing the gentle anchorfolk spraining their tongues in their mangled attempts at proper pronunciation, I was brought back to those endless hours in the cramped studio, relentlessly calibrating this "popo" and that "catep" and the other "etl" to the point of bleary stupefaction. Suddenly I remembered one of the noodling exercises by which I'd endeavored to keep myself awake through those long hours, a memory that sent me back to my files, where indeed I managed to retrieve the document in question, a painstaking back-of-an-envelope transliteration of my grandfather's *Geographical Fugue* into a more contemporary idiom—a medical fugue, to be specific, to wit:

## MEDICAL FUGUE
an elaboration of Ernst Toch's *Geographical Fugue*
by Lawrence Weschler

Trinidad and the big Mississippi
*Syphilis and the pig trichinosis*

and the town Honolulu
*and the tight tendonitis*

and the Lake Titicaca
*and that clap gonorrhea*

The Popocatepetl is not in Canada
*The psychosomatical are just hysterical*

rather in Mexico Mexico Mexico
*and not reliable liable liable*

Canada Malaga Rimini Brindisi
*Stamina famine and muscular dystrophy*

Tibet Yokohama Nagasaki
*Rickets euthanasia apoplexy*

Trrrrrrrrrrinidad!
*Ssssssssssyphilis!*

Huh, I find myself thinking. I wonder what that would sound like. Probably wouldn't need to change much to bring it up to date: maybe replace "and muscular dystrophy" with "immunodeficiency." Anyway, "psychosomatical" could serve as a good pronunciation guide for "Popocatepetl," in case anybody was asking.

In the meantime, the anchorpeople stammer and flail, and even further down below a grandson fancies and flits.

*POSTSCRIPT:*

IN THE SUMMER OF 2010, as part of an unexpectedly strong revival of interest in all things Tochian, the Jewish Museum in Vienna mounted a full-scale exhibition on the composer and his life, and I took my daughter, Sara—Toch's oldest great-grandchild—to see it. They were calling the show: "Ernst Toch: Life as a Geographical Fugue." And my daughter, who's something of a language and linguistics nerd, much in the style of her great-grandfather, praised the show's organizers on the pun in the show's title. They looked on, pleased but baffled. "'Fugue' and 'refugee,'" she elaborated. "The words share the same root in Latin, *fugio*, *fugere*, meaning to flee, take flight, or go into exile." I could sense Ernst up there, somewhere, smiling.[1]

# Some Probes into the Terrain of Human Rights

## SENTRIES
Photographs by Richard Avedon
(DECEMBER 1993)

> *Task: to be where I am.*
> *Even when I'm in this solemn and absurd*
> *role: I am still the place*
> *where creation does some work on itself.*
> > —from Tomas Tranströmer's "Sentry Duty,"
> > translated from the Swedish by Robert Bly

Tyrannies all over the world exist in the ironclad certainty that people are nothing more than meat on bones. Anything that their subjects are or have beyond that exists at the sheerest whim of the regime. Indeed, the notion that human beings have absolute rights simply by virtue of their humanity—the right, for instance, not to be tortured—arises initially as a wild, untethered assertion in the face of eons of stark evidence to the contrary. But it is a magical assertion.

"We hold these truths to be self-evident, that all men are created equal, that they are endowed by their Creator with certain unalienable Rights, that among these are Life, Liberty and

Bahey El-Din Hassan, Egypt

Florence Butegwa, Zimbabwe

Cecilia Jimenez, Philippines

Yuri Schmidt, Russia

the pursuit of Happiness." The truly revolutionary insight in that declaration is contained not so much in the words "truths," "self-evident," or "created equal" as in the calm self-certainty of those opening words: "We hold." The text does not launch out with "It is manifestly self-evident that" or with some similar construction, as strict logic might seem to dictate. In fact, the self-evidence of the assertion remains hidden, fugitive, immanent at best, until people rise up to embrace it, to hold fast to its insistence (mutually pledging their lives, their fortunes, and their sacred honor in the process). It is holding such truths to be self-evident that first makes them so—and, more specifically, doing so in concert, alongside others.

Forty-five years ago last month, the members of the General Assembly of the United Nations adopted and proclaimed a Universal Declaration of Human Rights. Most of that organization's member states, however, instantly took to dismissing the document's ringing assertions as so many dead words, and it was left to individual citizens in those states, often through public stands of almost preposterous courage, to realize the declaration's most basic premises. Theirs is a labor that remains far short of completion, of course. But fundamental to that work—the foundation on which everything else has risen—has been the simple, endlessly repeated act of bearing witness, of compiling accurate and reliable information on the fate of the victims of the human rights depredations of renegade regimes. Such monitoring has usually had to take place in the very midst of those depredations, and it is almost always very dangerous work.

Each December, the New York-based organization Human Rights Watch commemorates the anniversary of the Declaration of Human Rights by gathering together a dozen or so human rights monitors from countries throughout the world—the very people whose vigilance makes the rest of the human rights movement possible. (Often, their trips to New York constitute the first time these people have ever been out of their homelands. And not infrequently they are prevented from coming at all—as in the case,

Father Matías Camuñas Marchante, Venezuela

Sister Nohemy Palencia, Colombia

Srey Chanphallara, Cambodia

Mary Rock, Israeli-occupied West Bank

*Pieter Loggenberg, South Africa*                    *Monique Mujawamariya, Rwanda*

this year, of China's Liu Gang and Syria's Salama George Kila,
both of whom are in prison.) The sentries come from all walks
of life: lawyers, social workers, peasant organizers, priests. This
year's crew even included an actual sentry—Pieter Loggenberg, a
prison guard at Pollsmoor, South Africa, who helped to found
an organization that monitors living conditions in the depths of
the apartheid regime's security institutions. A fellow-monitor of
Loggenberg's, the Cairo journalist Bahey El-Din Hassan, oper-
ates within perhaps even narrower (and ever narrowing) confines.
The Egyptian Organization for Human Rights, which he heads,
regularly manages to alienate both the Mubarak regime and the
Islamic-fundamentalist movement, upon which that regime has
been lavishing its increasingly extraconstitutional attentions. The
regime shows little patience with Bahey's insistence on the rule of
law, and the fundamentalists have nothing but contempt for such
"cosmopolitan" ravings, either. Nevertheless, Bahey persists.

　　All the monitors have their stories. Rwanda's Monique
Mujawamariya's is typical of those of this year's crew. Trained as a
social worker, she helped found and now directs an organization

that has been painstakingly documenting a pattern of government-sponsored atrocity and slaughter across her small East-Central African homeland. When members of Human Rights Watch visited the country, she led them directly to a recent massacre site. Later, when the delegation was at the airport, preparing to leave, one of its members saw her being pulled aside by the regime's chief torturer. Subsequently reaching her by telephone, the Human Rights Watch people asked what he had wanted. "Oh, he just said that if he sees his name in your report he's going to have me killed," she told them. This was no idle threat: Her face already bears the scars of a car "accident." Understandably alarmed, they asked her what they ought to do. "Why, print it, of course," Mujawamariya replied, without a moment's hesitation. And they did.

Such bravado ought not to work. How can it? How can mere vigilance, the puny insistence on the rule of law in the face of armored, historically entrenched tyranny, ever make any difference? We hold these truths—these truths and nothing else: Aside from them we are naked before power. Nothing is there except the bold, scary insistence that something is there: this ineffable but essential thing called human rights. And yet, when enough people start insisting forcefully enough on those rights, then, over time, a light does begin to shine in the middle of the dark, a substantial light that not only illumines but actually begins to *melt tyrannies*. It's uncanny.

But one should be clear about the nature of that light: The Bible notwithstanding, the Truth by itself never made anyone free. It has always been *people*, sentries like these, witnessing and declaring the truth, who work that magic.

# SWALLOWED UP IN RWANDA
(APRIL 1994)

Monique Mujawamariya, of Rwanda, had always been the one that the people at Human Rights Watch worried about the most. She was in New York City only last December, one of a group of human rights monitors from countries throughout the world who were being honored by HRW on the occasion of the forty-fifth anniversary of the United Nations' Universal Declaration of Human Rights—and indeed, she was one of the monitors I wrote about at the time. She had an almost regal bearing and showed an unnerving poise, especially given the fact that her face bore the scars of an assassination attempt and she had received several death threats since. Because her personal danger was so great, she was chosen to represent the group during a symbolic call on the White House; it was thought that such a highly visible private audience with President Clinton might help shield her once she returned home. When Rwandans shake hands, they sometimes continue to hold the other person's hand; it's as if they were reluctant to abandon contact once it has been made. Monique, completely unaffected, held President Clinton's hand in her gentle clasp for the better part of the ten minutes of their entire meeting. Some people in New York suggested that it still might not be the best thing for her to return to her homeland right away, because of the ferocious tensions rapidly overwhelming her country. But she insisted that those very tensions necessitated her being there, doing her work, and she did go.

In many ways, Monique's conviction grew out of her personal circumstances. The daughter of a Hutu father and a Tutsi mother, she was married to a senior Rwandan Army officer, with whom she had three children. Monique's husband was in

*Monique Mujawamariya, Rwanda*

the habit of beating her savagely, she says, and ten years ago, in an extremely unusual move for a Rwandan woman, she walked out on him, taking her children with her. For several years, she struggled to earn an independent livelihood, finally getting a job as a social worker helping AIDS victims. (In addition to all its other problems, Rwanda is at the very epicenter of that disease's worldwide sway.) She also opened her home as a shelter for battered women and their families, and at one point was feeding seventeen people on her single paycheck.

Monique's involvement in human rights work began in 1990. By that time, Rwanda was in the seventeenth year of the increasingly dictatorial and corrupt regime of Juvenal Habyarimana, a Hutu given to inciting ethnic animosities between the country's majority Hutu and minority (though historically dominant) Tutsi as a way of maintaining his rule. Since a series of terrible massacres around the time of the country's independence, in 1962, hundreds of thousands of Tutsi refugees have been consigned to often squalid camps immediately outside the country's borders, and in October of 1990 the primarily Tutsi Rwandan Patriotic Front, the RPF, launched a military incursion into the country, demanding the liberalization of the country's governance and the right of repatriation for exiled compatriots. Habyarimana responded by jailing ten thousand of his domestic opponents (both Tutsi and Hutu) under horrifyingly primitive and often fatal conditions, and setting off a series of diversionary pograms against outlying Tutsi. It was then that Monique, who had long insisted that such ethnic distinctions swelled to troublesome dimensions among her otherwise pacific countrymen only at the recurrent instigation of venal politicians, threw herself into a struggle grounded in individual human rights—as opposed to, and transcending, group rights. She founded a series of monitoring groups and regularly tabulated the extent of the regime's depredations; when, for example, in early 1992, she heard of a developing massacre outside Kigali, she rushed to the site and then back to the capital, where she shamed a group of diplomats into returning with her to the scene. (Their presence probably saved scores of lives.) In the following months, she displayed ingenuity in forging alliances among human rights proponents both in her own country and throughout the region, and also in getting American and European organizations to coordinate their efforts at intervention. These efforts fueled the ire of the Habyarimana regime against her, and Monique became the target of ever increasing intimidation.

By the end of 1992, she had brought about the visit of an international commission of human rights monitors. A week before the delegation arrived, however, a truckdriver picked up Monique and, in a suspicious incident, proceeded to slam the passenger side of his speeding vehicle into a tree. She was thrown through the windshield, and her face was severely lacerated. But she survived, and a week later, swathed in bandages and still in obvious pain, she was at the airport in Kigali to greet the commission. She handled the logistics for the group throughout the two weeks of their investigation. It was at the end of this visit, as I reported a few months ago, that, as the delegates were boarding a plane to leave, they noticed that Monique was being pulled aside by a military officer, a man who, the delegates say, was notorious as the regime's chief torturer. Once they got to Europe, they called her to ask what he had wanted. "Oh, he just said that if he sees his name in your report he's going to have me killed," she told them nonchalantly. Alarmed, they asked what they ought to do. "Why, print it, of course," Monique replied, without a moment's hesitation. And they did.

Her work continued, and so did the death threats. The more tenuous Habyarimana's grip on power became, the more vigorously he endeavored to stir up ethnic prejudices and animosities toward specific scapegoats. After Monique's return from America in January, she received more threats than ever. A month ago, a regime-affiliated radio station in Kigali regularly began playing a love song about a girl named Monique, and each time the disk jockey cut in and noted that Rwanda had another Monique and she was a different sort altogether, that she had been defaming the country and didn't deserve to live. Monique is a well-known figure in Kigali and, because of the scars on her face, is easily recognizable.

As the situation in Rwanda continued to deteriorate, Monique provided her collaborators abroad with frequent reports. On March 26, she faxed HRW in New York the news that the regime was distributing huge quantities of firearms to its paramilitary "militia," gangs of thugs that Habyarimana had been deploying to carry out acts of violence ever since international monitoring had begun thwarting his traditional recourse to more official organs of power. (Until recently, the militia had been armed only with machetes.) She spoke with dread of the coming weeks, but still refused to consider leaving, even though large numbers of people were now abandoning the capital. (She did send her three children out of the city to stay with a European friend.) On April 3, Monique says, she received her most chilling death threat yet, from her former best friend, the wife of a senior military man, who recited to her, in lurid detail, all the tortures awaiting her—torments so terrible that she assured Monique she would end up taking her own life, which, the caller said, would be best for everyone. By Wednesday, April 6, even Monique was beginning to think that it might be best to leave for a while, but she stayed for one more meeting of her human rights organization. That is why she was in town, and at home, that evening when the presidential plane went down.

Just who shot down the plane bearing Habyarimana and also the new president of neighboring Burundi remains a mystery. The Rwandan Army blames the RPF, but no RPF forces were known to be in the vicinity; in any event, the Presidential Guard quickly sealed off the site and prevented UN forces from inspecting the wreckage.

There has been speculation that Habyarimana was assassinated by rivals in his own regime who were upset either with the way he seemed to be dragging the country back into war or, alternatively, with the possibility that he might finally be moving to implement a peace settlement agreed to last August. (The two presidents had been returning from a conference, brokered by Tanzania, about their respective internal conflicts.) At any rate, Monique immediately foresaw the consequences of the disaster, both for her country and for herself.

Monique's own neighborhood had now almost completely emptied out. She had no car and was suffering from a foot inflammation that left her unable to walk. She called the Canadian general in charge of the United Nations forces that had been billeted in the capital since last year—twenty-five hundred soldiers—and she called people she knew in various embassies, but all those she got in touch with said, perhaps understandably, that they were too busy to send anyone out to get her.

At ten thirty at night, she managed to get a long-distance call through to her friend and colleague Dr. Alison Des Forges, a Buffalo-based historian of Africa, who has been serving as HRW's principal point person on Rwanda. (She had been on the international commission.) Monique gave Alison an update on human rights developments and, incidentally, in passing, on her own situation. Alison urged her to seek shelter at a Jesuit compound about half a mile from her house, but Monique explained that because of her foot she couldn't even walk there. Alison then telephoned colleagues at HRW and elsewhere, and they began pulling out all the stops, trying to get someone to order someone to rescue Monique, but to no avail. Kigali was descending into chaos.

At four in the morning Buffalo time on April 7—ten in the morning in Kigali—Alison received another call from Monique. It appeared that the members of Habyarimana's Presidential Guard were on a rampage, targeting all the dead leader's perceived opponents, whether Tutsi or Hutu—and they were now pouring into her neighborhood. She could hear gunfire all around. Alison and Monique endeavored to maintain hourly contact after that, and Alison's call at five o'clock found Monique huddled in a corner: Members of the Presidential Guard were now methodically ransacking the neighborhood. A few minutes earlier, she had seen them escort three terrified people (one of them a colleague of hers) out of a house two doors away from her own and execute them at a nearby intersection, where their bodies still lay. The soldiers had then left, but who knew if they would be back?

"We continued desperately trying to reach someone who could pressure the UN into sending a personnel carrier over to retrieve her," Alison told me later that day. "But still to no avail. At 6:00 AM, when I reached Monique again, she whispered that the soldiers had returned and were now in the house next door, and that they were just then dragging a boy out. I myself was able to hear a rifle shot, and Monique confirmed that the boy had been killed. While we were still talking to each other—it was about six twenty my time now—she exclaimed, 'They're here! They're coming in!' I urged her to tell them that she was talking to the White House, and to have them talk to me; I urged her to open the door herself, to let them in, to offer them jewelry, money—anything. 'Oh, my God,' she said, interrupting me. 'Please take care of my children. I don't want you to hear this.' And she hung up."

Alison was silent for a few moments. "By coincidence, two of my Belgian colleagues phoned her during the next few minutes. The first got Monique. Then a man took the phone, said hello, and hung up. The second got a man who, hearing the foreign voice, immediately hung up. After that, we kept trying to reach her, but we only got a busy signal."

As of that afternoon, Alison and the people at HRW had almost given up hope that Monique had survived, and they seemed devastated. Monique's boundless energy and unquenchable good cheer had made a singular impression on her colleagues during her New York visit. When one of them asked her at that time how she managed to retain her spirits amid such desolation, she'd replied with an old Rwandan proverb: "Either you float with the foam or you sink in the beer." By Friday morning, papers throughout the world (including the *Times* and the *Washington Post*) were reporting that Monique had in all likelihood been killed.

But Alison hadn't given up. All through Thursday, she had kept calling—the line seemed to have gone dead. But then, at 11:00 PM her time, she got through. The man who picked up the phone this time turned out to be Monique's gardener, and he said that she had somehow managed to escape through her back door as the troops barged in and had hidden out in the bushes of her back garden for the rest of that day. After the soldiers left, that evening, she had crawled back into her house and hidden in its rafters. It took her a while to struggle down and speak to Alison, who now told her to stay put—that she would do what she could to rescue her.

Once again, HRW set about trying to find someone who could go get Monique, but with no better luck. Reports of near-indiscriminate slaughter were flooding the airwaves: The Jesuit compound that Alison had tried to direct Monique to had been raided, and almost all the Africans there had been butchered. UN forces had themselves come under fire: Ten Belgian soldiers were killed trying to defend the Rwandan prime minister, a well-known moderate, and she, too, was killed. Bodies were piling up by the hundreds and then by the thousands.

The phone lines to Monique's neighborhood once more fell silent, this time permanently. Several days went by with no further word of Monique, and again there was a growing sense that there never would be any word. Alison reached a priest in Kigali—a European who had run a modest democratic opposition journal—and as she ticked off the names of those she was most concerned about he said, "Stop, stop, they're dead, all dead." Monique's situation, considering her easily identifiable facial scars and her limp, seemed particularly hopeless.

But then, suddenly, on Monday morning, HRW received word from someone at the UN that Monique had been rescued and was on a plane, bound for Europe. The organization broke into an exultant celebration, the likes of which few of its members could recall. But just as suddenly, six hours later, the same person called back to confess: "Wrong name. Somebody different. We don't have any word on your person."

In some ways, this was the lowest moment of all for Alison and the rest of Monique's friends, at HRW and abroad. The RPF was marching on the capital and a horrendous battle appeared imminent. Hope gave way once more to anxiety. Early the next morning—Tuesday, again at four in the morning—Alison's phone rang. "Alison, I feel terrible." It was Monique, apologizing. "I'm always waking you up like this." She had somehow made it to a hotel in downtown Kigali and was momentarily safe, though the slaughter outside continued. Monique recounted how for three days and nights she had remained hidden in the rafters of her house, with soldiers coming in and out, rummaging around, shooting up the neighborhood. Finally, just a few hours earlier, when she realized that a few soldiers who were encamped in her backyard were starting to dismantle her fence for firewood—and who knew what they intended to torch next?—she decided to venture down. Seeing that the soldiers seemed quite young and were possibly inexperienced, she sneaked into her bedroom, pulled out an old photograph album, took out a wedding picture of herself with her officer husband, and went out into the backyard. She showed the young soldiers the picture, told them that her husband was an important officer who was away at the front, and asked them to take her to a hotel in the city center. The boys discussed the situation among themselves warily—though they didn't seem to recognize her—and then one offered to grant her request in exchange for a hundred thousand Rwandan francs (about seven hundred dollars). She went back into the house, where she had an emergency stash, got the necessary amount, gathered up some of her other possessions, and came back out. The boy loaded her into a jeep and headed downtown. He stopped after a few moments to rob her of all the rest of her possessions, but then, a true gentleman, went on to the hotel. "And, oh, Alison," Monique now said plaintively. "He took your grandmother's brooch, too!" (She was referring to an antique brooch—a legacy from Alison's Czech grandmother—that Alison had given her just before the meeting at the White House, so that she could secure her elegant ceremonial Rwandan gown. After the meeting, Alison had insisted that Monique keep it.)

Once again, Alison and HRW kicked into high gear. They received assurances from the Canadians, the Belgians, and the UN that if Monique showed up at the evacuation site she would be allowed to leave, but, they were told, nobody could possibly get to the hotel to bring her there. And with the battle for Kigali now beginning in earnest, spirits in New York once again began to sag.

Early the next day, Wednesday, April 13, Alison's phone rang: It was Monique, and this time her voice was much clearer. She was calling from Brussels, where she had just arrived, on one of the last evacuation transports out of Kigali. She had yet another astonishing story of bluster and scary improvisation to tell, this one involving a Canadian cleric; a Hutu businessman and his car; a final checkpoint manned with drunken young soldiers who let the car through only because it happened to be being driven by the priest, who had once worked in their home region; a moment's hesitation at the evacuation point; and then, to her great relief, her name showing up on the list of those few Rwandans with permission to join the evacuation. HRW's exertions had paid off after all.

When I reached her the next morning, Monique sounded rested, ebullient, thankful, and at the same time, filled with a sense of urgency. She had already launched into a tight schedule of meetings with international officials, trying to press the cause of her ravaged homeland, and she said she was planning to come to New York in a few days so that she could further press that cause at the UN. She said that what she had witnessed during the previous week was "horrible beyond words," but that it was not random or spontaneous or the inevitable product of age-old animosities. The vast majority of her countrymen were perfectly capable of getting along with one another. No, this horror had resulted from the premeditated policy of a dictatorial regime: "The vast majority of the slaughter in Rwanda this week was perpetrated by small bands of young men who'd been systematically transformed by the regime into killing machines"—*machines à tuer*—"and then unleashed upon the population." Now, she said, the great task was "to prevent the RPF from succumbing to the terrible temptations of vengeance." As for the future, she concluded, the way to prevent such carnage before it even begins is to force regimes to honor human rights in the first place.

*POSTSCRIPT:*

MONIQUE PRESENTLY SETTLED WITH her children in French-speaking Montreal, Canada, where in 1998, she founded a new human rights organization, Mobilisation Enfants du Monde, given over to advocating on behalf of threatened children all over the world.

Alison Des Forges continued to be one of the foremost human rights activists working on the Great Lakes region of central Africa. In 1999, the year she was awarded a MacArthur Fellowship, she published *Leave None to Tell the Story*, widely considered the definitive account of the Rwandan genocide. Her continuing even-handed activism on behalf of human rights in that benighted country earned her the ire of the Paul Kagame's RPF-installed successor regime: By 2008, she had been banned from the country all over again. On February 12, 2009, she died in that freak nightstorm crash of Continental Flight 3407, en route from Newark back to her hometown of Buffalo.

Monique gave one of the most moving talks at Alison's memorial celebration in New York City a few weeks later. "I lived through a very important period of my life with Alison," she declared, with her customary grace and poise. "I shared unforgettable moments with her. I learned from her and appreciated both her deep humaneness and professional qualities. I can say with confidence, now that she has passed over to the other side, 'Alison, you were and you are my angel.'

"When I was asked to speak at this memorial service, I had so much to choose from. I wanted to talk about everything, as if we were all sitting around a cozy fire on a cool autumn night, our hearts overflowing with nostalgia. You are for me a beautiful story, you are part of my story, and I often tell myself that you are my story."

# EXCEPTIONAL CASES IN ROME:
## The United States and the International Criminal Court
(1998)

## I. PRELUDE

*"The Mother of all Motherboards"*

"This is easily the most complex international negotiation I have ever been involved in," Philippe Kirsch, the chairman of the International Conference, convened in Rome in the summer of 1998 and aimed at promulgating, for the first time, an International Criminal Court, commented one afternoon during a rare break in the proceedings. The chief legal advisor to the Canadian foreign ministry, the youthful-seeming Kirsch could claim an improbably vast experience chairing such convocations (in recent years, he'd spearheaded, among others, conferences on maritime terrorism; the safety and deportment of UN workers in the field; refinements of various International Red Cross protocols; and, most recently, nuclear terrorism). As it happened, he wasn't even supposed to be anywhere near this particular process, having been dragooned into his current role, on an emergency basis, when the highly regarded Dutch legal advisor Adriaan Bos, who'd been chairing the painstaking four-year-long preparatory conference (Prep Con) process leading up to the Rome meeting, fell gravely ill a mere three weeks before the opening of the final convocation. "We have representatives here from 162 countries," Kirsch continued, "confronting—many of them for the first time—a draft document of over 200 pages, consisting of 120 articles, and containing 1,300 brackets. That is to say, 1,300 issues which the six Preparatory Conferences couldn't resolve, leaving multiple options to be tackled one by one by everybody gathered here. The 1,300 hardest issues.

"There's the simple linguistic complexity of the undertaking." (Earlier, the head of the drafting committee had related to me a confounding moment when the Chinese delegate had suddenly started objecting to the eventual court's seat being in The Hague—"although, as it turned out, it wasn't The Hague that was bothering him; rather, it was the shockingly inappropriate reference to—how shall I put it?—the court's derrière.") "There's the way we have to interweave all sorts of different legal procedural traditions," Kirsch continued, "for instance the Napoleonic civil law tradition on the one hand, and the Anglo-Saxon common law tradition on the other. The one enshrines an activist investigating judge as the finder of fact; the other favors an adversarial procedure, defense versus prosecution before a studiously impartial judge. The one allows trials in absentia; the other finds such trials utterly abhorrent. And so forth. And that's not even getting into, say, traditions of Islamic law. How does all that get channeled into a single statute?

"And precisely what law is the eventual Court supposed to be enforcing? The Geneva Conventions, the Hague law, the Genocide treaty, the Crimes against Humanity jurisprudence flowing out of the Nuremberg Tribunal—not everyone subscribes to all of those standards, and in any case, much of this body of law exists in so-called 'customary' form, which is to say the degree to which it is actually observed is subject to evolving customary practice, which is in constant flux. This statute, on the other hand, has to be precise, every detail spelled out, all the ambiguities clarified. For example, the law of war with regard to international conflict is considerably more developed than that applying to internal conflicts, even though most conflict nowadays comes in the latter form. There are some countries here that don't want the Tribunal having *any* say over internal conflicts, while others are pushing for a fairly stiff internal conflict regime. Some countries insist on the death penalty while others insist that they will walk out if the death penalty is included. Some countries want the Tribunal to be as much under the Security Council's control as possible—several of the Permanent Five, for example. Others—India, Pakistan—insist on its being completely free of any Security Council role." (There had been a marvelous moment in the Committee of the Whole just that morning when the Indian and the Pakistani delegates had taken to lavishly praising each other for taking precisely that stand. Translation: They both wanted to be entirely free to enter into savage war, no holds barred, with one another, at any moment, without having to worry about their case getting referred to the Tribunal by any meddlesome Security Council.)

"And it goes on and on," Kirsch continued. "How will the judges be chosen? Who will pay for the entire operation? With everything to be resolved in just five weeks. Some countries want the use or even the threat of using nuclear weapons included as a war crime—India, again, for instance—others, such as the United States, would storm out of the conference were that to happen. Trinidad and Tobago started this whole recent phase of negotiations back in 1989 by reviving a long-dormant proposal for a permanent International Criminal Court—only what they wanted it to address was drug crimes, and they still want that. Others want it to cover the crime of aggression, which nobody at the UN has been able to define in fifty years. Others want to include terrorism—but how do you define that?

"Some favor a strong, robust court; others say they do but clearly don't; while others say they don't and mean it. It often depends on who happens to be in power back home at the moment: A fledgling democracy that a few years ago might have been a dictatorship, or the other way around. A country just coming out of a civil war, or just about to go into one. They all look at matters differently, and differently than they might have a few years ago, or might a few years from now. It's incredibly dispersed."

"Like a 3-D chess game," one of Kirsch's lieutenants now interjected, "being played on a rotating board."

"On a rotating *fluid* board," elaborated another.

"And on top of everything else," Kirsch resumed, "this conference is transpiring under a truly unprecedented degree of public scrutiny. The NGOs"—nongovernmental organizations—"are here in force, incredibly well disciplined and coordinated. They've got representatives monitoring all the working groups and even inside the Committee of the Whole." (The General Assembly had passed a special measure earlier this year allowing NGOs unprecedented access into the Committee of the Whole, at which point the press had been allowed in as well.) "Everything is happening in full view. Nothing happens without everybody knowing about it instantaneously. It's really altogether unique."

"People compare it to the land mines process," Alan Kessel, the acting head of the Canadian delegation, who'd dropped by to check up on his compatriot, now interjected, referring to the international campaign that had culminated last year in Ottawa with a comprehensive land mine ban (which the United States, up till now, has pointedly declined to sign on to). "Some of the NGO people sometimes say, 'Well, we can do it like the land mines.' But Land Mines was—I mean, by the end that was a simple on-off switch. Either you were for it or you were against it. This, by contrast, is like a great big motherboard. You touch a switch here, and five lights blink off over there. You attend to one of those, and sixteen flash on over here. This conference has to be the Mother of all Motherboards!"

*Double Vision*

THERE WERE TIMES, SITTING there on the margins of the Committee of the Whole there in Rome, gazing out over the hall and squinting one's eyes in a particular way, that one could momentarily envision the hundreds of delegates and experts gathered there—the blue-black Africans, the turbaned Iranians, the Brits in their Savile Row finery and the Russians in theirs, the Chinese and the Japanese and the Indians, the Americans toting their ever present satchels and briefcases—as a vast convocation of the Family of Man, all gathered together in that one place at last, finally and once and for all, to face down the greatest scandal of the twentieth century, the galling impunity with which millions and indeed hundreds of millions of victims had been hounded to their deaths, and to proclaim, on the cusp of the new millennium, in the firmest possible voice, "Never Again!"—to proclaim it and mean it *and make it so*: that never again would victims be permitted to sink like that into oblivion, and never again would their tormentors be permitted to harbor such blithe confidence regarding their own indubitable inviolability.

It was possible, squinting one's eyes one way, to see it like that, but then, if you squinted them another, or if you cocked your ear such that you were actually listening to some of the speeches, suddenly the same convergence of delegates could transmogrify from stand-ins for the Family of Man to the representatives of 162 separate and distinct states, each one zealously husbanding its own righteous sovereignty: each one all for lavishing such vigilance on the other guy but damned if they were going to subject themselves or their compatriots to any such intrusive oversight. Not all of them, in fairness, and not all the time, but these were, after all, diplomats first and foremost, whose overriding brief, here as anywhere else (as one of the NGO representatives observed dispiritedly from the margins) was "to protect sovereignty, reduce costs, and dodge obligations."

I mentioned that double vision one afternoon to a young lawyer on an important Southern hemisphere delegation, a veteran of the Prep Con process and one of the most energetic presences in the working-group trenches, and he noted that many of the delegates experienced themselves in a similarly doubled light. "Especially among some of the younger, middle- and lower-ranking delegates," he said, "many of whom start out as the representative of Country X to the ICC Diplomatic Conference but slowly find their allegiances shifting, so that they become rather the delegate of the ICC Conference back to their foreign ministry, and presently, even, a sort of secret agent, burrowing toward a successful outcome. 'My minister says this,' they'll tell you, 'but I think if you propose it this other way, he won't notice, and we can still accomplish the same purpose.' That sort of thing."

I was struck by the similarity of that sort of drama to accounts I'd read of the American Constitutional Convention of 1787–8, and indeed I often had the sense of being witness to a parallel sort of historic undertaking. Just as back then fiercely independent states were being enjoined to surrender part of their precious sovereignty to an as yet inchoate united entity and were doing so at best grudgingly (insisting on the primacy of "state's rights" to the very end—an insistence that could arise out of an honest concern for the more authentic, responsive kind of governance available at the more localized level, but could just as easily arise out of more perverse imperatives, such as the desire to preserve the institution of slavery), so the nation-states gathered in Rome seemed driven by a similar amalgam of authentic and then more suspect misgivings.

## II. THE ROME PROCESS

*Conference Dynamics*
FOR THE FIRST THREE weeks of the Conference, Chairman Kirsch and his multinational associates in the Conference's executive Bureau maintained an almost studied aloofness, allowing the delegates to flounder in the complexities of the evolving document. Although many of the delegates were veterans of the Prep Con process, many more were encountering the draft statute for the first time there in Rome (many of the smaller countries simply hadn't been able to afford to send delegations to the earlier meetings), and

there was a cliff-steep learning curve. In addition, the Rome meeting had elicited the attendance of higher-ranking delegates, and as one of the Prep Con veterans noted wryly, "Such types aren't generally prone to humility. They are incapable, for instance, of saying, 'I don't understand this provision. Could you explain it to me?' Instead they launch into a long, flowery statement detailing their own manifest misunderstanding of the matter, all so as to provoke you, at the very end, into responding with the simple clarification they'd been trying to elicit all along. But it can take forever." The various working groups were plowing through the myriad brackets all the while, struggling toward occasional consensus and moving on. But the tough questions—the independence of the court and its prosecutor, the oversight role of the Security Council, what sort of jurisdiction the Court would be able to extend over precisely what sort of law—remained scarily unresolved, and time now seemed to be fast running out.

At the beginning of the fourth week of a five-week conference, expertly gauging the growing sense of anxiety in the hall, Kirsch launched a series of calibrated interventions—working drafts on major issues in which he attempted to narrow the contours of the sprawling debate, bracketing out extreme positions that weren't any longer likely to elicit consensus, narrowing the options on any given contentious matter to three or four, floating various compromises, narrowing the options still further. It was remarkable to watch the way he seemed to amass authority—stature he'd doubtless be needing to spend later on—simply by being the one who was at last seen to be moving the process demonstrably forward.

By the middle of the fourth week, a range of possible outcomes was beginning to arc into view. One afternoon around that time I worried out a sort of flowchart of such possible outcomes with a Latin American delegate. There seemed at that point to be basically three: On the one extreme, the Conference could completely collapse by the end of the next week, the delegates storming home in unbridgeable anger. At the other extreme, they might emerge with a truly robust court—"Not just a court," in the words of the Canadian Minister of Foreign Affairs Lloyd Axworthy, "but a court worthy of the name." A court with powerful jurisdiction over clean, clear law; a strong mandate; and the wherewithal to carry it out. Wasn't going to happen, was the simple verdict of my Latin American friend: no way.

In between, there were middle possibilities: One branch debouched in a sort of crippled court, a Potemkin court, a court in name only. Something that would look for all the world like a full-fledged court, but whose tendons—as to jurisdiction, independence, authority—would have been surgically severed from the outset. An excuse court: a court to which the Great Powers could refer intractable problems, as if they were actually doing something, confident that nothing would actually get done. The other branch led toward a fledgling court, a baby court, a court whose powers and prospects, at the outset at any rate, would be highly circumscribed. But with the capacity to grow. "Something like your own Supreme Court in the original Constitution," my Latin American friend volunteered. "I mean, if you look at the Constitution itself, the Supreme Court at the outset really had very little authority; it was very weak. For instance, the Constitution itself doesn't grant it the right of judicial review—the power, that is, to rule on the constitutionality of the acts of other branches or of the sovereign states. That was a power it only grabbed for itself, fifteen years later, with Justice Marshall's ruling in *Marbury vs. Madison*. And maybe one could imagine a similar development here. A baby court now that gradually gains the confidence of the world community through its baby steps and then, at some moment of crisis in the future, under appropriate leadership . . . On the other hand, that presupposes that it's given room to grow." This option in turn seemed to sprout two possible suboutcomes: a baby in a spacious crib, as it were—or a baby in a tight-fitting lead box. "Imagine, for instance," my Latin American friend ventured, "if the U.S. Constitution had specifically forbidden the possibility of judicial review." The baby in the lead box. "On the other hand," he smiled conspiratorially, "maybe it would be possible to build some hidden trapdoors into that lead box."

### America's Bottom Line

ONE AFTERNOON, ONE OF the most canny thinkers in the hall, a leading Asian delegate, was parsing some of the 3-D game's more intricate strategic considerations for me: "The thing is," he explained, "you want to create a court that the parties that might need it would still be willing to sign on to. I mean, face it, we're not going to need to be investigating Sweden. So, the treaty needs to be 'weak' enough, unthreatening enough to have its jurisdiction accepted without being so weak and so unthreatening that it would thereafter prove useless. It's one of our many paradoxes."

And yet, paradoxically, those last few weeks, the biggest challenge facing the process no longer seemed to be coming from such potentially renegade states (the ones that might someday "need it"). Rather, they were being presented, with growing insistence, by the United States, whose position was truly incongruous.

The United States had been one of the principal moving forces behind the Nuremberg Tribunal and more recently was a leading sponsor of the ad hoc tribunals on Rwanda and the former Yugoslavia (dozens of lawyers from the Justice Department, the Pentagon, and other government agencies had been seconded to serve stints in the prosecutor's office in The Hague, and several of those were now serving on the U.S. delegation in Rome as well). Secretary of State Madeleine Albright—herself a childhood witness to the Holocaust in Europe—had played a strong role in fostering the ad hoc tribunals during her term as ambassador to the UN and had made the apprehension and prosecution of accused war criminals one of the rhetorical touchstones of her tenure at State. In addition, on several occasions across the preceding years, President Clinton had himself issued forceful calls for a permanent war crimes tribunal, most recently in March 1998, when he addressed genocide survivors and government officials in Kigali, Rwanda.

The U.S. delegation—forty strong and easily the best prepared and most professionally disciplined at the conference—was spearheaded by David Scheffer, Albright's ambassador at large for war crimes issues, who'd clearly been consumed by the subject for some time. Over lunch one afternoon, on the rooftop cafeteria atop the conference proceedings, he became quite emotional, describing a trip he'd taken to Rwanda in December 1997, accompanying Secretary Albright: the horrors he'd witnessed, the terrible testimonies he'd heard. He grew silent for a moment, gazing out toward the Colosseum, before continuing: "I have this recurrent dream, in which I walk into a small hut. The place is a bloody mess, terrible carnage, victims barely hanging on, and I stagger out, shouting, 'Get a doctor—Get a doctor!' and I become more and more enraged because no one's reacting fast enough." He went on, passionately invoking the importance of what was going on down below and insisting on the necessity of its successful outcome.

And yet, increasingly as the Conference lumbered toward its climax, the American delegation seemed gripped by a single overriding concern. Senator Jesse Helms, the Republican head of the Foreign Relations Committee, had already let it be known that any treaty emerging from Rome that left open even the slightest possibility of any American ever, under any circumstance, being subjected to judgment or even oversight by the court would be "dead on arrival" at his committee. The Pentagon was known to be advancing a similarly absolutist line. The State Department, sugarcoating the message only slightly, regularly pointed out how, in Scheffer's words, "The American armed forces have a unique peacekeeping role, posted to hot spots all around the world. Representing the world's sole remaining superpower, American soldiers on such missions stand to be uniquely subject to frivolous, nuisance accusations by parties of all sorts. And we simply cannot be expected to expose our people to those sorts of risks. We are dead serious about this. It is an absolute bottom line with us."

Originally the American team thought it had addressed this concern with a simple provision mandating that the court only be allowed to take up cases specifically referred to it by the Security Council—where the United States has a veto (as do the other Permanent Five: Britain, France, China, and Russia). In effect, the Americans seemed to be favoring a permanent version of the current ad hoc Yugoslav and Rwandan tribunals, one all of whose authority would flow from the Security Council, but without the cumbersome necessity of having to start all over again (statutes, staffing, financing) each fresh time out. The rest of the Permanent Five tended to favor such an approach as well, for obvious reasons of self-interest, but also out of concern over the Security Council's own paramount mission, enshrined in Chapter VII of the UN Charter—the securing and maintenance of world peace.

### The Role of the Security Council

THE ENTIRE ROME CONFERENCE was transpiring under the motto "Peace and Justice," but, as proponents of the Security Council's primacy liked to point out, there would come times when the two might not necessarily coincide, at least not simultaneously. In order to secure peace, the Security Council might need to negotiate with technically indictable war criminals and might even need to extend pledges of full amnesty to them in the context of final peace agreements. At such moments, it couldn't very well have an unguided prosecutor careering about, upending the most delicate of negotiations. Therefore, if the Security Council was "seized" with an issue—as the term of art has it—it needed to be able to forestall, even if only temporarily, any such court interference.

Opponents of this line—many of the countries that didn't happen to have such veto power, and the preponderance of the

NGO observers—liked to cite a Papal remark to the effect that "If you want peace, seek justice," further pointing out that as often as not, historically, a Security Council "seized" with an issue was a Security Council seized *up* and paralyzed. The veto-encumbered Security Council was the very institution, after all, which for fifty years after Nuremberg had proved incapable of mounting trials in the cases of Idi Amin, Pol Pot, or Saddam Hussein (at the time of his genocidal Anfal campaign against his own Kurdish population). More often than not, indeed, over the past fifty years, war criminals have had sheltering patrons among the Permanent Five—Pol Pot, for instance, had the Chinese; the Argentine generals had the Americans (just as, more recently, as many of the NGOs were pointing out, U.S. Ambassador Bill Richardson had actively shielded the Congo's Laurent Kabila from the full force of Security Council oversight into the ghastly massacres involved in the campaign leading up to his installation). In this context, the Yugoslav and Rwandan ad hoc tribunals had been historic flukes (in both instances the product, as much as anything else, of Security Council embarrassment over its failure to take any more concerted action to stop the violence itself). "If we're going to have gone to all this trouble," my Latin American friend commented, "only to have ended up with a slightly more streamlined version of the very failed system we gathered here in the first place to overcome, it will hardly have been worth the bother."

As it happened, it was Lionel Yee, a lanky and self-effacing young government attorney out of Singapore, generally regarded as one of the most supple thinkers in the hall and a master of the 3-D game, who at one point during the Prep Cons came up with a possible route out of the impasse through the simple expedient of turning the conundrum on its head. Instead of requiring Permanent Five unanimity to launch a Court investigation, why not require Permanent Five unanimity in order to block one? More specifically, why not establish a regime where a simple majority

vote of the Security Council could at any time forestall any further Court action on a given case, for a renewable period of up
to twelve months (though any single Permanent Five veto could
derail the stalling effort). After all, Yee pointed out, if a majority of the Security Council, including all five Permanent Five
members, agreed on the peacekeeping necessity of temporarily
blocking Court action, there'd likely be something to it.

The Permanent Five were understandably dubious about
the so-called Singapore Proposal, but in what may have been
the single most important development during the Prep Cons,
in December 1997, Britain, under fresh New Labour auspices
(with their foreign minister Robin Cook's highly vaunted new
"ethical foreign policy"), swung around behind it. In so doing,
Britain became the first and only Permanent Five member to join
onto what was becoming known as the Like-Minded Group, a
loose coalition of some sixty countries (including, among others,
Australia, New Zealand, Canada, most other European countries
with the exception of France, and most of the newly democratiz-
ing countries in Latin America and sub-Saharan Africa) favoring
a more robust court.

### State Referrals and the Independent Prosecutor

TO SUGGEST THAT THE Security Council could *block* certain Court
initiatives was likewise to acknowledge that one might want to
include other ways, besides Security Council referral, of instigating
such cases in the first place. And indeed two further such proce-
dures had been broached during the Prep Cons.

The first would allow so-called state referrals, such that any
state party to the treaty (any state that had both signed and ratified
the treaty) could on its own and by itself refer a complaint to the
Court. Some argued that that ought to be enough: If not a single
one of the, say, sixty countries that were going to have to ratify the
treaty before it went into effect was going to be willing to lodge a

complaint—singling out, say, Hussein's Anfal campaign against the Kurds—then how much merit was such a complaint going to be likely to have?

The NGOs were supporting state-referral; however, from bitter experience over the last several years they'd come to feel that in fact it would not be enough. As it happened, Human Rights Watch had recently spent several years shopping around the very case of Hussein's Anfal campaign, trying to find a single country willing to lodge a formal complaint against Iraq with the International Court of Justice in The Hague (the ICJ lacks the authority to hear criminal cases against individuals but is still empowered to adjudicate certain sorts of claims against entire countries). Despite the widespread publicity and documentation regarding Iraq's manifest depredations (including the indiscriminate use of poison gas), HRW was unable to find a single state willing to pursue the matter. (Most fretted over issues of trade—if not now, in the future—or retaliation, and even some of the Nordic European states in the end backed off, citing domestic political complications.)

For that reason, the "soft coalition" of the NGOs and the Like-Minded Group were additionally advocating an independent prosecutor—a prosecutor's office, that is, empowered to evaluate complaints from any source (nonparty states, party states, NGOs, news reports, the petitions of individual victims)—and to launch investigations or prosecutions on its own (subject, granted, to majority Security Council postponement). Only an office thus empowered, it was argued, would be able to respond to the worst depredations in real time, as they were happening, efficiently and free of political coercion.

Nonsense, countered that proposal's adamant opponents (the United States chief among them). "For one thing," Scheffer suggested to me, "such a prosecutor would be inundated with complaints from Day One. His fax machine would be permanently jammed up. With no filter between him and the world, and no possible way of responding to all the complaints, his selection process would of necessity take on a political tinge. Why did he choose to pursue one matter and not another? Each time he passed on a given matter, he'd lose that much more of his desperately needed authority."

The proponents of an independent prosecutor argued that such dilemmas were no different than those faced by any other prosecutor anywhere in the world—all of whom face decisions like that every day.

"But those prosecutors exist in a framework of accountability," Scheffer pointed out when I rehearsed that argument for him. "States are accountable to their polities; the members of the Security Council are accountable to theirs. There are checks and balances. But who would this independent prosecutor be accountable to?" Scheffer himself didn't specifically raise the specter, but others did: What would prevent such an independent prosecutor from ballooning into a sort of global Kenneth Starr (the independent prosecutor back in the United States who had been hounding Bill Clinton with such arguably frivolous and politically motivated scandals as the Whitewater and Monica Lewinsky affairs)—if not worse. This office, after all, stood to become, as it were, the judicial branch of a world government that lacked an effective, functioning, democratically chosen legislative or executive branch to check and oversee it. An untethered international Kenneth Starr, floating free.

The proponents of an independent prosecutor, for their part, scoffed at the notion. For one thing, the prosecutor—like every member of the Court—would be answerable to an Assembly of State Parties and removable at any time for cause. Certainly at the outset, his budget would be minuscule and he'd be utterly dependent on the good will and cooperation of states (for instance, he'd have no police or enforcement resources of his own). He'd continually be having to demonstrate his upstanding character and evident fairness, since from the outset what authority he'd be able to muster would be largely moral. Beyond that, with regard to any specific case, the way the statute was evolving, he'd have to present his evidence and justifications every step of the way before a supervising panel of judges: He wouldn't even be able to launch an investigation without their authorization.

None of which assuaged the U.S. delegation, which remained fixated on the prospect of that lone American marine—a peacekeeper stationed, say, in Somalia—getting nabbed on some capricious charge and inexorably dragged into the maw of the machine, his fate at the mercy, as it was sometimes phrased, of some Bangladeshi or Iranian judge.

"What is the United States talking about?" an exasperated Like-Minded diplomat virtually sputtered at me one evening over drinks. "This prosecutor is going to have a lot more important things to worry about than some poor Marine in Mogadishu."

Earlier I'd tried a similar argument on one of those incredibly competent and respected midlevel delegates—in this case, a Pentagon lawyer attached to the U.S. delegation: Surely the prosecutor is going to have a lot more important things . . . I said. "Not necessarily," he countered, recalling some recent proceedings at the Yugoslav tribunal where, "At a certain point, word came down from the prosecutor that they really had to find more Croats to indict—there were too many Serbs getting indicted; it was too unbalanced. The prosecutor had to be able to project the appearance of fairness.

"And I can almost guarantee you," he continued, "that a similar thing will happen one day up ahead. Say, it's something like the end of Desert Storm, and the prosecutor has been able to round up and indict dozens of Iraqis. You just watch: The Iraqi government will be lodging all sorts of trumped-up, phony complaints about Americans, and the prosecutor will come under terrific pressure to indict a few of them as well, just to demonstrate his fairness."

I subsequently related the Pentagon lawyer's scenario to my Like-Minded friend, at which point he immediately shot back, "But that's what complementarity is for!"

*The Principle of Complementarity*

COMPLEMENTARITY WAS PERHAPS THE keystone of the entire draft statute, and one would have thought it would have gone a long way toward answering American concerns. For central to the entire enterprise was the notion that national judicial systems would be taking precedence over international ones, and specifically over this Court. That is to say that if a state could show that it was itself already dealing with any given complaint in good faith—investigating and if necessary prosecuting—then those national efforts would automatically trump the International Court's. "In fact," the Like-Minded diplomat continued, "in the best of all possible worlds, one day in the future, the International Court will have no cases whatsoever. Under the pressure of its oversight, all national judicial systems will be dealing in good faith with their own war criminals, at the local level. That would obviously be a better system, and getting to such a point is one of the goals of the entire exercise. In the meantime, democracies like the United States, with highly developed systems of military as well as civilian justice, would invariably be able to shield their own nationals by invoking complementarity." (To further buttress this doctrine of complementarity, the United States had demanded, and the Like-Minded seemed willing to accede to, an entire statute section requiring the prosecutor to notify any investigative target's home state at the outset of its investigation, so that the home state could apply to the Court on complementarity grounds from the very start.)

As it happened, Conference participants were being afforded a high-profile object lesson in the proper workings of a complementarity regime during the very weeks of their deliberations. Earlier that year, a U.S. Marine jet flying too low on training maneuvers in the Italian Alps had tragically sheared the cables on a ski lift, an accident that claimed twenty lives. The plane's crew had initially been charged with manslaughter in Italian courts.

But from the moment that U.S. military prosecutors filed court-martial charges against two of those officers (at the same time clearing two others)—as it happened in the very middle of the fourth week of the Conference—the Italian prosecutor dropped all his charges, exactly as he was required to in keeping with the complementarity provisions in the bilateral "status of forces agreement" governing the presence of U.S. forces in Italy.

"And on top of that," my Like-Minded drinking companion was continuing, "the Americans have the protection of the chapeau"—the preamble, as it were, of the section defining what sorts of crimes could come under the prosecutor's scrutiny. The chapeau stipulated that only "systematic or widespread" instances of such crimes would qualify. The Americans would have preferred "widespread *and* systematic," but still the former wording would likewise have seemed to radically narrow the exposure of any single Marine peacekeeper or group of them who wandered down the wrong alleyway in Mogadishu.

The Americans, however, were not satisfied. As far as they were concerned, there still remained a chance, however slim, that Americans could find themselves exposed on the wrong side of the line. And, as Scheffer insisted to me one afternoon in the halls, almost jabbing his finger into my chest with his intensity, "The exposure of American troops is *really serious business*, and bland assurances about the unlikelihood of any given outcome simply don't move the mail back where I come from."

*The Requirement of State Consent*
WHICH MAY BE WHY the American delegation chose to make its stiffest stand on the question of jurisdiction itself.

The legal issue involved went something like this: Suppose the prosecutor had reason to launch an investigation or prosecution regarding a particular case, either on his own or because he'd had the case referred to him by a state party or an NGO: What conditions, particularly with regard to states that had not yet cho-sen to join onto the treaty, would have to be met for him to be able to move forward?

The Germans favored giving the prosecutor the widest pos-sible latitude in this regard, which is to say *universal jurisdiction*. They pointed out, for instance, that according to the Geneva Conventions, every signatory (for all intents and purposes, all the countries of the world) had not only the right but also the obligation to pursue war criminals from any countries anywhere—and failing anything else, to deliver them up for trial in their own courts. (Granted, in practice, most countries had thus far failed to enact the necessary enabling legislation, but according to their signatures on the Conventions, as well as on the Genocide Treaty, they'd acknowledged such universal jurisdiction over war crimes.) All that was being asked here was that state parties together transfer the rights granted each one of them separately to the Court they were founding in concert. The Germans didn't need to point out that the doctrine of universal jurisdiction had been a cornerstone rationale at the Nuremberg Tribunals—the crimes the defendants there had been accused of were universal in nature, as hence so was the Tribunal's jurisdiction; otherwise all that could have been possible there would have been so-called "victor's justice" (which the Americans have always insisted was not what they were perpetrating). If such a principle was good enough for the Germans at Nuremberg, the Germans in Rome seemed to be saying, it ought to be good enough for everybody else now.

This viewpoint, however, so rattled international lawyers affiliated with several of the delegations—not just the Americans—that by the middle of the fourth week, Kirsch's Bureau had already shaved it from its list of four possible remaining options regard-ing jurisdiction. The broadest of these, the so-called Korean plan, stipulated that in order for the prosecutor to claim jurisdiction over any given case, at least one of the following four states would have to be a state party to the treaty (or at any rate have accepted the jurisdiction of the Court in that particular case):

a) the state where the crime took place

b) the state of nationality of the accused,

c) the state that had custody of the accused, or

d) the state of nationality of the victim.

A narrower second option mandated that the state where the crime took place would have to be a state party. A yet narrower third option stipulated that both that state and the state having custody would have to be state parties. Finally, a fourth option would limit the court's jurisdiction exclusively to accused who were themselves nationals of state parties.

Guess which one the United States was favoring.

*The Soundings Proceed Apace*

KIRSCH WAS INVITING ALL the delegations to stand up and, as briefly as possible, indicate how they were tending with regard to each of the contentious issues highlighted in his paper, including that of jurisdiction. In effect, he was conducting a poll without having to have recourse to any actual vote ("the dreaded V-word," as he'd characterized that prospect for me during our conversation), the polarizing consequences of which could have blown the conference apart at any moment. (He was trying to nudge the process along through a sequence of grudging consensual concessions, culminating only at the very end with a single up-or-down vote.) So, one by one the delegates were rising to lay out their preferences.

It was vaguely unsettling, once again, this tug-of-war between the claims of humanity and those of sovereignty, especially if, squinting your eye, you momentarily chose to visualize the proceedings from the point of view of a victim, or victim's survivor, who might one day be seeking recourse before this Court. For it is, of course, of the essence of genocide itself that it denies the essential humanity of its victims: They are not humans like the rest of us; they are vermin, swine, sub-beings worthy solely of extermination.

Granted, here the question wasn't so much one of humanity as one of standing: myriad seemingly arbitrary hoops an eventual victim would someday have to jump through before being deemed worthy of recognition by this Court (whether his violator was or wasn't a national of a state party, whether the war in which the violations took place had or hadn't been international in scope, and so forth). But in the end it came down to the same thing: victims whose core humanity had already been trampled upon in the crime itself having a good chance of seeing it denied all over again across an abstruse legal process in which, clearly, some stood to be counted as more fully human than others.

Having said that, it was striking how many countries were still coming out in favor of the broadest possible remaining jurisdictional option, and how many of these included countries only recently, if ever so precariously, emerged from their own totalitarian or genocidal sieges. Many of the Latin American delegates, for example, were lawyers whose own attempts to settle accounts with their countries' earlier military rulers had been stymied by amnesties those militaries had been able to wrest, on leave-taking, from their still timorous civilian successors. The president of Korea, whose country was offering that broadest remaining jurisdictional scheme, had himself been a longtime prisoner of one such regime— as had the president of South Africa of another. The pattern recurred throughout the hall. The delegate from Sierra Leone, whose country at that very moment was being ravaged by renegade bands of recently dislodged coup-plotters, got up and delivered a riveting plea for the most robust possible court. Afterward, he commented to me how "for many of the delegates here, these pages are just so much text. For me, they are like a mirror of my life. This article here," he said, flipping through the draft statute, "this is my uncle; this one here, my late wife; this one here, my niece. This is not just paper for me."

On the other hand, there were others—India, Pakistan, most of the Middle Eastern delegations—who were decidedly more suspicious of the Court. ("I had the chief of the Iranian delegation in here a few minutes ago," the head of the drafting committee told me at one point, "and believe me, he's just as spooked at the prospect of having one of his people dragged before an American judge as the Americans are the other way around.")

Kirsch's sounding continued apace—several delegations going for the Korean option, others going for the second or the third—until eventually David Scheffer got up to deliver the American response. On several issues (the degree of coverage of crimes committed in internal wars, for example), the U.S. was notably expansive. (Scheffer even indicated, for the first time, that under certain conditions the U.S. might even be willing to entertain something like the Singapore compromise.) But when it came to the question of jurisdiction, Scheffer was adamant: The U.S. was insisting on the fourth option (that the court be denied jurisdiction over the nationals of any country that had not signed the treaty). Not only, he said, would the U.S. refuse to sign any treaty that dealt with jurisdiction in any other manner, it "would have to actively oppose" any resultant court. Whatever that meant. On the other hand, Scheffer concluded, if this and all "the other approaches I have described emerge as an acceptable package for the statute, then the United States delegation could seriously consider favorably recommending to the U.S. government that it sign the ICC treaty at an appropriate moment in the future."

Scheffer's address sent a chill through the auditorium: Defy us and we'll kill the baby; accede to our terms and, well, we're not sure; we'll see.

More startling yet, though, was the seeming ineffectiveness of the American stand: It didn't seem to be changing anybody's mind. A few minutes after Scheffer's presentation, tiny Botswana got up and spoke of "the breathtaking arrogance" of the American position. And, ironically, it was precisely the sort of line represented by Jesse Helms back in Washington that so seemed to be undermining American authority there in Rome (as it had, last year, during the land mines process in Ottawa). "The U.S. struts around like it owns this place," one NGO observer pointed out. "It doesn't own this place: It *owes* this place." And indeed the fact that the United States was still well over a billion dollars in arrears in its debt to the UN was having a direct impact on the efficient operation of the conference itself: There was a distinct shortage of interpreters on site; documents were having to be sent back to Geneva for overnight translation; inadequate photocopying facilities were causing backups. America's UN debt, furthermore, had had a direct impact on many of the countries it was now trying to influence. Samoa's representative commented to me on how "the Fijians have peacekeepers scattered all over the world, too, and you don't see them worrying about their boys' exposure before this Court. What they do worry about is how, thanks to the U.S. debt, the UN has fallen behind in paying the salaries of those peacekeepers, leaving Fiji itself to have to pick up the tab, which, I assure you, it can afford far less than the U.S." America's implicit threat not to help finance the Court unless it got its way thus tended to get discounted by delegates dubious that it ever would even if it did.

By the same token, many delegates discounted the likelihood of the United States ever ratifying the treaty no matter what. "David Scheffer could draft the entire document, every single word of it," David Matas, a lawyer with the Canadian delegation, commented toward week's end, "and the Senate would never ratify it. It took America forty years to ratify the Genocide Convention. The United States still hasn't even ratified the Convention on the Rights of the Child. There are only two countries in the entire world that have failed to do so—the United States and Somalia—and Somalia, at least, has an excuse: They don't have a government. So, one has to wonder, why even bother trying to meet such demands?"

Beyond that, the logic of the U.S. position seemed all twisted in knots: Still obsessed over this question of the status of its own soldiers in the field, the U.S. was saying that it would endorse only a treaty that included an explicit provision guaranteeing that the resultant court would hold no purchase on the nationals of countries that hadn't signed on to the treaty. So, in other words, clearly, the United States appeared to be signaling the fact that it had no intention of signing on to the treaty—or, at any rate, of ever ratifying it. (Surely, Helms would be able to shoot down any treaty whose only conceivable, if ever so remote, threat to American soldiers would come if the Senate ratified the plan.) And meanwhile, in the words of Kak-Soo Shih, the exasperated head of the Korean delegation, "In order to protect against this less than 1 percent chance of an American peacekeeper's becoming exposed, the U.S. would cut off Court access to well over 90 percent of the cases it would otherwise need to be pursuing. Because what tyrant in his right mind would sign such a treaty? What applies to America also applies to Hussein, and simply by not signing he could buy himself a pass."

"No, no, *no!*" Scheffer insisted, when I brought this argument back to him. "Hussein would still be vulnerable to a Security Council referral under Chapter VII, by virtue of Iraq's being a signatory to the UN Charter."

Except, as my Like-Minded drinking companion subsequently pointed out, bringing the argument full circle, that was the very channel that, thanks to the blocking vetoes and with the sole exceptions of Yugoslavia and Rwanda, had failed to work every other time in the past. "Including, to take just one example, the very case of the Iraqi Anfal campaign, which, to this day, and even in the wake of Kuwait, the Security Council has been unwilling or unable to refer to an ad hoc Tribunal."

Scheffer was unswayed. Furthermore, he pointed out, the U.S. position was grounded both in common sense and in all prior international law, as codified in the Vienna Convention on the Law of Treaties, which stipulates that no state can be held to the provisions of a treaty it has not itself ratified. It would be patently unacceptable for Americans to be held to account before a court and under laws they had themselves not democratically endorsed by way of the actions of their legislative representatives.

But that, too, was nonsense, another Canadian lawyer delegate pointed out to me. "Americans are subjected to courts and laws they didn't vote for all the time. You think an American can come to Canada—or a Canadian go to the U.S., for that matter—break some local ordinance, and then claim, 'Well, I didn't have any say in passing that ordinance, or voting for this judge, so it doesn't apply to me.'" (For that matter, as Michael Posner, the head of the New York–based Lawyers Committee for Human Rights, reminded me, since 1994 the United States has had implementing legislation related to the Torture Convention on its books that allows an American court to go after a visitor from another country for acts of torture he committed *in that other country*, with penalties ranging from twenty years all the way through death.) "As for American military men on official business," the Canadian lawyer continued, "again, it's a moot point, at least as regards this Court, thanks to the complementarity provisions."

*The Option of Opting Out*
FOR HIS PART, THOUGH still unswayed regarding the basic argument, Scheffer, too, hoped the matter might prove moot, at least with reference to the United States, because, as he pointed out, the U.S. delegation was still trying to craft a treaty that the country would one day be able to sign on to, which is where a second jurisdictional issue came into play: the so-called opt-out clause. The United States, along with several other important countries (notably including France, which was just as concerned about the status of its Foreign Legionnaires in the field), was supporting language that would make court jurisdiction automatic for any state ratifying the treaty as regards the crime of genocide. However, at the

time of ratifying, states would have the right to opt out of coverage on war crimes and crimes against humanity, as applied to themselves or their own nationals. (War crimes generally get defined as occurring between warring parties, and in particular refer to the behavior of the established military units; crimes against humanity, by contrast, as first codified in positive law at Nuremberg, refer to specific acts of violence against individual members of a persecuted group, irrespective of whether the individual was a national or nonnational of the warring parties and irrespective, for that matter, of whether these acts were committed in times of war or times of peace. Genocide, in turn, requires that the violence perpetrated be part of a campaign to destroy such persecuted groups "in whole or in part.") Obviously, the United States had no plans for committing genocide anytime soon, and such a clause would provide yet another way of shielding American forces from the Court's scrutiny.

But the arguments here were virtually identical to those regarding the status of nonstate parties. What would prevent Saddam Hussein from opting out as well? For that matter, why would anybody opt in? And what kind of crazy Swiss-cheese jurisdictional regime would such a scheme lead to? William Pace, the head coordinator for the NGOs, parsed the matter in terms of numbers: "Having trouble holding the line with a forum in which five countries, including the U.S., could veto Court initiatives, the U.S. now wants in effect to extend veto power to 185 nations, such that in the end the only forum that would really retain the ability to launch Court action would once again be the one with five vetoes."

## III. THE ENDGAME

*The United States Digs In*

"LOOK," AN INCREASINGLY GRIM and embattled Scheffer was almost shouting at me by the end of the fourth week, *"The U.S. is not Andorra!"* He immediately caught himself up short. *"That's off the record!"* What, I asked—official State Department policy has it that the U.S. *is* Andorra? Laughing, he continued, "No" (by which I inferred that the comment was no longer off the record), "but the point is that the world—I mean, people in there, some of the people in there—have yet to grasp that the challenges of the post–Cold War world are so complex that, in some instances, the requirements of those few countries that are still in a position to actually do something by way of accomplishing various humane objectives simply have got to be accommodated. And you can't approach this on the model of the equality of all states. You have to think in terms of the *inequality* of some states. There have been times, there will come others, when the U.S. as the sole remaining super power, the indispensable power, has been and will be in a position to confront butchery head-on, or anyway to anchor a multilateral intervention along such lines. But in order for that to be able to happen, American interests are going to have to be protected and American soldiers shielded. Otherwise it's going to get that much more difficult, if not impossible, to argue for such humanitarian deployments in the future. Is that really what people here want?"

A few minutes later, Charles Brown, the official spokesman of the U.S. delegation, who'd been listening in on my conversation with Scheffer, pulled me aside. "We're coming to the endgame now," he suggested, "and basically, we're facing three possible outcomes: A Court the U.S. is going to be able to be part of. A Court the U.S. can't yet be part of but could still support—cooperating behind the scenes, assisting in detentions, sharing intelligence, and providing other sorts of background support—and which it might one day still be able to be part of. Or a Court the U.S. will find it impossible to work with and may yet have to actively oppose.

"And, frankly, I don't see how this Court is going to be able to flourish without at least the tacit support of the United States." He pointed to my notepad. "Remember that flowchart you were showing me the other day? The baby in the nurturing crib or the baby in the lead box. It seems to me there's a third possibility. A baby alone, unprotected, in the middle of a vast, open field."


"IT'S AS IF WE'RE being forced to choose," Kak-Soo Shin, the Korean delegate, sighed disconsolately late Friday of the fourth week. "A court crippled by American requirements with regard to state consent, or a court crippled by lack of American participation."

"The Court could definitely live without U.S. participation," insisted an NGO representative at their news conference that same afternoon. "If all the Like-Minded sign on, that's virtually all of Europe, with the exception of France. That's Britain, Canada, Australia, much of Africa and Latin America, all sorts of other countries—there's funding there, support resources, a definite start. And the U.S. in fact would still be pivotally involved through its Security Council referral role. The U.S. claims it wants a weak treaty that could be strengthened later on. But that's being disingenuous: For one thing, the U.S. itself, anxious at the prospect of the process spinning out of control later on, has placed incredibly high thresholds on amending the treaty— in some instances, seven-eighths of state parties would have to ratify any changes. Not just vote for them at the Assembly of State Parties but get their legislatures to ratify them back home. Almost impossible.

"But in any case," he continued, "the main point is a weak treaty won't work. And even more to the point—you've seen the soundings—a majority of those gathered here are calling for a strong treaty. It's a scandal that two of the major democracies—France and America—are the main ones standing against such an outcome."

Hans-Peter Kaul, the head of the German delegation and one of the most passionate proponents of a strong court, was meanwhile addressing a news conference of his own: "We desperately, desperately, *desperately* want the U.S. on board. We are not sure the

Court will even be workable without the U.S. We are willing to walk the extra mile, beyond the extra mile, to meet U.S. concerns. So the problem is not on our side, but on the side of the U.S. Will they be willing to move the slightest bit in order to meet us?"

"The trick," Chairman Kirsch explained to me, "is to emerge with a strong statute with incentives enough that down the line currently reluctant governments may yet want to join on. Because later on it will be far easier to get governments to change their minds than it will be to change the statute itself. And, anyway, no government is going to want to join onto a useless statute."

*Honing the Final Treaty*

BY MONDAY OF THE fifth and final week, Kirsch's Bureau was facing challenges on all sides. The United States was still fuming over state consent. India, dubious over the entire treaty, was itching to provoke a conference-busting vote on the question of the inclusion of nuclear weapons and lobbying the other members of the Non-Aligned Movement hard in preparation. Mexico was still restive over the Security Council's referral powers. Thailand and others were still trying to dilute coverage of internal wars. Faced with all of these challenges, Kirsch was painstakingly guiding the delegates through a second sounding—narrowing the options—and then a third, steadily aiming toward a Thursday night final vote. Informal meetings were burgeoning off to the side, and the truly hot ticket: the informal informals. Nobody anymore seemed to be pausing for sleep.

The United States, meanwhile, was stepping up the pressure. Albright and Defense Secretary William Cohen were known to be phoning their counterparts all over the world, and President Clinton himself was said to be placing some key calls. (A high American delegate assured me, that last week, that Washington was now focused on these negotiations, "at the very highest level," and over "the most specific details.") Some of that pressure was proving remarkably ham-fisted. When Defense Secretary Cohen warned his German counterpart that the treaty as it was currently evolving might force the Pentagon to reconsider the advisability of even stationing troops anywhere in Europe, the Germans, far from crumpling in horror, became righteously indignant and leaked word of the demarche back into the auditorium in Rome, provoking a brief firestorm of outrage and embarrassed denials. The Latin Americans, for their part, were still smarting over a March incident in which the Pentagon had convened a meeting of military attachés from throughout the hemisphere, urging them to pressure their home governments to bend to American treaty demands. Several delegates described for me their enduring annoyance over the ploy, how it had only been with the greatest difficulty, over the past decade, that their civilian governments had been succeeding, ever so precariously, in easing their officers back into thier barracks, and they certainly didn't need any Americans coming around, urging the officers back where they didn't belong.

On Monday night, the Russians hosted an exclusive private dinner limited to top delegates from the Permanent Five, at which tremendous pressure was brought to bear on Like-Minded renegade Britain. When the NGOs got wind of that meeting the following morning and began worrying over a possible wavering in the British line, they instantaneously swung into a typically impressive lobbying blitz, contacting all their affiliates back in England, who in turn started pulling all the right media and parliamentary levers. New Labour's "ethical foreign policy" had already been taking its share of hits earlier in the month (notably over a scandal involving the sale of arms to the warring parties in Sierra Leone), and faced with such a massive upwelling of vigilance, the Brits in Rome appeared to stiffen their position once again.

The Bureau had been aiming to release its final document—the result of hours of front-room soundings and backroom recalibrations—by midday Thursday, but midday came and nothing emerged. Sierra Leone was brokering a final compromise on the coverage of internal wars. The French were cutting a last-minute deal with Kirsch on their main concern: a seven-year opt-out clause, inside the treaty itself, limited to war crimes alone. (Since their interventions seldom included carpet aerial bombing campaigns, it was explained to me, they weren't that worried about the Crimes against Humanity provisions.)

Scheffer and Kirsch held several urgent parlays those last few days; both seemed equally desperate to find some way of bringing America under the Treaty tent. "And it was amazing," one of Kirsch's top deputies on the Bureau subsequently recounted for me. "Nothing could assuage them. We figured they'd be trying to negotiate, to wrest concessions from us in exchange for concessions on their part. Frankly, as of that Monday morning, we figured the independent prosecutor was toast, that we'd have to give him away in the final crunch negotiation. But they never even brought him up. They seemed completely fixated on that Helms/Pentagon imperative—that there be explicit language in the Treaty guaranteeing that no Americans could ever fall under the Court's sway, even if the only way to accomplish that was going to be by the U.S. not joining the treaty. We talked about complementarity, we offered to *strengthen* complementarity—for instance, a provision requiring the prosecutor to attain a unanimous vote of a five-judge panel if he was going to challenge the efficacy of any given country's complementarity efforts. In the unlikely event of their ever getting thus challenged, all they would need was one vote out of five. Not enough. In fairness, they seemed on an incredibly short leash. Clearly, they had their instructions from back home—and very little room to maneuver."

Thursday midday dragged into Thursday evening and then past midnight. Still the Bureau's final draft failed to emerge: In fact it only finally came out Friday at two in the morning. Kirsch was giving delegates less than twenty-four hours to digest the seventy-odd page tiny-typed document and consult with their capitals. They'd all reconvene for a final Committee of the Whole session that evening at seven.

*The Climactic Session: the Final Vote*
"FOUR WORDS. FOUR LITTLE words," Charles Brown, the spokesman for the U.S. delegation, was almost wailing the next morning. "It's incredible. They're within four words of a draft that, even if we couldn't necessarily join, we would still be able to live with. And they're not going to budge. They're going to stuff them down our throat."

On the question of state consent, the Bureau had ended up splitting the difference, stipulating that the Court could exercise its jurisdiction if "one or more of" the following states were parties to the Statute or had accepted the Court's jurisdiction in a given particular case: 1) the state on the territory of which the crime was alleged to have occurred; 2) the state of which the accused was a national.

The NGOs were none too happy with that compromise, either. "They took the Korean plan, split it in half, and left us with North Korea," the indefatigable and endlessly quotable Richard Dicker, of Human Rights Watch's Rome delegation, quipped almost immediately. "By leaving out the state of the victim, and even more crucially the state having custody of the accused, they've spawned a treaty for traveling dictators. Even if France, say, joins the Treaty, the next Mobutu or Baby Doc would still be able to summer blissfully undisturbed on the Riviera and to squirrel away his ill-gotten gains in the local banks."

Which, come to think of it, may have been one of the reasons the French were so avidly pushing for it. My source in the Bureau, on the other hand, told me that actually several countries besides France had been expressing profound misgivings about the custody clause. In Africa, for instance, former allies are crossing over into each other's countries all the time, and things could get quite messy.

But it was the Americans who, more than anyone else, were denouncing the provision, spooking themselves with sordid scenarios. "What if," Scheffer postulated, "the American army finds itself deployed on the territory of Iraq as part of a UN force. Now,

Hussein and his nationals are not subject to this treaty because he hasn't signed on, but what if suddenly he pulls a fast one, accuses some of our men of war crimes, and as head of the territory in question, extends the Court permission to go after them on a one-time basis? And one of the really weird anomalies in all this is that, thanks to the French provision, signatories are able to opt out of such exposure for seven years, but nonsignatories aren't afforded the same option."

"Well," said HRW's Dicker, when I relayed that observation over to him, "maybe then the U.S. had better sign on. For that matter," he continued, "if I were an American GI, I'd much prefer being held in a cell in The Hague to one in Baghdad."

The U.S. was going to have one last opportunity to upend the provision at that evening's final meeting of the Committee of the Whole, and all through the day urgent communiqués were coursing from Washington to capitals throughout the world.

Kirsch brought the meeting to order at seven fifteen in the evening, on Friday, July 17, 1998, and presented the draft text as a whole, hoping to fend off amendments of any sort. It was generally conceded that if even one provision was called into question, the whole intricately cantilevered structure could start coming apart.

India rose to propose an amendment, reintroducing the use or even the threat to use nuclear weapons as a war crime. Norway immediately moved to table the motion. (The Like-Minded had agreed among themselves that Norway would serve this function with every attempted amendment.) Then, in one of the most significant moments at the Conference, Malawi rose to second Norway's motion. In a brief speech of strikingly understated eloquence, Malawi noted how the treaty was a package, everyone had given up something and gained something else, that many of the delegates had sympathy for India's position, but that pursuing the matter any further would no longer advance the process and could threaten to blow everything up. As Malawi sat back down, everyone realized that the Non-Aligneds had fractured, and that India was not going to be able to rely on their votes to subvert the Conference. Chile rose to give another second to Norway's motion; a vote was taken on the question of whether or not to take a vote; and India lost overwhelmingly (114 against, 16 for, and 20 abstentions).

Scheffer now rose up. He looked ashen. "I deeply regret, Mr. Chairman," he began, "that we face the end of this Conference and the past four years of work with such profound misgivings and objections as we have today." Going on to note how tragically the statute was creating "a court that we and others warned of in the opening days—strong on paper but weak in reality," he proceeded to lay out the U.S. position one more time before proposing a simple amendment: that the words "one or more of" be stricken from the nonstate party provision, such that *both* the territory and the nationality would be required.

After Scheffer was seated, Norway immediately rose up to table the motion. Sweden seconded Norway's motion, and Denmark followed suit. A vote was held, and the United States lost in a similarly lopsided vote (113 against, 17 for, and 25 abstentions).

Kirsch looked over at Mexico and Thailand—both had earlier indicated their intention to file amendments, but both now shook their heads: No, they'd pass. There were no other amendments. A mood of heady celebration was rising in the hall. In that case, Kirsch announced, gaveling the meeting to a close, they would all reconvene in half an hour upstairs, in the flag-decked ceremonial chamber, for the final plenary session, for speeches and a final vote.

Filing upstairs, several of the longtime NGO activists were discussing Scheffer in remarkably sympathetic terms. Over the years many had had occasion to work with him, and few doubted the fervency of his commitment and concern. "His instincts were better than his instructions," Dicker surmised. "Would make a good epitaph," someone else observed.

The delegates streamed into the plenary chamber and took their seats amid the flags. There were broad smiles, fierce hugs, a growing swell of elation. Kirsch handed the gavel to the frail guest by his side—Adriaan Bos, the ailing Dutch legal advisor who'd piloted the four-year Prep Con process right up till a few weeks before the opening of the Rome Conference. Bos, beaming, banged the session to order, said a few words, and retired to the side. Kirsch called for a vote. It ended up 120 to 7 with 21 abstentions. Cuba voted for the Statute, as did Russia, Britain, and France. The United States was apparently joined by China, Libya, Iraq, Yemen, Qatar, and Israel in voting against it (at American request the particulars of the vote itself went officially "nonrecorded"). The hall erupted in applause, which grew louder and louder, spilling over into rhythmic stomping and hooting that lasted a good ten minutes, the room becoming positively weightless with the mingled senses of exhaustion and achievement.

"This treaty's flawed," Dicker was saying. "It's badly flawed." He cited another nasty little concession, effected at the last minute—how the chemical and biological warfare provisions had been deleted so as to undercut India's argument about these being poor men's nuclear weapons, unfairly singled out. He was quiet for a moment, gazing out over the scene. "But it's not fatally flawed."

Theodor Meron, one of the world's most distinguished academic experts on international humanitarian law, who'd been serving as a citizen-advisor on the U.S. delegation but now seemed almost visibly to be doffing that official role so as to revert to his private academic persona, walked over and seemed eerily content. "Oh," he said, "these last few hours have been unpleasant, of course. But flipping through the pages of the final document, there's much here that's very good, very strong. The articulation of war crimes: completely solid. And the section on crimes against humanity, which heretofore have existed primarily in the form of precedent and custom: Here they're codified, in a remarkably robust form, and in particular without any nexus to war. This was a big fight, unclear in the customary law, but here it's clearly articulated that crimes against humanity can even take place in the absence of outright warfare: a major development.

As is the section on noninternational war, the most frequent and bloody kind today. The section on gender crimes—rape, enforced pregnancy, and the like—all rising out of recent developments at the Yugoslav and Rwanda tribunals, but codified here for the first time. There's excellent due process language, mens rea, all of this reflecting a strong American influence. The requirement for a clear articulation of elements—what exactly, in clean legal language, constitutes the elements of a crime. Command responsibility, superior orders: American fingerprints are all over this document, and with just a few exceptions, America's concerns were largely accommodated."

"We'll see," my contact in the Bureau was now saying. "It will take three or four years for the Treaty to garner the required number of ratifications and then come into force. Maybe things will change in the U.S.—they'll be able to give it a second look. Or else, once the Court is up and running, sure enough, a few of those nuisance complaints will get lodged against American soldiers and the U.S. will invoke complementarity and, *boom*, they'll be popped right out of there—and the U.S. will cease feeling so threatened. Or there will come some great crisis, and suddenly the U.S. will want to make use of the Court. Time will tell. In the meantime, the Court will be able to start growing."

Jerry Fowler, one of the NGO lobbyists affiliated with the Lawyers Committee for Human Rights, was taking an even longer view: "We didn't get Korea, but what we got is still important: the territorial requirement. Because one of these days there's going to come a Baghdad Spring, and one of the first things the reformers there will want to do is to sign on to this treaty—as an affirmation of the new order, but also as a protection against backsliding. One by one, countries will go through their Springs, they'll sign on, and the Court's jurisdiction will grow. A hundred years from now—who knows?"

A bit later, Fowler's boss, Michael Posner, was gazing back the other way. "Do you realize how long the world has been straining toward this moment—since after World War I, after World War II.

It's extraordinary. Who'd have thought it, even ten years ago, that you could get 120 countries to vote for holding their militaries personally liable before a prosecutor with even a limited degree of independent initiative? I mean, it's unprecedented, it's absolutely unprecedented. One day it may even be seen to have been the birth of a new epoch."


## IV. CODA

*The Father of All Exceptions*
"TODAY, FOR THE FIRST time in history," Forrest Sawyer, sitting in for Peter Jennings, led off that evening's *ABC World News Tonight*, just a few hours later New York time, "a Secret Service agent testified before a grand jury as part of a criminal investigation on a sitting U.S. president." That and adjacent stories regarding Kenneth Starr's ongoing pursuit of the Monica Lewinsky scandal took up the next seven minutes of air time. The developments in Rome never even got mentioned. Nor were they broached on NBC or CBS. Nor did they receive a single column inch in the following Monday's *Time* or *Newsweek*. Monica and Kenneth Starr were everywhere.

It occurred to me how surely the siege by this independent prosecutor must have been coloring president Clinton's own responses to the developments in Rome, leaving him especially wary at the very moment the toughest decisions were having to be made.

On the other hand, surely, there was more to it than that. At various times, there in the halls of Rome, various people would invoke the League of Nations. "If the U.S. walks out on this court," the Syrian delegate assured me, his eyes twinkling with grim satisfaction (he was all for it, he could hardly wait), "it will be like the League of Nations."

Perhaps, I remember thinking, but in that case ought President Clinton be cast in the role of Woodrow Wilson or that of Henry Cabot Lodge?

Of course, the answer, in retrospect, is both. With regard to the Court, Clinton wanted to play both Wilson and Lodge. And not half and half: not a wily Wilson disguising himself as a grimly realistic Lodge, or vice versa. Rather, Whitmanesque, Clinton wanted to contain multitudes. He saw no contradiction in being both Wilson and Lodge, each 100 percent and both simultaneously.

Which is to say that he was approaching the International Criminal Court in much the same way he'd approached just about everything else—gays in the military, national health insurance, campaign finance reform, land mines, Bosnia, global warming—in his presidency.

LESS THAN A WEEK later, on Thursday, July 23, back in Washington, D.C., David Scheffer was called to appear before Jesse Helms's Senate Committee on Foreign Relations. He might have been excused a certain feeling of conceptual whiplash.

For if he was being treated, by the end there in Rome, as a sort of pariah or leper, now back in Washington he was being unanimously praised as a kind of returning hero. Positions that had provoked nary a chord of resonance in the conference hall in Rome were almost drowned in a rising chorus of defiant triumphalism on Capitol Hill.

Senators Helms, Rod Grams, Joseph Biden, and Dianne Feinstein each addressed Scheffer in turn, congratulating him on the fortitude of his resolve and pledging their undying contempt for that monstrosity spawned in Rome. Not one of them mentioned Bosnia or Rwanda or Pol Pot or Idi Amin or the Holocaust or Nuremberg. (Senator Feinstein did wonder about the possible implications for Israel.) They all seemed utterly and almost uniquely transfixed by the Treaty's exposure implications for American troops, vowing to protect them and fight it. Scheffer indicated the administration was reviewing its options. For starters, it would be reexamining the more than one hundred bilateral status-of-forces agreements governing the legal status of American servicemen just about anywhere they might be posted around the globe, with an eye toward tightening them in such a way as to preclude the possibility of any extradition to the ICC.

At that Senate hearing, it became possible to identify what may have been the true underlying anxiety of the American delegation all along, never broached by any of them back in Rome but veritably pullulating just beneath the surface even there. Helms wasn't afraid to name it outright. The status of individual peacekeepers in some Mogadishu alleyway had never been the real concern. Rather, as Helms picked off the examples defiantly, he was going to be damned if any so-called international court was ever going to be reviewing the legality of the U.S. invasions of Panama or Grenada, or the bombing of Tripoli, and holding any American presidents, secretaries of state, defense secretaries, or generals to account.

"I've been accused by advocates of this Court of engaging in 'eighteenth-century thinking,'" Chairman Helms concluded his statement. "Well, I find that to be a compliment. It was the eighteenth century that gave us our Constitution and the fundamental protections of our Bill of Rights. I'll gladly stand with James Madison and the rest of our Founding Fathers over that collection of ne'er-do-wells in Rome any day."

At some level, of course, Helms was way off the mark in his choice and characterization of antecedents. James Madison, for one thing, was a Federalist—with Hamilton, the principal author of *The Federalist Papers*—and as such ranged himself passionately against the nativist states-rightsers of his day and in favor of a wider conception of governance.

But at the same time, it seemed to me that Helms was onto something. "We hold these truths to be self-evident, that all men are created equal, that they are endowed by their Creator with certain unalienable rights": Thomas Jefferson strikingly pitched his Declaration of Independence in an assertion of *universal* human values, an assertion that, cascading down through the ages, from the Declaration of the Rights of Man (1789) through the Universal Declaration of Human Rights (1948), constitutes one of the principal wellsprings of the law feeding into the International Criminal Court.

But at the same time, Jefferson cast those assertions in what was, after all, a declaration of *independence*, of separateness, of American exceptionalism—stirring, defiant themes that had been very much in evidence there in Rome as well.

*POSTSCRIPT:*

WITH THREE WEEKS LEFT to go in his administration, Bill Clinton signed the Rome Statute on December 31, 2000, the last day countries could become parties to the treaty without ratifying it, though, indeed, he made no move, then or at any other time, to try to get the Senate to ratify the document. And two years later, on May 6, 2002, his successor George Bush formally unsigned the treaty, renouncing any American obligations as a signatory. (During the same period, Israel engaged in a similar dance with an identical outcome.)

Notwithstanding such contortions, the International Criminal Court came into being on July 1, 2002, the date its founding treaty, the Rome Statute, entered into force, a sufficient number of states having signed on and ratified the document.

As of March 2011, 114 states had signed and ratified the treaty (including virtually all European, Latin American, and African countries); a further 34 (including Russia) had signed but not yet ratified it. Notwithstanding these impressive numbers, a majority of the world's population remains unrepresented at the Court (not all that surprisingly, when one realizes that China, India, and the United States all remain outside its purview).

The official seat of the Court is in The Hague, though its proceedings may take place anywhere. Under the leadership of its founding prosecutor, Argentinian lawyer Luis Moreno-Ocampo, the Court has pursued investigations into five situations, all of them in Africa: northern Uganda, the Democratic Republic of the Congo, the Central African Republic, Kenya, and Sudan (Darfur). The most high-profile of Moreno-Ocampo's indictments, that of Omar al-Bashir, the president of Sudan, for his alleged involvement in the depredations in Darfur, has also proved the most controversial. African states in particular felt especially put upon and mounted a move to try to get the Security Council to block the prosecutor's efforts in this regard, at least for a year, as per provisions of the treaty, but in the summer of 2008, the Bush administration (having come full, or at least half, circle) let it be known that the United States would veto any such effort.

The Court itself—not to mention America's exceptional attitude toward it—remained very much a work in progress.

Baby steps: baby steps.

# GAZING BACK: THE DISAPPEARED
## (Preface to an Exhibition)
### (2005)

*When she showed me her photograph,*
*she said,*
*this is my daughter,*
*she still hasn't come home*
*She hasn't come home in ten years.*
*But this is her photograph.*
*Isn't it true that she's very pretty?*
*She's a philosophy student*
*and here she is when she was*
*fourteen years old*
*and she had her first communion*
*starched and sacred.*
*This is my daughter*
*she's so pretty*
*I talk to her every day*
*she no longer comes home late, and this is why I reproach*
*her*
*much less*
*but I love her so much*
*this is my daughter*
*every night I say goodbye to her*
*I kiss her*
*and it's hard for me not to cry*
*even though I know that she will not come*
*home late*
*because as you know, she has not come*
*home for years*

*I love this photo very much*
*I look at it every day*
*it seems that only yesterday*
*she was a little feathered angel in my arms*
*and here she looks like a young lady,*
*a philosophy student*
*but, isn't it true that she's so pretty,*
*that she has an angel's face*
*that it almost seems as if she were alive?*

THAT FROM THE CHILEAN poet Marjorie Agosín, in a poem entitled "Buenos Aires."[1] As I write, the citizens of Buenos Aires are
marking the thirtieth anniversary of the launch of Argentina's
devastating Dirty War, which would presently come to see the
disappearance of over thirty thousand of the country's citizens—
the term "disappearance" being both a euphemism and as such
an evasion (for these people didn't just disappear, they were *disappeared*, they were made to disappear) and also a cannily accurate
description of their fate as seen from the point of view of their
surviving friends and relatives: Suddenly, horrifically, unaccount-
ably (and this last was key), these dear people had just vanished
without a trace and were no more. (The thirtieth anniversary of
the launch of such campaigns of repression elsewhere in Latin
America—Guatemala, Brazil, Uruguay, Chile, and so forth—is
already several years past.)

It was a diabolically effective tactic. If, as has sometimes
been noted, repression is the effort by the Forces That Be to
take people who had started behaving like subjects (instead
of the abject objects into which role history had theretofore
long relegated them), to take such people and turn them back
into good little mute and neutered objects once again, one
could hardly have come up with a better one. For the regime
was simultaneously able to eliminate some of its most vividly
effective opponents, to discombobulate the wider opposition

as such (sending friends, relatives, and coworkers who might otherwise be working to overthrow the regime into ever more desperate and futile and isolating efforts at search and rescue), to demoralize the wider society through the whiff of terror such disconcerting tactics evinced—and all the while to deny that it had been doing anything of the sort. These people, after all, had just "disappeared"—how was the regime supposed to know what had happened to them?

As the years passed and one by one the regimes encountered other sorts of difficulty (military defeat, financial debacle, institutional disarray) and began ever so gingerly exiting the scene, they invariably took care to lavish amnesties upon themselves, further shielding their officers from prosecution for any of the depredations they in any case steadfastly denied ever having been party to. And by and large, with certain exceptions, such retrospective amnesties held, and kept on holding, till the point where the statute of limitations kicked in, further shielding any wrongdoers.

A sort of civic normalcy began to take hold, albeit a peculiarly riddled one. For as the great Polish poet Zbigniew Herbert had once parsed things, regarding this sort of situation, in his poem "Mr. Cogito on the Need for Precision,"[2]

*and yet in these matters*
*accuracy is essential*
*we must not be wrong*
*even by a single one*

*we are despite everything*
*the guardians of our brothers*

*ignorance about those who have disappeared*
*undermines the reality of the world*

And a democracy could be many things—could countenance all sorts of special arrangements to secure the cooperation of its various contending interests—but at very least it would seem that it needed to be grounded in reality, a reality continuously undercut by any willed (albeit enforced) ignorance (or amnesiac amnesty) as to the fate of those disappeared.

And yet here is where things began to get interesting, where the tactic of disappearing people doubled back on some of its progenitors. For legally speaking, while torture and mayhem and maybe even manslaughter and murder could be subject to a retrospective amnesty or a statute of limitations, disappearance was different. Disappearance was an ongoing crime: Its victims were still disappeared and hence as subject to legal recourse today as they ever had been. Or so one judiciary after another began to hazard. And at long last accountability of a sort began to seem possible . . .

Still, this legal sort of accountability—this systematic holding of malefactors to account in a court of law—only addressed a part of the putrefying legacy of the era of disappearances (and even that, fitfully and sporadically at best). The culture of these countries as a whole had also been undermined and laid waste by those campaigns, and in this sense it was going to be up to others besides lawyers and judges to begin the labor of reclamation: up to artists and playwrights and novelists and filmmakers.

And that is where this remarkable show comes in—an exhibition (improbably) gathered up and undertaken by a little museum in just about the most northern reaches of a distant (if heavily implicated, notwithstandingly resolutely oblivious) United States, surveying some of the most powerful and unsettling efforts by Latin American artists to come to terms with the toxic legacy of those terrible years.

The exhibition largely speaks for itself, and tremendously eloquently at that. Kudos, brimmingly grateful kudos, to Laurel Reuter and her entire team at the North Dakota Museum of Art, and of course to all of the artists they were able to enlist in their survey.[3] In passing I would note how the truly remarkable thing about Ms. Reuter's curation of the show may not lie in the astonishing caliber of the works she managed to include so much as in the vast range of things she finally resolved to leave out: Across countless trips south over the past decade, Reuter (a rank amateur in the field at the outset, with no special knowledge either of the political history or the languages involved) was exposed to hundreds upon hundreds of responses to the Dirty Wars, many every bit as authentic and heartrending as the ones upon which she finally alighted, though not perhaps as artistically distinguished or convincing. Hers was a truly heroic labor of sensitivity, tact, and discernment.

Beyond that, I would just call attention to certain abiding themes that recur from one artist and country to another and throughout the show. The power, for starters, of brute facticity (of *this* bicycle, *that* x-rayed jaw) in the labor of reclamation. And likewise the force of names—specific names, carefully compiled and respectfully nested. And likewise, and somehow especially evocatively, the power of faces.

I have had occasion elsewhere to call attention to Jean-Paul Sartre's luminous little essay on the face,[4] with its careful elaboration of the complex dynamics of the human look and gaze. Here I would just highlight his concluding remarks, to the effect that "If we call transcendence the ability of the mind to pass beyond itself and all other things as well, to escape from itself that it may lose itself elsewhere; then to be a visible transcendence is the meaning of a face."

By contrast, though, look at what is going on here. For time and again in this show (as with the photo in Marjorie Agosín's poem), we are being confronted with a squandered and truncated gaze, a forward-looking, future-tending gaze that has nevertheless been interrupted, cut short. We, of course, here and now (for the time being, as it were), are forced to embody the future toward which that gaze was directed, but it becomes up to us to reach out, to gaze back, to fulfill and redeem that haunted gaze.

The redemption involved, however, is of a complicated sort. In the immediate wake of the Second World War, in an essay entitled "La guerre a eu lieu" (translated as "The War Has Taken Place," though the title might more accurately and tellingly have been rendered "The War Has Had a Place"), the French philosopher Maurice Merleau-Ponty noted how

*We have learned history, and we claim that it must not be forgotten. But are we here not the dupes of our emotions? If ten years hence, we reread these pages and so many others, what will we think of them? We do not want this year of 1945 to become just another year among many. A man who has lost his son or a woman he loved does not want to live beyond that loss. He leaves the house in the state it was in. The familiar objects upon the table, the clothes in the closet mark an empty place in the world . . . The day will come, however, when the meaning of these clothes will change: once . . . they were wearable, and now they are out of style and shabby. To keep them any longer would not be to make the dead person live on; quite the opposite, they date his death all the more cruelly.*[5]

And I'm likewise reminded of a luminous parable of W. S. Merwin's, his prose poem, "Unchopping a Tree," which begins, ever so self-evidently, "Start with the leaves,"—continuing—"the small twigs, and the nests that have been shaken, ripped or broken off by the fall; these must be gathered and attached once again to their respective places." And it goes on like that ("It is not arduous work, unless major limbs have been smashed or mutilated . . . It goes without saying that if the tree was hollow in whole or in part, and contained old nests of birds or mammal or insect . . . the contents will have to be repaired where necessary, and reassembled, insofar as possible, in their original order, including the shells of nuts already opened.") And so forth for paragraph after hallucinatorily precise paragraph: Every single leaf is reattached, every single branch; tackle and scaffolding are hauled in so as to facilitate the final reattachment of the reconstituted bore to its stump, at which point the tackle and scaffolding start getting pulled away:

*Finally the moment arrives when the last sustaining piece is removed and the tree stands again on its own. It is as though its weight for a moment stood on your heart. You listen for a thud of settlement, a warning creak deep in the intricate joinery. You cannot believe it will hold. How like something dreamed it is, standing there all by itself. How long will it stand there now? The first breeze that touches its dead leaves all seems to flow*

*into your mouth. You are afraid the motion of the clouds will be
enough to push it over. What more can you do? What more
can you do?*

    *But there is nothing more you can do.*
*Others are waiting.*
    *Everything is going to have to be put back.*[6]

Everything put back indeed. But surely the point is the leaves in question are dead and will never again not be dead, the clothes in the closet out of style and shabby, the angel's face in Agosín's poem just that, and only seemingly alive.

The challenge in these societies is to find a way of reclaiming the dead and honoring their presence in a manner that nonetheless still allows room for, indeed creates room for the living. It is a challenge that, time and again, the artists in Reuter's show, and the curator who brought them together, appear to meet and master.[7]

# A BERLIN EPIPHANY
(2006)

ONE COULD SEE HOW it might have been intended to work.

I was in Berlin a few months back for a concert featuring a pair of my grandfather's—the composer Ernst Toch—works, a cello concerto that during the height of the Weimar era had been one of the most celebrated and performed pieces of its time there in that capital of avant-garde music, and then a defiantly vivid and unbowed piano quintet, which he had composed only a few years later, early on in the California exile that would nevertheless, with time, come to entail the slow occlusion of his once vibrant reputation ("I still have my pencil!" he had declared near the outset of his life as a deracinated refugee, though it presently became clear that just having one's pencil wasn't by itself ever going to prove quite enough)—anyway, there I was, witnessing the stirrings of a not insubstantial revival of that reputation (in Berlin of all places!), and I was taking advantage of a break in the rehearsals at the celebrated Kammermusiksaal of Philharmonic Hall off Potsdamer Platz to saunter through the clean, clear late spring afternoon in the direction of Peter Eisenman's recently completed Memorial to the Murdered Jews of Europe, a few blocks away, just off Hannah Arendt Strasse, on the leeside of the lush Tiergarten park, in the shadow of the Brandenburg Gate, a few blocks down from the Reichstag itself, and having read so much about it, I was brimming over with expectation.

And indeed, now there it came looming into view: an austere blockwide low-slung hive of graphite-gray monoliths, monoface rectangular plinths arrayed in a regular perpendicular grid over gently undulating terrain—over three thousand of them spread over nearly five acres, some (near the perimeter) as low as a foot and a half, some further into the hive, where the terrain fell away

into some of its deeper undulations, as high as ten feet, the entire expanse crisscrossed by narrow paths between the parallel rows of vaguely pitched concrete plinths, paths that veritably beckoned those passing by on the busy city sidewalks above into this uncanny maze of vaguely determinate remembrance.

And, as I say, the thing ought to have worked. One could see how, being drawn in, one might thereupon have been expected to experience a sobering sense of solitude, much like the experience of getting lost in a rippling field of sky-high wheat, which the seventy-one-year-old American Eisenman (himself the American son of refu-gees) has cited as one of his very own inspirations for this memorial scheme, "an experience," as he has said, "close to what it's really like to be alone in some place." (And I must say, I do like that source of inspiration, a rippling wheat field with its Homeric undertow of a bountiful harvest ripe, alas, for wholesale scything.)

Maybe it was the sublime afternoon: the crisp cerulean blue of the springtime sky. Though it shouldn't have been that: I mean, perhaps the single most viscerally gut-wrenching representation of the Holocaust I ever experienced came in the 1974 East German film *Jakub der Lunger* (Jacob the Liar), a scene from inside a cattlecar packed to the rafters with foredoomed Jews, trundling relentlessly toward the extermination camp, and at one point the camera assumes their point of view, peering out through the narrow slats of the cattlecar's confining walls, and the view outside turns out to be one of gleaming, lush springtime: teeming green meadows and breezy blue skies. I don't know, somehow I had just always magically assumed that Europe clouded over one terrible morning in September 1939 and the smoke-choked skies hadn't then cleared for nearly six years.

Or maybe it was the oblivious bustle in the busy streets outside, for though Eisenman had spoken, in advance, of his memorial field as being a place where a visitor could fall away from the city and into the solitude of his or her own bare thoughts, in fact, the clean perpendicular vantages rendered the city visible (and audible) at every moment and to every side, and what you in fact kept being forced to vision were the tour-buses lumbering to a stop along the memorial's perimeters and disgorging their cargo of dutiful tourists (talk about echoes of cattlecars!) or the aggressively colorful advertising billboards, blissfully celebrating Germany itself that springtime afternoon (on the eve of the coming World Cup) as "The Country of Ideas!" (I'll say, I couldn't help but think: and some Really Big Ideas at that.)

But what really undercut the effect was all the kids scampering about, the schools having apparently just let out a few moments earlier—the blissed-out teenagers chasing each other all about in a cheery tag team version of hide-and-seek, as come to think of it, how could they have been expected not to (this being the virtual equivalent of an amusement park arcade specifically designed for the purpose), with some of the older ones nipping behind this plinth or that for a furtive hug or peck, moans and giggles and general merriment all around, with here and there heedless German erupting in giddily happy snatches?

"Campo dei Fiori," I found myself muttering. Campo dei Fiori cubed. Which come to think of it might have made a nice title for the entire enterprise.

One evening in the spring of 1943, in Warsaw, the thirty-two-year-old Czeslaw Milosz witnessed the agony of the Warsaw Ghetto Uprising from the city side of the wall, where a carnival fair happened to be in full swing, a chance happenstance that became the occasion for one of the most powerful acts of witness of the bloody century now past. "In Rome," Milosz began his poem, recalling a prior visit to that other town,

> on the Campo dei Fiori
> Baskets of olives and lemons,
> Cobbles spattered with wine
> And the wreckage of flowers.
> Vendors cover the trestles
> With rose-pink fish;
> Armfuls of dark grapes
> Heaped on peach-down.
>
> On this same square
> They burned Giordano Bruno.
> Henchmen kindled the pyre
> Close-pressed by the mob.
> Before the flames had died
> The taverns were full again,
> Baskets of olives and lemons
> Again on the vendors' shoulders.

"I thought of the Campo dei Fiori," he now continued, turning to this more recent experience,

> In Warsaw by the sky-carousel
> One clear spring evening
> To the strains of a carnival tune.
> The bright melody drowned
> The salvos from the ghetto wall,
> And couples were flying
> High in the cloudless sky.

*At times wind from the burning*
*Would drift dark kites along*
*And riders on the carousel*
*Caught petals in midair.*
*That same hot wind*
*Blew open the skirts of the girls*
*And the crowds were laughing*
*On that beautiful Warsaw Sunday.*

"Someone will read as moral," he goes on, anticipating the almost too-easy and evident response (which, frankly, is to say my own),

*That the people of Rome or Warsaw*
*Haggle, laugh, make love*
*As they pass by martyrs' pyres.*
*Someone else will read*
*Of the passing of things human,*
*Of the oblivion*
*Born before the flames have died.*

"But that day," Milosz asserts, speaking for himself,

*I thought only*
*Of the loneliness of the dying,*
*Of how, when Giordano*
*Climbed to his burning*
*There were no words*
*In any human tongue*
*To be left for mankind,*
*Mankind who live on.*

"Already they were back at their wine / Or peddled their white starfish," he now concludes,

*Baskets of olives and lemons*
*They had shouldered to the fair,*
*And he already distanced*
*As if centuries had passed*
*While they paused just a moment*
*For his flying in the fire.*

*Those dying here, the lonely*
*Forgotten by the world,*
*Our tongue becomes for them*
*The language of an ancient planet.*
*Until, when all is legend*
*And many years have passed,*
*On a great Campo dei Fiori*
*Rage will kindle at a poet's word.*[1]

So, yes, there you see why I was thinking, a building rage barely suppressed, of the Campo dei Fiori, the Campo dei Fiori cubed, as I sat there that glorious afternoon, on one of the lower plinths near the perimeter of the Eisenman memorial.

But presently I found myself thinking of another poem, another Polish poem at that, one composed almost exactly fifty years later by that other sublime Polish Nobel laureate, Wislawa Szymborska, and composed (I suddenly came to see) as if in direct response to Milosz's looming masterpiece—"Reality Demands":

*Reality demands*
*that we also mention this:*
*Life goes on.*
*It continues at Cannae and Borodino,*
*at Kosovo Polje and Guernica.*

*There's a gas station*
*on a little square in Jericho,*

*and wet paint*
*on park benches in Bila Hora.*
*Letters fly back and forth*
*between Pearl Harbor and Hastings,*

(How I love that line! Who else but Szymborska would ever think such a thought?)

*a moving van passes*
*beneath the eye of the lion at Chaeronea,*
*and the blooming orchards near Verdun*
*cannot escape*
*the approaching atmospheric front.*

*There is so much Everything*
*that Nothing is hidden quite nicely.*

(And that, too. Quintessential Szymborska, with a side-nod, it seems to me, to W. H. Auden, who in his 1939 elegy to the late W. B. Yeats had famously proclaimed that "poetry makes nothing happen," a line most people read as a cautionary and almost despairing—given the moment of its pronouncement—gloss on the inefficacy of poetry in the actual political world, though one which I for one have always chosen to read slightly differently, which is to say more actively, as if Auden were declaring, precisely, that poetry, and maybe poetry alone, can and occasionally does Make Nothing Happen—a reading with which in turn, it seems to me, Szymborska is herein concurring, though she now trumps that insight with a further one to the effect that even so, the lifeworld, "Everything," is so teemingly rich and various that that poetic Nothing can itself be quite easily breached and overwhelmed.)

*Music pours*
*from the yachts moored at Actium*
*and couples dance on their sunlit decks.*

*So much is always going on,*
*that it must be going on all over.*
*Where not a stone still stands,*
*you see the Ice Cream Man*
*besieged by children.*
*Where Hiroshima had been*
*Hiroshima is again,*
*producing many products*
*for everyday use.*
*This terrifying world is not devoid of charms,*
*of the mornings*
*that make waking up worthwhile.*

She goes on like that, for a few more stanzas ("Perhaps all fields are battlefields, / those we remember / and those that are forgotten") before concluding, in a line that seems to address Milosz directly,

*What moral flows from this? Probably none.*
*Only the blood flows,*

Which is to say, no moral flows, only blood does

*drying quickly,*
*and, as always, a few rivers, a few clouds.*

*On tragic mountain passes*
*the wind rips hats from unwitting heads*

(again here a direct countervailing allusion to Milosz)

*and we can't help*
*laughing at that.*[2]

So that I don't know, I didn't know, sitting there on the perimeter plinth among the whoops and shrieks of those happy German kids: Maybe life does just go on, and that is its blessing (as well as its curse). I mean, there I was in Germany to help witness a renewal of interest in the work of my grandfather Toch, work after all that had been spawned right there in Germany and out of Germany (right alongside everything else).

I reached into my pocket and pulled out a sheet of paper onto which I'd photocopied a letter Toch himself had written to his friend and patron Elizabeth Sprague Coolidge, back in January 1942 (just a bit over a year before Milosz's terrible epiphany by the ghetto wall)—I was intending to quote from it later that evening in my introduction to the coming concert. He was reporting excitedly on some recent investigations he'd himself embarked upon in anticipation of a stint of lecturing at Harvard: "I never expected so much fascination to come from investigations on the nature of musical theory and composition," he wrote.

> Aspects unfolding to me show why the rules of established musical theories could not be applied to "modern" music, why there seemed to be a break all along the line, either discrediting our contemporary work or everything which has been derived from the past. To my amazement, though, I find that those theories are only false in reference to contemporary music because they are just as false in reference to old music, from which they have been deduced, that in correcting them to precision you get the whole immense structure of music into your focus.

Such that, I don't know, as per my grandfather and as per Szymborska, maybe with time, as the whole immense structure of history swings into view, it is the continuities and not the breaches that render themselves most manifest.

But then again, then again . . .

When it comes to Germany, as probably with most people in my generation (and still rightly so?), I will likely always be of two minds.

As to whether kids in the next generation should likewise always be of two minds as regards Germany, as regards that I am also of two minds.

Or then again (the kids in the plinth hive were still playing gleefully as the sun now began to dip toward the horizon) maybe, just maybe not.

# Four Walkabouts

## I.
## WAKING UP TO HOW WE SLEEPWALK
(1982)

ONE AFTERNOON EARLY LAST fall, Knud Jensen[1] opened the gates
of his Louisiana Museum, in Humlebaek, Denmark, on a bluff
overlooking the narrow Oresund Strait, with the Swedish coast
glistening in the distance, to activists in the Danish and Scandi-
navian antinuclear movement. "I'm getting a certain amount of
flak for this from people at other museums," Jensen told me in
his office. Down below, the museum's wide lawn teemed with
visitors in all kinds of attire, carrying banners and posters, gathering around booths, collecting literature, sampling pastries, and
listening to a poetry reading. One group, near the edge of a small
grove, huddled about a folksinger; others meandered through the
museum's glass corridors, from one special exhibit to another.
Everything was part of a calling out for peace, specifically for
nuclear disarmament (this in the context of President Reagan's
insistence that he would soon be stationing a new generation
of Pershing missiles on the European mainland). Thousands of
visitors had converged from as far away as Oslo, Stockholm, and
Hamburg for this day of vigilance and celebration.

"I keep being told," Jensen continued, "that it's not a good thing to mix museumship and politics like this. But I don't know. My coworkers here at Louisiana and I have gone to a tremendous effort to create this sanctuary for art, to see to its long-term preservation, so that it will be here for our children and grandchildren; I guess we consider it part of our curatorial responsibility to do whatever we can to make sure that they will be here to enjoy it."

As we walked among the Calders and the Arps, I noticed that some of the visitors carried black plastic bags filled with air, the necks tied with string. Several people had them, and there didn't seem to be any organizing principle as to who did and who didn't. If you asked what the bags signified, their carriers simply said they'd been given them at the entrance, and then moved on.

The air was beginning to cool, although the sun was still high in the sky when we heard the bells of the neighboring church ring six o'clock. We continued to stroll about, talking and listening. It must have been five after six before we began to notice: First one person and then another, and then dozens all over the grounds, stood frozen, stock-still. Children with their mothers, businessmen, teenagers, farmer types—isolated individuals all over the grounds stood deathly still, limp black bags hanging by their sides.

Only not so still after all. Looking away and then looking again, you'd see that they'd have moved, infinitesimally. They were all moving, in suspension, maybe a few feet each minute—but moving nonetheless, toward the bluff. Afternoon of the Living Dead. By six fifteen, the "zombies" had coalesced into three vague groups: one proceeding out from the cafeteria terrace to the north, another down the gully that bisects the sculpture park, and the last setting out across the wide lawn to the south. All moved slowly toward and then down the face of the bluff. The rest of us looked on; some giggled nervously. Little kids ran up to the zombies and tried to distract them, to no effect. They simply crept on—not even grim exactly, just absent, emptily compelled. The rest of us jock-eyed for position; some took photographs, while others seemed to

become even more transfixed than the zombies and stood motionless, staring at their glacial advance.

By about six forty-five, the three columns had begun to converge at the foot of the bluff. Now they continued on out across the narrow lawn toward the sand and the sea strait, seeming utterly deliberate, utterly mindless. There were about two hundred of them. Their black bags hung limp. Any laughter from the onlookers had stopped. The silence was immediate; it wasn't that we didn't know or weren't thinking about what would happen next—time itself seemed to have congealed. Our anticipations had become as suspended as their gait. We watched.

The walkers kept advancing, inevitably; still, it came as a shock when the first one entered the water. Or, rather, failed to stop at the water's edge. The wavelets slapped across the man's shoes—a few minutes later he was immersed to his knees. All the rest followed him in, mindless but determined; the sea received them. The water must have been cold, but they continued on. As the small waves rose and fell, wet clothes clung to limbs and torsos not yet entirely submerged. This death march became erotic. Cloth outlined sinew: thigh, groin, arm, breast, hair.

One child broke into tears as the water reached his waist. Unable to continue, humiliated, he bounded free of his trance and out of the water into the arms of his grandmother, who'd been watching from the shore—the strangest figure of hope I've ever seen. The others were in the sea up to their necks before they began to turn. The black bags bobbed alongside their heads; now, moving parallel to the shore, the zombies let them go. Downshore a bit, a low canoe dock jutted out from the beach, and the heads now drifted underneath it, beginning finally to arch back inland on the other side. Slowly, one by one, the sleepwalkers emerged from the water and filed—still trance-slow, dripping, shivering violently—through the doors of a large converted boathouse.

While they were still filing in, I entered the boathouse to talk with some of these walkers. Once inside, one by one they snapped to; friends offered them towels and cups of hot rum. It took over half an hour before the last made it through the doors and back to life. Kirsten Dehlholm, the leader of one of the columns, a woman in her midthirties with sharp features, punkishly styled, was drying her hair. "So," she asked, "what did you think of our trained snails?" We were presently joined by Per Flink Basse, a tall young man who'd headed the cafeteria group, and

Else Fenger, a somewhat older woman who'd led the lawn contingent. The three of them, along with architect Charlotte Cecilie (who wasn't present on this occasion), have been working together since 1977, when they pooled their artistic resources (Dehlholm had previously been a sculptor, Basse a set designer, and Fenger a lithographer) in founding the Billedstofteater. "That translates roughly as 'picture theater,'" explained Basse, "or 'theater of the image'. We are basically a group of performance artists interested in a theater built out of spaces, rooms, occasions, images, rather than literary sources. We often try to involve others in our conceptions—we usually stage them in public spaces around Copenhagen. We almost always work in slow motion, usually exploring themes from everyday life—eating, sleeping, walking—slowing things down to help people notice them. In a way that's what we were doing here—trying to find an image, a way of helping people to notice what is going on."

I asked how the performance had come about. "We were contacted several months ago by the people here at Louisiana who were organizing this Peace Festival," recalled Fenger. "We came out to look at the site, since all of our performances arise from the occasion provided by the site. After we got our idea, we sent out about three hundred letters to people who had worked with us before or expressed interest after seeing our work—we've developed quite a network. We said we were planning a performance for the Peace Festival and that the one criterion was that they must not be afraid of water. As you can see, about two hundred people responded."

"We had two meetings at the beginning of the week," Dehlholm took up the story, "and then we performed our snail walk today. Most of us are strangers, but it's incredible the intimacy and fellow feeling this kind of thing brings out. Look at everyone." Throughout the large room people were hugging each other, laughing, stripping out of wet clothes, and putting on dry ones. Any anxious feelings of propriety seemed to have given way.

I walked over and asked one young man, who was punching his head through a turtleneck sweater, why he'd joined the performance. "You know," he said, "a few months ago even, I was more or less ignoring this issue. But Haig and Reagan have really frightened us. When they said it is possible to win a limited nuclear war, we suddenly realized what they're talking about—they meant a war limited to Europe."

"It's funny," said a woman who'd been listening to us, "I had all kinds of associations during the walk besides nuclear war. For one thing I found myself thinking of the boat people in Vietnam. And then it was so strange—I realized that this is one of the narrowest points between Denmark and Sweden, and that it was out of the little village harbors up and down this coast that the Danes smuggled their Jews across to neutral Sweden during the early days of the Nazi occupation."

"I don't consider myself particularly religious," another listener offered. "But I kept thinking of baptism—and death and resurrection." "For me," another woman said, "the whole thing became incredibly compelling—almost primal. It stopped being political and became biological. I felt the pull of the sea: I felt primordially alive, and then this feeling of feeling so alive came back on itself and became powerfully political. Because that, after all, is what we must fight now to save. Nuclear war is a threat, precisely, of primordial proportions."

A few minutes later I was standing out on the wood-plank porch of the boathouse, facing the water, talking with Jensen once again. "It's very difficult, you know," he said, "to find new images which can wake people up to the horrible reality of this nuclear war danger; this is vital work which artists are especially qualified to take on, since their very livelihood is image-making. The whole world seems to be sleepwalking toward a holocaust. Maybe the image of such sleepwalking paradoxically can help to wake people up."

"Do you realize how long we were out there?" said Dehlholm as she joined us on the porch. "Almost two hours! It's incredible: It felt like maybe ten minutes. It was strange," she continued. "At first I felt incredibly alone, cut off, isolated. It was a scary kind of feeling. But then there came this very strong feeling of being with others, of togetherness, of communion. When two hundred people concentrate that strongly, it gives off an aura. Ordinarily you have a thousand ideas kicking around, and at first we were having our various associations, but as time went on, it became like an emptiness for us. Everything became suspended. It was like a meditational exercise.

"No," she said, and paused for a moment, searching for the right word. "No, it became like a prayer."

Twilight was descending. The strait was flat and silver, and on the water two hundred black balloons drifted out toward the gathering night. Dozens of ships, their lights gradually flickering on, coursed north and south through the narrow strait. It occurred to me that this very place—a crucial choke point for Soviet shipping out of the Baltic and into the North Sea—could well be one of the first targets for irradiation were a nuclear war ever to begin, and that the folk laughing and partying in the hangar behind me could well be some of that war's first victims.

"TWO PATHS LIE BEFORE us," Jonathan Schell recently concluded in his remarkable essay, *The Fate of the Earth*. He continued,

> *One leads to death, the other to life. If we choose the first path . . . we in effect become the allies of death, and in everything we do our attachment to life will weaken: our vision, blinded to the abyss that has opened at our feet, will dim and grow confused; our will, discouraged by the thought of trying to build on such a precarious foundation anything that is meant to last, will slacken; and we will sink into stupefaction, as though we were gradually weaning ourselves from life in preparation for the end. On the other hand, if we reject our doom, and bend our efforts toward survival . . . then the anesthetic fog will lift: our vision, no longer straining not to see the obvious, will sharpen; our will, finding secure ground to build on, will be restored; and we will take full and clear possession of life again. One day—and it is hard to believe that it will not be soon—we will make our choice.[2]*

To say that artists and writers today have a particular responsibility with regard to this choice is to acknowledge that in this particular crisis the specter of obliteration bleeds into all areas of human life, and most profoundly into those very areas that have always constituted the life source of culture and civilization. Being, time, vision, presence, copresence, tradition, posterity—the fundamentals out of which art has always sprung—today all of these are in jeopardy. It's simple: Artists are inexorably implicated in the current crisis of vision.

## II.
## DARIO FO ON BROADWAY
(1984)

"IF THEY WEREN'T SO late, we might have been able to get in ten, maybe even a dozen," the producer Bernard Gersten was commenting the other Saturday afternoon as he checked his pocket watch nervously—its digital face was switching over to two twenty-seven. "As it is, we'll be lucky to catch six."

Broadway shows, that is—in two hours.

We were standing in Shubert Alley waiting for Dario Fo, the noted Italian playwright, whose farce *Accidental Death of an Anarchist*, adapted by Richard Nelson, was in previews down Forty-fourth Street, at the Belasco Theatre. Fo and his wife and frequent collaborator, the actress Franca Rame, were apparently still at lunch, but the fact that they were in New York at all was something of a breathless, last-minute plot twist.

"For several years now," Gersten explained, "Fo has been denied a visa to come to this country." Fo and Rame are two of several dozen world figures who have run afoul of a vaguely worded but vigorously enforced subsection of the 1952 McCarran-Walter Act that gives the State Department wide latitude in prohibiting entry into the United States to foreigners whose visits might be deemed detrimental, in principle, to the mental well-being of the nation (or, in practice, to the political well-being of whichever administration happened to be in charge at the moment). There has been a good deal of activity lately aimed at getting the provision repealed—notably an October conference in Washington on Free Trade in Ideas—but Gersten explained that his own recent appeals to the State Department in the specific case of Dario Fo had been more commercial than broadly idealistic.

"Forget the free trade in ideas," he elaborated. "We appealed on the basis of free trade, period. You see, we knew that Fo had been denied a visa twice in the last four years. So, when we applied earlier this fall for permission to bring Fo here to assist in the rehearsals for our Broadway production of *Accidental Death*, we appealed as businessmen: My associates Alexander Cohen and Hildy Parks and I insisted on behalf of our backers, who were bankrolling *Accidental Death* with a $650,000 capital investment, that, even though this might seem a paltry sum by the government's standards, we were claiming the same rights to pursue our business—unrestrained by unwarranted, arbitrary government interference—that are enjoyed by international bankers, arms brokers, or any other buccaneers. After all, living playwrights are almost always present during the early stages of major productions of their plays, and their contributions are invariably vital to the eventual success of the production. For example, last year Arthur Miller traveled to Peking to participate in the Chinese premiere of his *Death of a Salesman*, and that government let him in. The Czech playwright Vaclav Havel recently tried to come to New York to assist in an Off-Broadway production of one of his plays—it turned out he wasn't able to, though, because the Prague dictatorship wouldn't let him leave Czechoslovakia. But here we were dealing with a case where the block was coming from our own supposedly democratic government, and this was seriously jeopardizing our investment."

Gersten's supply-side logic apparently worked, because early last month Dario Fo was granted a one-time visa to assist in rehearsals of his play. But now he was almost fifty minutes late for Gersten's Broadway jaunt. "Dario and Franca are only able to stay here for five days this time; the visas came so suddenly that they couldn't arrange for more time off from rehearsals of their current production back in Italy. But, as theater people, they were eager to see other Broadway productions. There's no guarantee whatsoever that they'll ever be allowed in again, so this seemed the best way of exposing them to the whole range of Broadway." Once again, Gersten anxiously checked his pocket watch.

Finally, a taxi pulled up to the curb, and Fo, Rame, and two interpreters poured out. *"Scusi,"* Fo said, approaching. *"Mi dispiace.*

*Mangiavo*." He is a solidly built gentleman in his late fifties, with a peculiarly malleable face: When dour, he can affect the dignitas of a Roman imperial marble bust (high forehead, jowly cheeks), but this countenance is continually melting into antic, goofy clownishness. Rame, for her part, both projects and consciously parodies the manner—swept hair, elaborate glasses, wicked heels—of a grand Italian starlet. Gersten quickly explained the ground rules of the jaunt, and by two fifty-nine we were all striding toward the Broadhurst Theatre, with its marquee beckoning us to *Death of a Salesman*. "Ah," crooned Rame. "Dusteen Hoffmannn! Oh lah."

Inside, the theatre was dark and the audience hushed. Willy Loman was exhorting Biff, "Go to Slattery's, Boston. Call out the name Willy Loman and see what happens." "All right, Pop." The ensemble was meshing like jeweled clockwork. "You know sporting goods better than Spalding," Loman was insisting. "Ask for fifteen . . . And don't say 'Gee.' 'Gee' is a boy's word." None of which Fo understood (his English is at best rudimentary), and yet he stood there, the light playing across his intent face, his volubility stilled: He was totally in the play. After a few minutes, Gersten walked over, gently tapped him, breaking the trance, and gathered up the rest of us, and then we were back on the street, quickly heading around the block toward the Booth Theatre.

On the way, Rame was explaining to us, with the aid of her interpreter, that she is by nature "a shy and insecure person" but that the State Department's repeated visa denials had made her feel "more secure, stronger." She went on to say, "The fact that such a powerful country was scared of me made me feel better, in a way—better about my work and efforts." Her work with Fo, principally on behalf of Italian prisoners dealing with questions of their legal representation and the conditions of their incarceration, which the two have undertaken in conjunction with an organization that is roughly the Italian equivalent of the American Civil Liberties Union, appears to have been the cause of their visa troubles in the United States. Rame was just starting to describe

Italian prison conditions as we strode through the doors at the Booth—all of us fell silent—and into *Sunday in the Park with George*. George, at work behind a painted scrim, was at the same time trying to persuade a dubious colleague to lobby his La Grande Jatte into the next big exhibition. The colleague presently departed, and George's mistress entered stage right, pregnant and perturbed. She warned him that she was about to go to America. "You are complete, George," she sang, "you are alone . . . Tell me not to go." But it was we who left at that point, hurried along by Gersten. "This is fun!" Fo exclaimed as we headed for the John Golden Theatre, down the street. "Like changing channels on TV."

Inside the Golden, the cast of David Mamet's *Glengarry Glen Ross* was embroiled in high dramatics and gutter slurs: What are the police doing here? Slight burglary last night. Your check was cashed yesterday afternoon. Cashed? Yesterday afternoon? You stupid (a flood of expletives), you just cost me six thousand dollars and a Cadillac. Here, again, the audience seemed completely engrossed. The jaunt was getting to be like walking in on the middle of other people's dreams: the vividness of their experience, the raptness of their attention, a veritable monadology of reverie. We were once more out on the street.

Three thirty-eight. Intermission was just concluding across the way at Michael Bennett's *Dreamgirls*, and we joined the late stragglers as they drifted back into the Imperial Theatre. While we waited for the lights to dim, we asked Fo whether the Italians ever denied entry visas to American writers—and, for that matter, whether in Italy the concept of "un-Italian" existed the way "un-American" does here, as a potent moving force.

"Ah, no," Fo replied, through his interpreter, laughing. "You don't understand. We are just the periphery, and the periphery cannot stay the desires of the Empire." He continued, "Once, long ago, we were the capital of an empire. In the second century AD, a poet from Syria named Luciano di Samosata came to live in Rome and started to complain about things. He had to be taken aside and informed, 'Remember, you are in the heart of the Empire, and you will always be a poet of the periphery.' In many ways, America today reminds me of Rome in the second century—its highest point of economic and territorial expansion but at the same time its highest point of cultural isolation. A curious combination."

As if on cue, the theater darkened and suddenly—wham! bam!—Las Vegas. Horn jabs, drum snares, the glitz and glitter of a lavish stage show: chorus boys and strutting women, sleek black figures swathed in sequins, entire staircases gliding silently by.

"Ah!" Fo exclaimed enthusiastically, back on the street a few minutes later, as Gersten rushed us along. "Such a high level of professionalism, the pacing so exact, everything so clean! Musicals hardly ever succeed in Italy, and it's too bad. They're wonderful."

Diagonally back across Forty-fifth Street, we barged into Tom Stoppard's *The Real Thing*. Jeremy Irons was visiting his former wife: "What you should have said is, 'Duragel; no wonder the bristles fell out of my toothbrush!'" "It's no trick loving someone at their best, the trick is loving them at their worst." Irons moved toward the door—"Henry, you still have your virginity to lose"— and exited stage right. And now the entire stage began to rotate counterclockwise on a huge hidden turntable, seamlessly revealing the set for the next episode, a process repeated a few moments later for another scene change. It occurred to me that Irons and company were going to have to be exceedingly careful backstage not to rotate themselves right into the last scenes of *Death of a Salesman*, which, I realized, were simultaneously being played just beyond the wall before us. Indeed, I was visited by this sudden sense of the entire block between Forty-fourth and Forty-fifth, Broadway and Eighth Avenue, with thousands of people divvied up into seven or eight discrete halls, in many cases facing each other—audiences separated by a thin double membrane of the sheerest contrivance. For a moment, I visioned some god coming down and simply filleting the block of this double spine: The audience at *Sundays* would be left staring at the group assembled for *A Chorus Line*; the throng at *The Real Thing* would find itself gaping across the ravine at Willy Loman's brood.

But before I'd had much time to play out this fantasy, we were once again interrupted by Gersten. "It's three fifty-five," he said. "We've only got a few minutes to make it to the finale of *Chorus Line.*" We veered around the corner, heading toward the Shubert, and then noticed that Dario Fo himself had disappeared. Gersten turned back in exasperation. What had happened? A few dozen yards away, Fo was surrounded by, of all things, autograph-seekers—bungling extras, loose cannons, as far as Gersten's script was concerned. The producer rushed back, apologized to the fans, and retrieved his tardy ward. We all entered the Shubert just as one actress was kissing today goodbye and pointing herself toward tomorrow, and already the entire company was being lined up so that a magnified voice from the audience could single out the audition's winners and losers. The audience was hushed as the choices were revealed: a tide of saddened disappointment, a countertide of excited satisfaction, and then—magic!—the entire company was back, transformed, all spangly and decked out, vaulting into the rousing finale. Fo and Rame soaked it in, smiling broadly. The curtain descended: four eleven. The jaunt was finished.

"Marvel-lous!" Fo exulted, through his interpreter, when we reached the street. "So exciting. The most impressive thing about your theater here is how it is rooted in reality, in the actual world of experience. This is something we often miss in Europe. I am a surrealist, but even the madcap must start out from the real."

I asked Fo whether this fast tour had whetted his appetite—whether he'd like to come back to New York someday, visa permitting, and see some of these plays all the way through.

"Ah, *si*," he exclaimed, not even waiting for his interpreter. "*Si, si!*"[1]

## III.
## TOMISLAV GOTOVAC: NAKED IN ZAGREB
(JANUARY 1991)

TOMISLAV GOTOVAC IS A fifty-three-year-old Yugoslav artist whose work often requires him to get naked. He doesn't particularly enjoy this—"I'm just as shy as anyone else," he was telling me the other day—but he has found nudity to be an essential element of many of his performances, which have established his reputation among the art lovers, bohemians, law-enforcement officials, consulting psychiatrists, party bureaucrats, and general populace of his native Zagreb. The success of his performances—their trenchant wit and subversive spirit—attracted the attention of Milena Kalinovska, a guest curator who's put together an exhibition of politically charged conceptual art, "Rhetorical Image," that is currently on display at the New Museum, in SoHo. A series of photographs in the exhibition show Gotovac stark naked, parading in broad daylight, trancelike, his arms outstretched, through Zagreb's quaint cobblestone streets and squares.

When I called on Gotovac there at the museum, a few days before the opening of the show, he was busy attaching those images and dozens of other pictures, along with certificates and clippings and official papers, to the museum's walls—his contribution is actually a vast collage entitled *Dokumenta (1956-1990)*—but he seemed happy to take a few moments off to talk. Indeed, Gotovac seemed happy about practically everything. This was his first time in New York City, he told me, and the town was giving him a wonderful buzz. "New York's one great big pulsating work of art," he said when I asked whether he'd had a chance to visit any of the other museums. "Who needs museums? Who needs galleries? Everything—the way time moves here, the speed, Central Park, the way light falls on the avenues, the black and white people hurrying down the street—it's like I've walked into a movie."

In addition to doing performance pieces, Gotovac occasionally makes highly rarefied avant-garde films; references to far more conventional movies are scattered through all his work, however. For example, the title of one of his pieces pictured at the museum is *lying naked on pavement, kissing the asphalt (zagreb, i love you!)*, but its subtitle is *homage to howard hawks' hatari! (1962)*. Gotovac explained that "Parading around naked like that, with all the people gawking and the police finally running up to ensnare me, I often feel a lot like the rhino in that movie."

Much of Gotovac's work comes out of the Dadaist ethos of the sixties. "Happenings were especially popular in Eastern Europe, because it was precisely state policy in our countries that nothing ever be allowed to happen," he said. "Those occasions were ways of getting things going." One naked walkabout recorded in the photographs at the New Museum landed him in a police station and eventually provoked a trial: He was sentenced to ten days in jail or a fine. Gotovac appealed the sentence, on the ground that he was an artist and such performances constituted his métier. That's all very well, the appellate judges ruled, but we're artists, too, and fining you or throwing you in jail is *our* métier.

The naked walks are actually quite powerful performances beyond their immediate silly-scandalous aspect. To confront a state built on mass conformity with an assertion of absolute, pristine individuality is, of course, a political gesture, and this one is rendered all the more compelling by the way it offers the individual up to the state in a spirit of raw vulnerability. Performing such a ritual in the middle of Europe, where two generations ago people were being marched naked through town squares on their way to death camps, affords the piece a profound historical dimension. And in contemporary Yugoslavia, where bitter regional and ethnic tensions are proliferating by the week, such a performance has an eerily prophetic aura as well.

Gotovac's entire *Dokumenta* piece, it turns out, is similarly charged. "In the capital of every republic of the Yugoslav federation, there's a Museum of the Revolution, through which schoolchildren, for example, are ritually marched," he recounted. "The museums feature yellowing photos of photos, bad copies of copies of documents, the birth certificates and gradebooks and passports and other official papers of eventual heroes, and documents showing how they were arrested or tortured or martyred, and clippings from newspapers where they are mentioned in passing, and so forth—everything lined up on the walls in a dreadfully boring jumble. In 1986, I simply decided to create a museum of my own revolution, with bad copies of my own documents similarly arrayed." Thus, once again, *Dokumenta* reads as a clever, almost sarcastic provocation—a parody of all those dreadful museums of martyrology—but it's also in dead earnest: What could be more subversive in a Communist mass culture like Yugoslavia's than to insist that an ordinary individual's life might be worthy of an entire display?

Gotovac had to get back to work. I thanked him for taking the time to talk with me, and, as I was leaving, asked if he had thought about performing a naked walk anywhere in Manhattan. He laughed, said no, and added that it probably wouldn't work here. "In Zagreb, when I tell them I'm walking around naked because I'm an artist, they think I'm crazy and seriously consider having me committed," he said. "Here, I'm afraid, if I were to go completely crazy and start walking around naked they'd probably just say, 'Oh, must be some kind of artist.'"

*POSTSCRIPT:*

A FEW WEEKS LATER, Gotovac returned to Zagreb. Within six months, Yugoslavia began tearing itself apart, the Serbian siege of the Croatian town of Vukovar, launched that August, marking the beginning of the most gruesome phase of the carnage, which would then go on, presently spreading to Bosnia, for the next three years.

## IV.
## SHARON LOCKHART: THE NŌ FILM
(2004)

LIKE EVERYBODY SAYS, THAT was a particularly fine Whitney Biennial, the best in years. There were all sorts of pieces I kept returning to—Zak Smith's 755 Pynchon drawings arrayed, row upon row, in a vast, obsessional passion; Eve Sussman's mesmerizing Velasquez film (everybody seemed to love that one); Anthony McCall's projected light forms; Peter Hutton's enthralling evocation of Icelandic land- and seascapes; Rona Horn's photo placard forest (ice floes, bird heads, water, that moody girlboy); some terrific etchings by James Siena; those sumptuous Hockney watercolors. But the piece that's been haunting me the longest, the one I keep returning to in my mind's eye to lounge and dally and drown in, is that damn Sharon Lockhart film, Nō.

Lockhart's offering was one of those films running on a continuous loop in a darkened sideroom that you sometimes come upon at these sorts of shows—the kind that people walk in on, gaze upon indulgently for a minute or two, and then, shrugging with benign indifference, indifference bordering on exasperation if not disdain, abandon for more-entertaining fare. Too bad, because while it's true that nothing much seems to be going on in this one—or rather, whatever's going on certainly seems to be taking its own good time to be on and going—seen in the right way (which is to say at the right pace, which is to say, allowing the time to let the film's stately pace reconfigure your own), it's hard to imagine a more engrossing spectacle.

The camera never moves: The vantage remains the same throughout, becoming progressively more confounding. We are gazing out, at the outset, on a field of rich black loam, stretching back several dozen yards (and about two-thirds of the way up the picture plane) to a wildgrass border, some low trees, and beyond that more fields stretching back toward distant hills

and overtopping it all a fairly bleached out overcast sky. Ambi-
ent sounds: insects, birdcalls, distant traffic . . . And for a good
while, not much else.

Then, at a certain point, from the right side of the far end of
the loam field, a Japanese peasant enters the scene (or anyway, a
man garbed in seemingly timeless Japanese peasant dress), tramp-
ing across the entire far border of the field, from right to left, bearing an armful of hay, which he now proceeds to drop—plop—in a
pile on the far left side of the field. He turns around and starts to
traipse back. And now, a few yards behind him, a Japanese peasant
woman, similarly attired, enters from the left side, carrying her own
burden of hay and traversing the field to the far right side, and just
before reaching the edge of the picture plane (beyond which he,
in the meantime, has disappeared), she drops her hay pile, turns
around and heads back, disappearing beyond the left side of the
plane. Two beats, nothing, and now the man emerges again from
the right side, bearing another armful of hay, which he proceeds,
this time, to drop in the center of the field, equidistant between the
two other piles and right in the middle of our line of vantage. He
heads back, and now she emerges from the left with another armful of hay, traipsing all the way across the field past the left stack
and the middle stack, dropping her load onto the right stack. As
she turns to head back, he follows her from the right, again heavy
laden with hay, and passes the right stack and the middle stack,
depositing his load on the far left stack, and then turns around to
head back. And so forth. From the left and the right the two emerge
time and again, armful upon armful of hay plopped onto one or the
other or the other of the three piles in some intricate if not immediately evident pattern of activity, till all three of the piles have been
graced with the same number of armfuls (six or seven? something
like that)—and then both the man and the woman disappear (right
and left respectively) and for a few beats, nothing . . . .

. . . until suddenly the man emerges, once again from the
right side, though this time maybe ten yards closer to us, traipsing

right to left across the empty field and starting a whole new pile on the far left side (in a straight line, from our point of view, with the first pile ten yards further back); he turns around, heads back; she emerges, also ten yards closer to us, ambling across the field to deposit her armful in a new pile on the right side. And so forth: three new piles in a straight horizontal row, only not quite so massive (only four or five armfuls each this time), and then nothing, two or three beats, and the guy emerges from the right maybe ten yards closer yet to us, bearing his armful, starting a new pile in line (from our point of view) with the others, as does she, and they repeat their dance (only fewer armfuls still this time around, maybe only three or four)—and the effect gets to be intriguing because though the piles are clearly of different volume, from our point of view, the one receding behind the other in foreshortening perspective, they all seem to take up roughly the same amount of visual space, as is true of the next (fourth) horizontal row, even though those three piles (right, middle, and left) contain only two or three armfuls each—and the last, right up close to the bottom of the picture plane (and the peasants have become giants now, traipsing across the foreground of the picture plane right in front of us) contain only one armful each.

There: five horizontal rows of three yellow piles each, or rather three vertical rows of five piles each receding to the far border of the black loam field, seemingly parallel, one along the left edge of the picture plane, one along the right, and the last coursing right down the middle.

Only, wait. That surely can't be right. For while the picture plane is indeed a perfect rectangle, our vantage, obviously, constitutes a triangle, receding in perfect one-point perspective, from the apex of our (and the camera's) point of view. Those seemingly parallel lines of haystacks are in fact converging on us. Triangles bowing into rectangles being one way of thinking about the perplexing maw that is perspective.

Or rather, wait again, for we are speaking here of reverse

perspective. In standard Renaissance perspective, the triangle extends from the right and left base of the picture plane (railroad-track-like) to a single point at the far horizon. (Streeter Blair, the marvelous old outsider painter, a sort of Grandpa Moses still active in the fifties and sixties, once told an interviewer how he used to believe that people had always known about perspective, which, he affirmed, just showed how ignorant he was, since in the old days, obviously, nobody had had railroad tracks so how could anyone have figured it out?) And here, this is the opposite, the lines converging from the far left and right of the infinite horizon coursing across the horizontal middle of the picture plane onto the infinitesimal point that is our point of view there at the base—and, for that matter, come to think of it, there at the top of the picture plane as well. It is as if in terms of this bulging diamond of vision, the infinitesimal points (our viewpoint) at the bottom and top of the picture plane have been stretched and the infinite horizon across the middle of the plane has been compressed, so that we're now left with this finite rectangle, with top, middle, and bottom all being the same width. Strange, odd: and yet how it is all the time!

And now, the two peasants, who have been absent again for a few beats (while we've been trying to puzzle all this out), reemerge, this time from behind us, each carrying a long rake, and they proceed to rip into the first row of haypiles, the one closest to us, scattering the hay in even billowing puffs, all about the foreground of the picture plane. Indeed, by the time they've finished spreading that first row about, the bottom third of the picture plane has been fully blonded over. And now they head back to the next row, and start scattering those three piles: Naturally, it takes them considerably longer. And then the next row, and it takes them longer still—the farther back they go, the narrower (seemingly) the remaining strip of black loam, and yet the longer (of course) it is taking for them to spread it over with hay.

And what had been Brueghel or Millet is now fast becoming Rothko: Talk about color field painting!

Only, of course, the opposite of painting: for though the back and forth raking gestures of the two peasants naturally recall the fine brushwork of a committed painter, with a painting it's the perspectival foreground that soaks up the most paint (across the vastest acreage), while the background, receding toward the horizon line, requires (indeed allows) progressively less and less, verging on nothing at all. And there our two protagonists still toil, at the far end of the field, slaving and slaving away to cover over that merest wisp, the thinnest hint of a remaining band of black loam.

Until, there, finally, it is done: a blond field, not a hint of black loam, stretching all the way back toward the horizon. Forty minutes have passed, with us, completely absorbed, entirely oblivious to their passage. Our sense of what space is, what time is, what perspective is, what painting is, what film is, all turned utterly inside out.

Neat trick.

# Five Further Adventures in the Narrative

## SPLENDORS OF DECAYING CELLULOID:
On Bill Morrison's *Decasia*
(2002)

ONE DAY A FEW months back, a close-cropped, sweet-natured, looming hulk of a young man named Bill Morrison tentatively poked his head into my office and mentioned that a mutual friend had suggested that I just might find his predicament of passing interest. He was a filmmaker, he explained, and had recently completed several years of intensive work on a project that had gone on to find favor in Europe, at Sundance, and even at the Museum of Modern Art. But suddenly it was beginning to seem as if the project had played itself out; it was proving impossible to secure distribution for his film, and he was stymied as to what to do next. Could that possibly be all there was going to be to it? Years of passionate, solitary work, a few well-received screenings, and then nothing—oblivion? He handed me a video and asked, if I ever had a spare moment, that I take a look at it, whereupon, passing me his card, he politely took his leave.

A few nights later I popped Morrison's video into my VCR and within a few further minutes I found myself completely absorbed, transfixed, a pillow of air lodged in my stilled, open mouth.

Now, I'm no particular authority on film, but I do know some-one who is—Errol Morris, the director of such highly acclaimed documentary features as *The Thin Blue Line; Fast, Cheap and Out of Control;* and *Mr. Death.* A short time later, when I happened to be visiting him, I popped the video into his VCR and proceeded to observe as Morrison's film once again began casting its spell. Errol sat drop-jawed: At one point, about halfway through, he stammered (I think only half-facetiously), "This may be the great-est movie ever made."

"MADE," OF COURSE, BEING the operative word.

And not exactly by Bill Morrison, either.

For, as it turned out, my soft-spoken giant of a visitor hadn't exactly shot a single frame in the whole thing. Rather, his film *Decasia* was fashioned entirely out of snippets of severely distressed and heartrendingly decomposed nitrate film stock: decades-old footage, wrested, it seems, from archives all around the country—and at the last possible moment. The sorts of things you hear about all the time from crusading preservationists like Martin Scors-ese, understandably desperate to rescue our nation's rapidly self-immolating film heritage—a worthy goal, to be sure, but who knew the stuff was so beautiful? That decay itself—artfully marshaled, braided, scored, and sustained—could provoke such transports of sublime reverie amid such pangs of wistful sorrow?

A dervish, whirling. A massive bank of film projectors relent-lessly unspooling their reels into long canals of developing fluid. A volcanic crater, belching smoke—a craggy shore, the waves break-ing (and in turn being broken over as waves of decomposition sweep over the image). An indecipherable welter of rotted, cours-ing shapes, and presently, through the pox-veil, a geisha gingerly approaching a screen. A butterfly pinioned against the coruscating surface. A mottled, pullulating mass: the frenzy of moths at twi-light. Semen. Cells dividing.

And then later: a procession of camels making its slow way across a desert horizon. Nuns leading their young wards through a mission colonnade. A man rescued from drowning. A grown woman being dunked into a river for baptism. A crouching Central Asian man, spinning wool. A hand-driven Ferris wheel, somewhere in India. And a merry-go-round. A Luna Park rocket car exploding out of disintegrating chaos. A hag pointing a threatening finger at an appalled judge, and then turning back to us, metamorphosing into sheerest monstrosity. Lovers, melting into embraces that are themselves melting and coming undone. A babe emerging from a womb, and then cradled in a tub of water (developing fluid?). A mine collapse, a shack gone up in flames. A young boxer, gamely jabbing at boiling nothingness. A lonely old man ambling through a mission colonnade.

The empty sky, dappled over with corrosive specks from which gradually emerge sputtering aircraft, droning on, circling, and presently releasing further specks—sperm? no, parachutists, who slowly float down to earth. The projectors unspooling.

The dervish, whirling.

AN AWARENESS OF THE magical photosensitivity of certain salts
has been documented as far back as the thirteenth century, with
Albertus Magnus, but it wasn't until 1839 that William Henry Fox
Talbot was able to announce a method whereby a latent image
could be captured, developed, fixed, and stabilized in a permanent
manner—the Caliotype (progenitor of the modern negative/posi-
tive process). In 1871, an English doctor named Richard Maddox
proclaimed a method whereby a light-sensitive emulsion—photosen-
sitive crystals such as silver nitrate suspended in a warm gelatinous
solution—could be spread over glass plates; and in 1889, George
Eastman in Rochester, New York, trailblazed a further innovation,
replacing the glass plates in his amateur cameras with a base made
out of a thin film of plasticized cellulose nitrate—under the trade
name Celluloid, the first industrially manufactured plastic in the
world. The following year, Thomas Edison used Eastman's nitrate
filmstock as the basis for his Kinetograph, the prototype for the
modern motion picture camera.

Now, cellulose nitrate was marvelous stuff. It was first discovered in 1846 when a vat of organic material—cotton, to be specific—was nitrated in the presence of sulfuric acid. The resultant goop could be extruded into thin transparent strips that subsequently made an almost ideal base—transparent and highly flexible—for mechanical cinematic projection.

The nitric cellulose medium, however, suffered from two serious drawbacks. For starters, it was highly explosive—a close cousin of nitroglycerine, and the basis for gun cotton. Even once its explosive potential had to a certain extent been tamed back, the material remained extremely flammable, and ever more so with the passage of time and its myriad corrosions. Actually, Celluloid filmstock didn't necessarily catch fire more readily than, say, paper—but once it did, it burned far more fiercely (in fact twenty times faster than wood): Twenty tons (the equivalent of eight thousand reels of one thousand feet each) could easily incinerate itself to pure ash in just three minutes! The fact that the burning material gave off copious quantities of oxygen meant that it was virtually impossible to put out—it even burned underwater—and the fact that it also gave off vast quantities of nitric gases meant that those unfortunate enough to inhale its smoke could easily perish from something akin to an acute case of the bends. And these sorts of disasters happened on a fairly regular basis: In 1937, for example, a massive nitrate explosion and fire in Little Ferry, New Jersey, consumed almost all of the silent films ever produced by the Fox Film Corporation. And a similar calamity, in 1977, at the National Archives storehouse in Sutland, Maryland, took out the preponderance of the Universal Newsreel legacy.

But for all their momentary drama, such catastrophes pale in comparison to the slower-motion conflagration afflicting virtually all nitrate filmstock (and nitrate filmstock formed the basis for most filmmaking into the 1950s). Because it is based on that organic cellulose ester—cotton—cellulose nitrate filmstock begins decomposing from the moment it is manufactured, a process that accelerates with the passage of time. As the base decomposes, it releases nitro-gen peroxide gases that, in combination with the moisture from the gelatin, produce acids that both bleach the silver crystals suspended in the emulsion and further hasten the decomposition of the base itself. The silver image—the singularly rich and deep and luminous image that is the glory of nitrate projection—undergoes a brown-ish discoloration, the emulsion becomes sticky, presently exuding a brown frothing foam (known to conservators, quaintly, as "honey") and provoking a pungent exhalation ("the smell of dirty laundry," as one conservator delicately parsed the matter for me). Presently the plastic depolymerizes and the entire film reel begins to congeal (moving through a so-called "donut" into the final "hockey puck" phase), after which the brittle mass disintegrates further into an acrid-smelling reddish powder that is in fact at that point extremely combustible (and has been known to spontaneously ignite at ambi-ent temperatures as low as 105 degrees).

And that's not even to get into the problems caused by the gelatinous foundation of the emulsion, an entirely other sort of organic compound derived from animal skin and bones, not that different from the sorts of mediums used in the petri dishes of biol-ogy labs, and like them, superb conduits for the spread of bacteria and fungi, which naturally have their own pernicious effects.

And all of this is inevitable—it cannot be avoided (although as conservators now realize, the processes of decomposition can be significantly forestalled if the archives are maintained at low tem-peratures and humidity). Sooner or later—and generally speaking, far sooner than we would like—all films crumble into dust.

Not a pretty picture—and one that in fact has already been estimated to have cost the nation's archives more than half of the twenty-one thousand feature films produced prior to 1950. (Curiously, some of the earliest titles have fared better than those produced in the late teens and then across the forties, presum-ably because during those years the higher quality materials and personnel were being diverted to the war effort.) The great and

marvelously sexy twenties film icon Colleen Moore, for example, was fated to outlive virtually all of her films—and such seminal performances as Greta Garbo's in *Divine Woman* and Theda Bara's *Cleopatra* have been relegated to powder, smoke, and rumor. They simply exist no more.

And yet—and this was to be Bill Morrison's key discovery-for all the sorry ugliness of the situation, the actual pictures this relentless process of disintegration was pouring forth could be more than just pretty. Sometimes, indeed, they were ravishingly, achingly beautiful.

BILL MORRISON WAS BORN in 1965 into a middle-class household—his father a lawyer, his mother a schoolteacher—in the Hyde Park-Kenwood area, the integrated neighborhood girdling the University of Chicago and in turn surrounded by severely impoverished, deeply segregated ghettos. The youngest of four and the only boy, he was cherished and doted upon, though somewhat isolate, or rather, withdrawn and self-contained. He was particularly fond of an old grandfather—named Jim Morrison, of all things—who'd rode the rails and explored the West as a youth, occasionally boxing for money. "I had an entirely blessed upbringing," the grandson says nowadays, "such that the seemingly dour nature of much of the art it subsequently engendered is all but inexplicable to me. People who've seen my work usually expect to meet someone in his sixties, all nostalgic for the nineteenth century, and obsessed with death and decay; when they do meet me, they're surprised to find me quite a bit younger, of fairly good humor, and not overly concerned with death at all."

With death, maybe not—but with decay: From his earliest days, Morrison reports, he reveled in the splendors of the urban detritus ranged all about him, enchanted by all sorts of vistas others found ugly or mundane. He loped about, lollygagging, lost in thought ("I remember, once, lying on my back in an abandoned, junk-strewn lot, gazing up at the sky, and a jet came coursing high overhead; I could make out its drone, and I experienced this overpoweringly vivid sense of time's passing, and passing me by"), challenging barriers. A tall kid, early on he took to frequenting late-night jazz clubs, sipping glasses of warm beer spiked with ice (he was never carded). A passable student, he also loved to draw; pen always in hand, he would festoon his notebooks with images of old men. "My parents grew concerned," he recalls. "Who were these people? I didn't know. They'd just appear, and appear everywhere—all over my margins, my desks, my room . . ."

A bit of a latter-day hippie, he presently enrolled at Reed College in Portland, Oregon, a last vestige of the counterculture, where he gravitated toward courses metaphysical ("The last semester of freshman year, I noticed that three of my term papers were dealing with proofs for the existence of God"). But after two years he ditched Reed ("I realized that the doodles to the left of my margins were growing far more interesting than the stuff to their right"), heading off instead to Cooper Union in New York, where he embarked on a four-year course of art studies, double-majoring in painting and filmmaking, reveling in the texture, the tactility of both media. His paintings limned solitary Hopperesque landscapes. Meanwhile, in his filmwork, he began experimenting with subtractive animation—degrading found images (for example, painting over the individual frames with excess developer fluid) until they were barely recognizable.

Graduating from Cooper Union in 1989, Morrison presently gave up painting, because, as he says, "I felt I was experiencing more exciting ideas in film." He secured a small flat and a job washing dishes at the Village Vanguard ("a great job," he insists, "same position Sam Shepherd maintained for years early in his career"), and presently fell in with an innovative young avant-garde performance cooperative, out of Pittsburgh's Carnegie Mellon—the Ridge Theater Company, who were at that time busy mounting a Manson Family opera as part of Lincoln Center's Serious Fun series. The short film, "Night Highway," that Morrison produced as a backdrop to the otherwise fairly lamentable production marked the launch of a marvelously prolific collaboration with the Theater's director Bob McGrath and set designer Laurie Olinder, which has lasted to this day. (Indeed, earlier this summer, Morrison and Olinder were wed.)

Across the next decade, in tandem with such other Ridge theater collaborators as the playwright Mac Wellman, the cartoonist Ben Katchor, and composers like John Moran and the Bang on a Can collective, Morrison fashioned nearly a dozen backdrop shorts, each more ambitious and challenging than the one before. "It's been an ideal situation," Morrison recently said of his collaboration with the Ridge. "I've regularly been afforded a small budget, loose subject matter, superb original scores, an occasion and a deadline, and then as well, an audience and a scene." And, he might well have noted, the opportunity for a steadily growing reputation, especially among avant-garde film cognoscenti and film archivists (whose vaults he was regularly raiding in search of obscure stock footage).

The relationship with these latter deepened even more markedly, later in the decade, when Morrison embarked on his most ambitious project up to that point, an independent short fiction entitled "The Film of Her." Somewhere along the line, Morrison had stumbled upon the story of an obscure, squirrely Library of Congress clerk who, during the early forties, had himself stumbled upon one of the most significant finds in the history of film preservation. For it turns out that copies did in fact still exist of many of the earliest nitrate films, movies whose original negatives and celluloid copies had in the meantime all disintegrated to powder. Owing to a time lag in the evolving copyright laws, there had been no provision for registering proprietary rights to motion pictures as such before 1912—for still photographs, yes, but for motion pictures, no. So producers began filing paper reels with the Copyright office—rolls containing miniature stills of every single frame in their movies. These rolls came to fill entire vaults in the Library of Congress and were about to be thrown out en masse one day in the early forties, when this nebbishy clerk, named Howard Walls, happened upon the scheme and singlehandedly averted disaster, devoting the rest of his life to painstakingly cataloging the collection. (Naturally, someone else subsequently garnered all the credit—and the honorary Academy Award.) The entire saga appealed to Morrison and formed the basis for the dreamy, melancholy short subject, "The Film of Her," with which he emerged in 1997.

And it was while screening that film the following year at the First Annual Orphan Film Symposium meeting, convened at the University of South Carolina in Charleston—home, as it turned out, of a veritable trove of decomposing Fox Movietone newsreels (deposited there a few years earlier by the Twentieth Century Fox corporation, which had been seeking a tax write-off to compensate for the huge profits it was raking in owing to the ridiculous success of its Indiana Jones series, itself a loving homage, when you think about it, to exactly that sort of film)— that Morrison first began thinking about film decay itself as a possible subject, and more than that, as the raw material for a future project.

AS IT HAPPENED, JUST around that time, Michael Gordon, one of the principal composers in the Bang on a Can collective (with whom Morrison and the Ridge Theater Company had recently finished collaborating on the Ben Katchor opera, "The Carbon Copy Building") received a commission to compose a major orchestral piece for premiere by the Basel Sinfonietta as part of the European Music Month in the fall of 2001. Gordon was in some ways Morrison's acoustic doppelganger, entranced by traces of decay and decomposition in music itself. He was fascinated by the slightly out-of-tune and yet more so by the more-out-of-tune-yet, and likewise by every sort of rhythmic distortion or distress. "I am attracted by something really pretty that's at the same time really ugly," he recently related to me, "so that you hear the pretty and you hear the ugly. In my own work I aim for an effect of sweet and

sour—to be able to evoke the sweetness through the sour. I like to take something really beautiful and to mess it up a bit."

Morrison and Gordon caught wind of each other's converging interests and resolved to embark on a cinematic-symphonic collaboration, invoking the model of *Fantasia*, only this time around keying to themes of decay and dilapidation. Morrison returned to Charleston and almost immediately struck it rich. "I managed to dig up the Boxer" (shades of his beloved grandfather) "and the Nuns with their wards at their Arizona mission the very first day. The Boxer footage in particular was unbelievably evocative: The guy—according to the reel's label, his name was Richie—had clearly been jabbing at a punching bag, only for some reason the chemical content of the bag imagery had deteriorated far in advance of the rest of the frame, so that it looked for all the world as if Richie were engaged in a desperate struggle with the roiling Abyss itself. But the whole place was a veritable gold mine—or rather a silver mine; I'd tapped into the deep seam, and I simply kept coming back for more."

In most cases, Morrison was looking at video copies of the underlying negatives, copies harvested several years back, and sometimes when he tried to pull up the negative itself, it would in the meantime have rotted away completely. He got so he could anticipate the treasured damage: early indications on the video portending more-advanced riches on the negative itself. (In any event, this was a less hazardous and time-consuming process than the sort of stratagems he'd been resorting to lately in some of his Ridge work, for example, slathering Drano over individual frames, one by one, in an attempt to achieve an artificially decayed look.) He kept returning to Charleston, and across a total dig of well over one hundred hours, he managed to excavate footage (including the camel caravan, the Indian Ferris wheel, the Central Asian wool-spinner, the planes and the parachutists, and an uncanny sequence of a high diver hoisting himself skyward up a silhouetted ladder that itself looked for all the world like a strip of film) that would come to comprise thirty-six minutes, a good half of the eventual completed film.

He ventured down to Walls's old haunts at the Library of Congress and from there out to a remote bunker on the Wright-Patterson Air Force Base outside Dayton, Ohio, where, in the wake of the Sutland catastrophe, the Library had chosen to house its phenomenal (and phenomenally volatile) collections, in caves once given over to high munitions. Here Morrison tracked down the silent melodrama footage of the judge and the harridan, the waves breaking on the shore, "My dash through Vesuvius," and the solitary man traipsing across the mission courtyard (further shades of his grandfather). "It was a bit of a challenge," Morrison concedes. "After all, I was looking for the stuff most archivists tend to hide." But he gradually got the archivists to warm to his daffy quest. "Many visitors are amazed at the sorts of decay you come upon around here," Ken Weissman, the head of the Library of Congress's Dayton operation, subsequently told me with a sardonic drawl. "But few seem to *enjoy* it as much as Bill does."

"I wasn't just looking for instances of decayed film," Morrison recalls of his three-year project of excavation. "Rather, I was seeking out instances of decay set against a narrative backdrop, for example, of valiant struggle, or thwarted love, or birth, or submersion, or rescue, or one of the other themes I was trying to interweave. And never complete decay: I was always seeking out instances where the image was still putting up a struggle, fighting off the inexorability of its demise though not yet having entirely succumbed. And things could get very frustrating: Sometimes I'd come upon instances of spectacular decay but the underlying image was of no particular interest. Worse was when there was a great evocative image but no decay."

MEANWHILE, MICHAEL GORDON WAS busy detuning his orchestral palette. For example, he scripted five pianos—one in perfect tune, the second 50 cents (which is to say a quarter tone) sharp, the third 23.7 cents sharp, the fourth 33.9 cents flat, and the last one 44.9 cents sharp. He was going to be requiring the services of three flutes, one in tune, the second an eighth of a tone sharp, the other an eighth of a tone flat (believe me, these do not cancel each other out). He was invoking eight brake drums being scraped. And so forth.

He began by composing the last fifteen minutes of the piece—or rather a stretch so powerfully climactic that nothing could possibly follow it, so that instead he spent the rest of his time tearing apart its themes and unpacking them one by one in the hour leading up to the climax.

When he first played a synthesizer version of the climax for Morrison, Bill says he was immediately put in mind of that overpowering overflying jet epiphany from his teenage years, and suddenly he knew what he was going to do with the scratchy planes-and-parachutes footage. Gordon and Morrison began trading material, though as they both agree, it was now more a case of Morrison lining his film clips up to Gordon's score. ("I'm the luckiest film composer ever," Gordon would subsequently tell an after-screening audience at BAM, "because this was a case of a film being scored to my music.") Their aesthetic was in any case about as identical as one could hope for.

With the November 4, 2001, premiere date bearing down on them, Gordon presented Morrison with a seventy-minute synthesized version of the final score in mid-August, and Morrison in turn set to work jiggering his final alignments. And then, of course, on September 11, everything suddenly changed. Or rather, imagery that had carried one set of associations one day—planes coursing through the sky, parachutists, the collapse of burning buildings, desperate mine shaft rescues, turbaned Central Asian wool spinners, and so forth—suddenly became freighted with even more powerfully poignant subliminal connotations.

The premiere in Basel proved to be an especially elaborate affair. "It wasn't theater exactly," recalls Morrison. "And it wasn't opera. Nor was it cinema in any conventional sense. It was more like a highbrow rave. In Europe, even the twenty-year-olds with purple spiked hair come decked out in suits."

In the wake of that performance, Morrison had an actual orchestral recording to work with for the first time. He returned to his cramped Lower East Side studio to further tinker with the pacing and the alignments in anticipation of the film's (more conventional) screening at Sundance ten weeks later, the second week in January. And then he completely reconceived the pacing and the alignments one more time for the film's New York premiere, at MOMA, on May 12.

As it happens—and the curators at MOMA aver as to how this was no coincidence—May 12 was the last day for screenings in the museum's celebrated Titus auditorium prior to the venue's three-year closing as part of MOMA's general renovation. *Decasia* was the second-to-last film screened—followed by a sumptuous, rarely seen silver nitrate print of Casablanca.

A MEMBER OF THE audience at MOMA came up to Morrison following the screening, slapped him on the back, and crowed, "Congratulations! You have created the world's first post-postmodern film." Bill rolls his eyes as he tells the story.

And yet, in a strange way, the guy was onto something. Because for all its antique sources and resonances, *Decasia* is a film absolutely of the moment. In fact, it couldn't have been made a minute sooner: It took precisely this long for time to exert its magnificently inspired ravages upon the source material. This is what this stuff looks like today—and now here it is, preserved for all eternity.

"Oh yeah?" Morrison smiles, when I try this notion out on him. "Just wait a few years."

Fig. 1

## STILL NOT FINISHED:
On Vincent Desiderio's *Sleep*
(2005)

HE WAS HAVING a terrible time giving the thing up.

The painting—a stunningly ambitious tableau, eight feet high, fully twenty-four feet long, and portraying twelve mostly naked figures, as visioned from above, arrayed, recumbent, one beside the next, knotted up in sheets and tossed by sleep (or maybe unconscious, or maybe even dead, it was hard to tell)— had been one of the stand-out triumphs of Vincent Desiderio's singularly impressive show at Manhattan's Marlborough Gallery in January 2004. (Fig. 1) Despite its forbiddingly unwieldy dimensions, the piece had sold off the floor, to a private museum in Connecticut, on condition, however, that Desiderio would first be allowed to take the canvas back with him to his Ossining

studio. For all its highly burnished finish, the work had been listed as still "in progress" in the exhibition's catalog. And now, over a year later, with its new owners clamoring for the painting's already frequently postponed final delivery, it was still very much a work in progress, changing dramatically from day to day. Dramatically, and yet hardly at all: for Desiderio had achieved one of those images of such layered complexity and tautly interwoven cross-reference that the slightest tweak—here, say, the new way light was being made to fall across this woman's shoulder, or there, the manner in which that man's arm had been stretched ever so slightly higher—reverberated across the entire panel, as if across a tightly stretched drumskin.

Which Desiderio was far from finished pounding.


THE PAINTING HAD HAD me nailed from the first time I'd come upon it at the Marlborough show. The image seemed eerily strange and yet at the same time preternaturally right. Magritte used to talk about the way that the process involved in conceiving his uncanny alignments—his so-called "elective affinities"—was often surprisingly arduous, although the solution, once found, was always "self-evident, with all the certainty of fact and the impenetrability of the finest conundrum." Just so, here, as well. An image that was baldly itself and yet veritably pullulating with associations.

In this latter sense, it reminded me powerfully of José Saramago's astonishing novel *Blindness,* the way in which (in that book's instance) a simple premise—this city suddenly gripped by a plague of blindness (white blindness, mind you, not the more conventional black kind), a blight horrifically conveyed from one victim to the next by the imploring gaze of the recently afflicted (imagine the implications for family life, for neighborhood, for medical care, for civility itself, for every possible relation!)—quickly ramified in every direction, shimmering with real world referents

FIG. 2: Gilles Press, *Grave near Pilice Collective Farm near Srebrenica,* 1996

FIG. 3: Henry Moore, *Tube Shelter Perspective, The Liverpool Street Extension,* 1941

(AIDS, Rwanda, Kosovo, you name it) but then somehow transcending the shimmering. Here, too, with Desiderio's painting: One experienced that same sense of shimmer and indeed to many of those very same referents. Were we gazing upon the sated aftermath of an orgy, or rather the gruesome coda to a massacre? The Playboy Mansion or Srebrenica fields? (Fig. 2) As it happens, *Blindness* itself includes a scene in which the bedraggled quarantined victims are spread about a giant hangar, sleeping, huddled, one beside the next—a scene that at the time had put me in mind, as Desiderio's painting now did as well, of Henry Moore's drawings of the thronged nighttime tunnels of London's Underground during the Blitz. (Fig. 3) A particularly pertinent association to be making now, in the lee of 9/11, especially there in Manhattan, with all the foreboding of more to come: civil defense, indeed.

And, then again, maybe none of those. One looked to the painting's label for a clue: *Sleep*. The first time, I'd misremembered the title as *The Sleepers*, and later that evening, rolling the image over and over again in my mind, I found myself wondering whether it might not better have been dubbed *The Dreamer*.

THE POINT IS, I couldn't get the image out of my head. Nights, in bed, as I lolled between wakefulness and sleep, it would come floating back to my consciousness and start ramifying, ramifying away. So one morning I decided to seek the artist out. I tracked him down to that Ossining studio, and I began making a point of visiting him there every few weeks.

The studio turned out to be a vast, capaciously windowed space on the top floor of a onetime opera house, just outside the center of the small town about thirty miles north of Manhattan, and the tableau took up virtually an entire wall. The artist, boyishly intense though in fact at the very middle of middle age (just turning fifty) proved both lively and loquacious.

As we gazed upon the painting, Desiderio began to recount for me the canvas's origins, and it turned out that an image so uncannily balanced along the knife-edge between life and death had had origins no less mortally fraught. In 2000, following a series of quite successful earlier shows at Marlborough, he had been felled by a rare nasal pharyngeal cancer that had landed him bedridden for months, prone, sapped weak from the various chemo- and radiotherapies, staring up at the ceiling. (In the middle of the journey of his life, I found myself thinking, he came to himself in a dark wood where the straight way was lost.) "And I began being visited," he recalled, "by this image of a continuous band of sleepers" (funny the way that what for us gets experienced as a looking-down-upon began for him as a looking-up-at). "Initially I was thinking I might try to realize that vision by way of a giant video loop, something one might project, say, onto the vaulted ceiling of Grand Central, stretched out in real time, perhaps with individual sleepers getting up and then returning, it all got quite elaborated in my head. I mean, it's not all that mysterious how such a notion might have originated for me, all alone like that, feeling so terribly vulnerable and separated from the world of healthy people, this primitive longing for company, the fantasy affording me a sort of comfort. But rather quickly I began to turn the idea around in my mind, and it started filling up with more and more associations, almost like a pressure cooker, it began to effervesce."

Curiously, though then again perhaps not so curiously as all that, the splay of those initial associations for Desiderio went not so much to the sorts of real-world referents that had first consumed me (AIDS, Rwanda, presently 9/11, and the like) but rather to earlier imagery and technical issues in the history and practice and crisis of art. Desiderio is a formidably intellectual, at times hyperintellectual and intellectualizing, artist ("Motherwell once famously said, 'It's an intellectual decision to paint emotionally,'" Desiderio recalled for me one day, "but I think it's an emotional decision to paint intellectually," whereupon he went on to celebrate the determination with which one of his foremost nineteenth-century heroes had deployed the intellectual in order to navigate the emotional. "Delacroix," he insisted, "was made of sterner stuff; he was attempting to use paint to fashion real models of states of being, evoking mind itself, the restless mind, in the immediate heat of the imagination.") The vast majority of that churning, tumbling intellectuality, in Desiderio's case, gets brought to bear, not so much on the world as such—its politics and its history—as on the world of art, its politics and its history, and the place of his own project within all that history.[1]

It's no accident that the other major image in the 2004 Marlborough show, the one that appeared on the cover of the catalog, was of a draped, steeply angled, circular table (again, seen from above), sporting the remains of some sort of banquet and in turn surrounded, on the floor below, by a veritable sea of art books—hundreds, thousands of them—spread open to a seeming flood of iconic images from the history of art: a surfeit of associations. (Fig. 4) *Cockaigne*, he'd titled this work, enigmatically—enigmatically, that is, until one recalled Brueghel's *Land of Cockaigne* from 1567, (Fig. 5) with its similarly angled circular table, likewise topped by the remains of a banquet, and in this instance, surrounded by three lying (!) figures (sleeping? unconscious? dead?), presumably victims of their own rampant gluttony in a mythical land where everything came too easily to hand, the birds flying around already cooked, the pigs scampering about with ready—sharpened knives sashed to their bellies . . .

Fig. 4, (ABOVE): Vincent Desiderio, *Cockaigne*, 2003

Fig.5, (RIGHT): Pieter Brueghel the Elder, *The Land of Cockaigne*, 1567

FIG. 6, (LEFT): Jan van Eyck,
*The Last Judgment,* ca. 1430, detail

FIG. 7, (BELOW): Willem de Kooning,
*Excavation,* 1950

With regard to his own fantasy of a continuum of naked bodies, Desiderio recalled for me how his own first associations had been to the similar array of such bodies ranged, panic-stricken and forlorn, below that giant leering skeleton in van Eyck's *Last Judgment* of 1430, (Fig. 6) a thoroughly unsettling image that he himself had first come upon, memorably, transfixedly, as a child rifling through his parents' art books. To that painting, he went on, effervescing, "but almost as immediately to Jackson Pollock's 1943 *Mural,* (Fig. 8, next page) the breakthrough canvas he'd made for Peggy Guggenheim. I mean, the thing is, as much as I am drawn to images of the *Last Judgment,* I am myself not all that judgmental, I don't like to think I am anyway, and with the Pollock, by contrast, you have this sublime evenness, all very muscular—this is still before the drips—that marvelous repetition of those strong vertical arabesques punctuating the lush all-overness of the whole, the sense that they could go on forever in either direction. Isn't it Derrida who defined

FIG. 8: Jackson Pollock, *Mural*, 1943

a dictionary as an infinite array of signifiers? Which is to say, words defining words. Something of that feeling as well."

And so forth. Another time, Desiderio told me how if *Cockaigne* had for him constituted a sort of homage to de Kooning's *Excavation*, (Fig. 7, previous page) with the same layered and over-layered archeological feel and subtext, then *Sleep* was no less his homage to Pollock, and to *Mural* in particular. Indeed, the dimensions of the two paintings are virtually identical (exactly the same height, with *Sleep* being slightly longer). *Excavation* and *Mural* constituted for Desiderio a kind of twined high point of the Western painterly tradition, just before painting, as he says, seemed to fall into a trance, stupefied under the thrall of conceptual and pop art, those years when everybody was so happily busy declaring painting good and dead. "What I love about the Pollock," he told me another time, as we were gazing upon *Sleep*'s latest iteration, "is the way it is an all-over picture, implying as that does this sense of an infinite even grid, which nevertheless manages to reintroduce a slight indication of incident and intentionality, almost of narrative, kind of like Philip Glass, who likewise seems to be trying to transcend the blind alley of minimalism—you get the evenness of that repetitive melodic drone, but within that, the slightest changes, which in turn register as completely thrilling."

He showed me a series of preparatory studies for the painting—dozens, scores of them, in every conceivable medium: photos of

FIG. 9: Vincent Desiderio, photo collage study for *Sleep*

models, pencil drawings, quick-daubed slatherings on paper cross-hatched over with ink, detailed oils on sized canvas, cut-and-pasted collages xeroxed to homogeneity, Photoshopped computerized renderings. There were studies of the draped sheets alone. "The lower half of the painting devolves almost into sheer abstraction," he explained to me, "and that's in turn part of what the painting is about, abstraction butting up like that against figuration, the way that the more exactly the sheets get rendered, the more they read as abstracts, and for that matter, the more I bring out the abstract, as it were melodic, interrelations between the figures in the top half, the more palpably the individual figures read as incarnate individuals." With one of the computer renderings, he'd blurred the figures and then tinted the whole thing toward the red end of the spectrum, the imagery seeming to devolve into flames. (I was put in mind of Bachelard's *The Psychoanalysis of Fire*.) *Last Judgment*, indeed.

It turned out that in some of the earlier versions of the image, there had been thirteen figures (when they were numbered from One through Twelve, left to right, there had been an extra figure slotted between Ms. Ten and Mr. Eleven), which in turn had quite fundamentally altered the way the picture read (Fig. 9): With thirteen figures, the man in the middle was more emphatically centered (with six figures to either side) such that the whole ensemble seemed more to rhyme with Leonardo's *Last Supper* (Fig. 10) than with anyone else's *Last Judgment*. Whereas in the final—or should I

say, current?—version, with its twelve figures, while the central man
retains his preeminence, the woman nuzzled to his right seems to
rise in importance, with five figures to either side of the couple,
the central man and woman now reading precisely as a couple,
both of them prominently pillowed, and the image thereby becoming, at least in part, about marriage, and maybe even, with the pil-
lows almost reading as nimbic halos, about holy marriage. Having
said that, the earlier *Last Supper* version, with its thirteen figures,
had at the same time included a more emphatic *Last Judgment* echo
as well, for the central man's right arm had been upraised, in a
conspicuous allusion to Michelangelo's *Last Judgment* in the Sistine
Chapel (Fig. 11), where, parenthetically, the Mary figure, next to
the muscular Jesus, is portrayed, her cusped hands nested into the
crook of her neck, in much the same pose as the sleeping woman
tucked next to Desiderio's central figure. The woman retains that

FIG.10, (ABOVE): Leonardo da Vinci,
*The Last Supper,* 1495-1498

FIG. 11, (RIGHT): Michelangelo,
*The Last Judgment,* detail of Christ
and the Virgin, 1535-1541

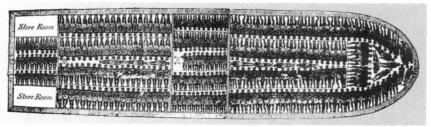

FIG.12: Slaveship

pose in the current version, while the man's hand has been recast downward, straightened, and wedged now along his side. "The echo was just too intrusive," Desiderio surmises, when I ask him about the revised placement of the man's arm. Notwithstanding which, in the final weeks leading toward the painting's current incarnation, Desiderio was subtly accentuating the tonal contrasts from side to side, the figures arrayed to the left glowing in a raking light that never quite makes it to the other side of the canvas, whose figures get progressively subsumed in gloom. "The saved and the damned," he joked one day.

Not that all the associations were to religious iconography. Another afternoon, Desiderio averred as to how another one of his sources had been the graphic imagery of slaveships (Fig. 12), with their shackled recumbent cargo sardine-packed one against the next. "There being a link somehow between sleep and slavery," he surmised, "and specifically privileged, pillowed, cushioned sleep—the culture asleep, enslaved, straining toward the liberation of wakefulness."

"I'M A PAINTER, A working man, a tradesman . . ."

I happened to be reading Joyce Cary's *Herself Surprised*, the first volume of the trilogy that culminates in *The Horse's Mouth*, for a while during those months when I was visiting Desiderio at his Ossining studio. And at one point Cary has his buoyantly exuberant protagonist Gulley Jimson explode in consternation: "I wish the very name of artist was abolished. It's simply a bad smell, it's not even good English. Painter is the English word, or limner."

Limner! How perfect, I remember thinking. An archaic word for painter wending all the way past Shakespeare and then forward into the Victorian era, and surely somehow tied to the word "liminal," from limen, the Latin word for threshold. How resonant of Desiderio's entire project with this painting planted so firmly as it was at the border crossing between enslavement and liberation, sleep and wakefulness, consciousness and unconsciousness, awareness and obliviousness, abstraction and figuration, peace and war, life and death.

Vincent Dividerio the Limner, I found myself thrumming, in the mode of that other great Irish Joyce.

I dove into the OED for confirmation, but, alas, I'd gotten it wrong. Not so much the word (1398: "Grauours, lymnours and payntours eteth Rewe to sharpe theyr sygthe." 1594: "The fine and subtil earth of the hearbe or flower, out of which some curious Limner may draw some excellent colour." 1875 Jowett, Plato: "The drawing of a limner which has not a shadow of a likeness to the truth") as its imagined etymology. For it turns out that the word grows not out of the Latin limen ("threshold") but rather the French lumière ("light," as in to illuminate, as in an illuminator of manuscripts). Still and all—light and dark, life and death—Desiderio remained in my mind a quintessentially liminal limner, who'd staked his claim right there on the verge of coming-to, at the edge of becoming.

Tomas Tranströmer, the sublime Swedish poet, has a poem where (in Robert Bly's elegant translation) he evokes his experience on all-night sentry duty, presumably while serving out his term of mandatory military service, guarding some remote outpost on the Finnish border or some such. "I'm ordered out to a big hump of stones," he says. "The rest are still back in the tent sleeping / stretched out like spokes in a wheel." Uncanny though it is (I'd forgotten that touch about the arrayed sleepers), that was not the echo that was drawing me back to the poem. "Task," he intones later on: "to be where I am. / Even when I'm in this solemn and absurd / role: I am still the place / where creation does a little work on itself." Not that either, though that is damn good. "Dawn comes . . ." There, now we were getting there:

> *To be where I am . . . and to wait*
> *I am full of anxiety, obstinate, confused.*
> *Things not yet happened are already here!*
> *I feel that. They're just out there:*

> *a murmuring mass outside the barrier.*
> *They can only slip in one by one.*
> *They want to slip in. Why? They do*
> *one by one. I am the turnstile.*

There: *that.* To be the turnstile.

I show the poem to Desiderio. He reads it to himself and then lets out a deep sigh. "Yes," he says. "Exactly. To wake up to that: to being present in the present."[2]


I KEEP VISITING, AND he keeps tweaking.

"Putting the light in in one place," he explains to me one day, "knocking it down in another. Scumble and glaze. Scumble, which is to say light over dark—and glaze, dark over light. Like tacking in sailing. Every gesture seeming to disrupt the balance ever so slightly, thereby necessitating other gestures elsewhere. A sequence of finely minced decisions. Do I believe it? And now do I believe that? But not just me, rather the universal self momentarily embodied in me. I am nothing but the image's first viewer. Like Diderot says somewhere, 'Painting is best when the artist stands slackjawed before the canvas.'"

Another time. "I am playing with the staging. Like in Baroque art—Gentileschi, Caravaggio. How they'd blind you with a flash in one area so that you didn't see the other stuff right away, the important stuff, thereby allowing a sequential exposition of detail, of revelation, a series of successive unveilings.

"There," he pointed, delphically (I must have been looking a touch bewildered). "The drapery work wrapped round her in the center."

FIG.13: Michelangelo, *Battle of the Centaurs and Lapiths,* 1492

Another day he was working on the punning arms. How the arms of Ms. Two and Mr. Three blend into each other. The same, even more confoundingly, with Mr. Four's right arm, which seems to be reaching across Ms. Five's belly—only, no, that's her forearm. How Ms. Eight's right arm seems to burrow under her pillow and then out from under Ms. Seven's head—or wait, is that Ms. Seven's own right arm? The doubling at the jointed elbows of Ms. Ten and Mr. Eleven. All of it subliminally helping to define the flow of energy through the whole painting, to keep the eye moving. "As in that amazing early marble of Michelangelo's of the *Battle of the Centaurs,*" he tells me. (Fig. 13)

Another day he is working on Ms. Ten and Mr. Eleven. Although shunted off to the side and into the gloom, their gestures are somehow the most operatic. Though mustachioed, he seems the most babylike, lying there prone, diapered in his boxers. And though she is in fact the most fully dressed, at the same time she seems the most nakedly vulnerable, her arms raised up as if fending off a nightmare blow.

Another day he is working on Mr. Four and Ms. Nine—a daub on one precipitating a compensating stab at the other. "Parentheses," he explains. "They frame the central group."

And week after week it is the central group and especially the

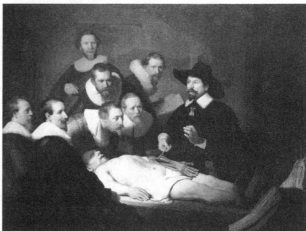

FIG. 14: Jan Vermeer, *The Lacemaker,* ca. 1665

FIG. 15: Rembrandt van Rijn, *The Anatomy Lesson of Dr. Tulp,* 1632

central couple who are coming into increasing focus, with the lateral figures falling progressively away. As in Vermeer's *Lacemaker* (Fig. 14)—how everything in the image falls out of focus, either too close or too far, except for the very thing that the girl herself is focusing upon, the V of threads stretched taut against the M cast of her hands: a painting, in short, all about concentration.

And Desiderio, too, continues to focus his concentration—almost as if, were he just able to focus intently enough, he could jar the figures awake. ("Do you know what it's like to wake up every morning to the news that painting is dead and over?" Desiderio asked me another time, not even quite hearing the terms in which he himself was casting the question. "To wake up, time and again, to that news, when you know that it just can't be true?")

Concentrically he hones in, and increasingly the locus of all that focus seems to be the hand draped across the central man's belly. As in Rembrandt's *Anatomy Lesson* (Fig. 15), where the central group are gawking, dumbfounded, not at the cadaver's flayed arm but rather at the professor's living hand, at the way he is explaining how with those muscles there you can move your hand this way, here. A miracle. The paired wonders of vision and manipulability:

a painting, in the end, about all the marvels that make painting itself possible. And just so, as well, with the hand of that central man, who Desiderio one day acknowledges is none other than he himself, although, as he insists again, not as himself but rather as a stand-in for everyman.

Thus, the self-generating, the self-creating hand. But also the hand that will reach out, any moment now, suddenly startled, grasping at the air, at the instant of coming awake.

SO FAR I HAVE been making Desiderio sound a little clearer than he sometimes does. As I say, he's a deeply intellectual guy, often quite maddeningly, hypertrophically so. There are moments when he seems to get himself all tangled up in sheet upon billowing sheet of postmodernist, structuralist, deconstructivist, semiotic, post-Lacanian, high Foucauldian verbiage. Wake up, you want to reach out and shake him—damn it all already, will you wake the hell up? And yet, amid the fog of all that verbiage, he is clearly struggling toward something vital, and in any case this is manifestly the background pulse to his astonishing creative flow.

For example, "emblemazation" and "sequentialization," two words he kept unfurling across our weeks of conversations (and which he likewise deploys repeatedly in the largely impenetrable essay that he folded into the end of his catalog for the 2004 Marlborough catalog). They have something to do with the crisis of modern painting, a crisis that, in his mind, spreads well beyond the world of painting.[3]

"Is a painting a wall or a membrane?" he asks me one day. "That's what it all comes down to. Picture the artist on one side, the object in between, the viewer on the other. As the painting increasingly stultifies to the status of a mere emblem, which is to say a sign and nothing more than a sign, it becomes more and more like an impenetrable barrier, almost a mirror, the viewer gazes in but all he gets back is a sort of ironical wink, often, in a lot of conceptual work, in a kind of one-shot punch: the illustration of a wink. There's that, and nothing more. But it's possible to imagine a different order of things—the loss of faith in the possibility of something more is a distinctly twentieth-century affliction—an order in which painting acts as a kind of veil across which, through which, the painter and the viewer arrive at some sort of communion across a sequential experience, a reinvigorated, authentic, viscerally felt sense of narrativity, breaking through to that place where we are all conjoined. That's the dream, anyway, that I'm trying to waken to.

"I mean," he went on, "I could do anything—in fact, I started as an abstract painter and for a time even trafficked in my share of conceptualist stunts—but now I choose to do this: a painting that unfolds, that purses out its information gradually, beyond glib ironic hipness and, I hope, toward a sort of enigmatic mystery."

He paused for a moment, gazed over at the tableau, and tried again. "At one level, what you see before you here is just a normal mind relentlessly, maybe even a little obsessively, working on a normal dream, trying to replicate the luxury of deep sleep, deep surrender, pure reverie.

"You know how when you dream, all those tendrils, those emblems, seem to float about independently, disjointedly, haphazardly, but the moment the alarm goes off, it's like there's a rush to assemble all those stray tendrils into a sensate sequence—*a narrative*. Suddenly all that random stuff comes together and momentarily coheres. For a moment, at that moment, everything, everyone connects, it all makes sense. That's where I'm trying to get with this."

But isn't that, I found myself wondering later that evening, precisely what dying is said to be like as well?

TIME WAS UP. THEY were coming for the painting the next day. Although he'd managed to extract a further assurance of his own: that, while displayed at the private museum, it would still be labeled as "in progress," and that from time to time, on off-days, he'd be allowed into the galleries to work on it some more.

How would he eventually know, I asked him, when it was finally finished?

"When it starts firing on its own," he replied assuredly, before immediately undercutting himself. "Then again, maybe it will always be unfinished—maybe that's its charm. Although I can still see some more specific things that need to be done. I'd like to be able to resolve it, to bring it to a resolution, and then to open it up all over again." He smiled.[4]

It seemed as if with this painting anyway, Desiderio might always be finding himself right there, at the very cusp.

Although, then again, you know how sometimes you wake up just before the alarm goes off?

# VALKYRIES OVER IRAQ:
Walter Murch, *Apocalypse Now, Jarhead,*
and the Trouble with War Movies
(2005)

EARLY IN 2003, A little more than ten years after the conclusion of
the First Gulf War—which is to say the short, fast, clean, clear, and
ever so painlessly triumphalist one—and on the very brink of what
was rapidly seeming the inevitable launch of its far more complicated sequel, Anthony Swofford, a Marine sniper veteran of that
first conflict, published *Jarhead,* a powerfully bleak memoir of his
experiences there in the Kuwaiti amphitheater back in the early
nineties, a bitterly cautionary screed, utterly pithed of illusion or
easy consolations. Of all the revelations in Swofford's brisk chroni-
cle, one of the most startling occurred near the book's very outset,
as he described how Marines on the verge of being sent into battle
goosed themselves into a blissed-out state of readiness by screening
videos of movies depicting earlier wars, and in particular battle
scenes from several of the bleakest Vietnam movies of all—some
of the most thoroughly illusion- and consolation-pithed films ever
made—scenes, for example, like Robert Duvall's celebrated and
notoriously blood-drenched Valkyrie helicopter raid in Francis
Ford Coppola's *Apocalypse Now.*

   "There is talk," Swofford noted, "that many Vietnam films
are antiwar, that the message is that war is inhumane . . . But actually, Vietnam films are all pro-war, no matter what the supposed
message, what Kubrick or Coppola or Stone intended." Swofford
went on to allow as how Mr. and Mrs. Johnson in Omaha or San
Francisco or Manhattan might well watch such films "and weep
and decide once and for all that war is inhumane and terrible,
and they will tell their friends at church and their family this, but

Corporal Johnson at Camp Pendleton and Sergeant Johnson at Travis Air Force Base . . . and Lance Corporal Swofford at Twentynine Palms Marine Corps Base watch the same films and are excited by them, because the magic brutality of the films celebrates the terrible and despicable beauty of their fighting skills. Fight, rape, war, pillage, burn," Swofford went on, starkly. "Filmic images of death and carnage are pornography for the military man; with film you are stroking his cock, tickling his balls with the pink feather of history, getting him ready for his real First Fuck. It doesn't matter how many Mr. and Mrs. Johnsons are antiwar—the actual killers who know how to use the weapons are not."

"The supposedly antiwar films have failed," Swofford concluded, a few paragraphs later, characterizing his euphoric state that distant afternoon. "As a young man raised on the films of the Vietnam War, I want ammunition and alcohol and dope, I want to screw some whores and kill some Iraqi motherfuckers."

One might have thought that such a bald appraisal would have given a new generation of filmmakers pause: Maybe trying to set such an account as Swofford's to film might not be such a good idea after all, especially in the midst of the buildup to a new war, with its fresh cadre of young men and women likewise being prepped for battle; maybe the viscerally immediate (mediumless) medium of cinema is simply incapable of projecting such measured and tentative reconsiderations.

And yet—such cautionary warnings be damned—a new team of filmmakers was taking on precisely this challenge. As that then impending new war became fully engaged, producers Douglas Wick (*Gladiator*) and Lucy Fisher commissioned Vietnam-vet screenwriter Bill Broyles Jr. (*Apollo 13, Cast Away*, etc.) and English stage director Sam Mendes (*American Beauty* and *Road to Perdition*) to attempt to transfer Swofford's deeply distressing vision to the screen. With filming already complete and postproduction well under way, the team had chosen to confront the challenge head-on, positioning that scene of battlebound young Marines goaded into a lusty frenzy by a screening of that Valkyrie helicopter raid right near the beginning of the film as in some ways its central fulcrum, the very hinge of their entire new effort. And the result was indeed proving one of the most deeply affecting and disconcerting scenes in recent film history, thanks in no small part to the lavish ministrations of the film's editor, the legendary Walter Murch (*The Conversation*, the *Godfather* movies, *The Unbearable Lightness of Being, The English Patient*, etc., etc.), who in this context was himself having to harrow the distinctly unsettling task of revisiting and revisioning a scene he'd labored over for months almost thirty years ago as a crucial member of the original *Apocalypse Now* team—this time, alas, in an entirely new and even more disturbing light.

"At times I get to feeling like I'm inside my own Escher drawing," Murch admitted to me one evening. One hand, as it were, drawing the other into being: his past decisions shaping his current ones, and vice versa.

I was somewhat sympathetic to Murch's plight. After all, I was reporting for a magazine (*Harper's*) that had itself run an excerpt from Swofford's book during the run-up to the current war in the hope that it might help people come to their senses (a gambit that hadn't ended up proving all that effective either). At any rate, I'd begun dropping in on Murch at the film's postproduction studios in Manhattan's West Village (conveniently located roughly halfway between his own usual Northern California haunts and those of

Mendes in London), where Murch—tall, slim, hunched, unflappable (as if Zen centered)—presided over his computerized flatbed, riffing through the original sequence from *Apocalypse Now*, looped onto one of the little monitors above, and then Mendes's rich trove of reaction shots, looped onto another monitor, meticulously interleafing the two for eventual projection onto the larger plasma screen over to the side (a screen in turn flanked by two diminutive paper silhouettes of standing humans, there to remind him of the actual scale of the film's eventual theatrical projection).

The original scene: Duvall, playing Colonel Bill Kilgore, darling of the First Air Cavalry, preternaturally dapper, gung-ho, buff, completely uninterested in his new assignment (to deliver the Navy speedboat ferrying Martin Sheen's Willard character to the VC-infested mouth of the river they in turn would presently be needing to ascend as part of their Conradesque mission)—completely uninterested, that is, until he finds out that Sheen's team includes a spacey young Navy seaman who just happens to be a Southern Californian surfing phenom, and that the delta beach in question, furthermore, just happens to sport the cleanest-breaking waves up or down the entire Vietnamese coast. Kilgore is a true aficionado, and as he memorably shoots back, self-evidently, when one of his junior officers counsels against an assault on such a well-defended Viet Cong stronghold, Why should they care about any VC defenders? "Charlie don't surf." The next morning, his fleet of choppers idling at the ready, Kilgore has one of his boys let rip with the traditional bugle charge from every cavalry Western you have ever seen. The helicopters peel off, thrillingly, and a few miles out from the village, Kilgore orders another of his men to engage the psyops loudspeakers, from out of which will soon come welling Wagner's "Ride of the Valkyries." "Scares the hell out of the slopes," Kilgore shouts out, by way of explanation, to his new surfing buddy. "My boys love it."

And how could they not? The music swells with the throbbing menace of propulsive inevitability. Suddenly, though, the Wagnerian soundtrack cuts out, and we are in a calm, almost

pastoral, seaside village, peasants and teachers and their school charges padding about, intent on their various morning rituals, when VC guards come barreling into the village's central square, raising an urgent alarm. Everyone tries to scatter, as back to the fast-scudding chopper fleet we go, the Valkyrie theme in full lusty throttle, rockets opening out as the village comes into view over the horizon, machine guns flaring—all hell breaking loose. Carnage and mayhem, the scene goes on for what seems like ever, the VC and their peasant hosts suffering relentless casualties, as presently do some of Kilgore's men as well ("Fucking savages," mutters Kilgore, surveying the scene from above, outraged at the gall of an enemy that deigns to oppose him). Talk about horror: In Conradian terms, this is the horror before The Horror—and Coppola and Murch are completely unflinching in their gaze.

Meanwhile, over on the other monitor, Murch samples some of Mendes's no less unflinching reaction footage, and if anything it is more horrifying yet. Bush père has just announced that Hussein's invasion of Kuwait will not be allowed to stand, and the Marines screening the Valkyrie scene there in their base auditorium (scores of extras, alongside Jake Gyllenhaal in the role of Swofford) are in a veritable paroxysm of ecstasy.

It's like a midnight showing of *The Rocky Horror Picture Show*: They know every line, they mime every gesture (one grinning grunt, for example, taps a box of Hot Tamales against his shaven skull as, up on the screen, an airborne soldier taps a magazine of fresh ammo against his helmet), they scream out encouragement ("El niño!" one of the boys cries out disconcertingly as a Vietnamese toddler momentarily hesitates in the midst of his class's hurried evacuation), they marvel at the technique (hand-banking along with the swerving Hueys) and exult at the exploding bodies, they soar with the swelling music (psyops, indeed—though, one is given to wonder, on just whom is it intended to ops?)—ecstatically they imbibe the smell of napalm in the morning, and yes, it does, it does: it smells like . . . victory.

And patiently, meticulously, Murch keeps interleafing the scenes. "It's probably best that I'm the one doing this," he avers one evening. "If it weren't me, some other editor would either be overly protective of the original—wary of breaking any of the precious china—or else just treating it all like raw material." Every transition evokes a rush of memory. For instance, that sudden cut to the village, the music momentarily falling away: "Originally," Murch recalls, "Francis wanted to have the tape in the copter-borne player simply snap, the spool flailing spasmodically as the music went suddenly silent and the soldiers rushed frantically to repair the damage. I pleaded with him not to do that, it felt too clunkily contrived, and we went round and round ourselves with that one—but I could see his point, he was dead right in his basic intuition, and eventually we were able to come up with this alternative momentary change

of focus and shift in sound density." Now, though, in the Mendes/ Murch version, the music goes silent, and uncannily, the auditorium- ful of Marines simply takes up the slack, chanting along in the place of the momentarily absent melody. And as a vertiginous member of the current audience, in 2005, you don't know whether to be roused or appalled: In fact, you are both at once (and both at each other).

"The essential armature of that original scene," Murch recalled for me another evening, "that combination of the surfing mania and the Wagner, came directly out of John Milius's script, though there it was only a few pages at most, and Francis elaborated it all into that vast extended battle sequence, largely by incorporating the stories

he was hearing out there on the set in the Philippines from some of
our vet extras." Murch went quiet for a moment, rejiggering the cut
between two of the takes he'd just been studying, forward and back.
"It's a funny thing about Francis and Sam," he resumed. "Both of
them were thirty-nine at the time they were shooting their respective
films, films that in both cases were attempting to come to terms
with military actions ten years prior that were only just then beginning to emerge, in part thanks to the films themselves, from an
extended period of public occlusion.

"And there are other odd funny coincidences. For example,
back in the late seventies, I was responsible for the sound design
on the Valkyrie scene, and for months I'd been using the Georg
Solti version with the Vienna Philharmonic. We were just about
to lock on the sequence when somebody had the sense to ask

whether anybody'd secured permission to use that particular version. Maybe because the whole editing process had been a bit of a slapdash madhouse, in fact we hadn't, nobody had bothered, and presently it became apparent that Decca Europe had no intention of granting permission for its deployment in such a potentially controversial context. Disaster.

"We rushed over to Tower Records and brought back nineteen separate versions, only one of which remotely tracked with the rhythms of the editing we had done with the visuals: Leinsdorf, with the L.A. Philharmonic. But after we feathered Leinsdorf's version in and projected the results, it too turned out to be all wrong, not so much because of the meter as because of the coloration: Leinsdorf emphasized the strings whereas Solti had brought the brass to the fore, and the scene really cried out for that acidic brass. So eventually Francis himself flew out to meet with Solti, and Solti said, 'Of course, dear boy, why didn't you ask me in the first place?' He ordered Decca to release the rights, only this all happened so late in the process that we weren't able to make use of the master tapes, we had to lift the music off a disc, which, actually, I suppose, is appropriate, since Kilgore probably did the same.

"But, as I say, funny coincidences: Because initially Francis was refusing the *Jarhead* team the right to use any footage from out of *Apocalypse Now*—he apparently wasn't pleased at the prospect of his complex film being reduced so narrowly to the aspect of its use as military pornography—and in the end, Sam had to plead with him personally to secure his tentative approval for use of the Valkyrie sequence. Though Francis still retains the right to refuse its use in the end, which would be a real disaster." Murch winced briefly, before resuming his customary Zen calm: "I expect it will be okay."

WALTER MURCH MAY BE one of the smartest people in America. Or so, anyway, I sometimes tell the students in my graduate writing classes ("In fact," I tell them, "that will be on the test. The question will be, 'Who is the smartest man in America?'—and the expected answer is 'Walter Murch.' Ten points toward your grade.") It's not just the evident intelligence of his editing choices, though those can at times be staggeringly apt, nor is it even the grace and erudition of his thinking and writing. Rather it's the constant dapple of insight and penetration you experience in his casual presence, the continuous free play of inference and association.

"It's funny about eye contact," he was telling me one day, for example. "The actual amount of eye contact in real life is quite low. In fact, to be looked at in the eyes, as it were, makes us quite uncomfortable: We expect our interlocutors to turn away, in the same way we instinctively turn away from gazing directly at them. But newscasters on TV look right at us, that's what teleprompters were invented for, and we expect that. When they don't, when they turn away, that makes us uncomfortable: It makes them seem shifty to us. Television is the opposite of real life. We look at them, and they look at us, and our rate of blinking goes way down—they've done studies—from a normal rate of twenty or thirty blinks per minute down to just two or three. If you stare at a wall and try to blink just two or three times, you'll see: It's real hard. But with TV you do that all the time. Whereas the rate of blinking in a movie theater is the same as real life." Murch does not own a television set. "Blinking in general is misunderstood. Most people think it has to do with lubricating the eyes, or something like that, but if you spend time watching people, you'll realize that our rate of blinking is somehow geared more to our emotional state and to the nature and frequency of our thoughts than to the atmospheric environment we happen to find ourselves in, the blink being something that either helps an internal separation of thought to take place or else consists in involuntary reflex accompanying a mental separation that is taking place anyway. And not only is the rate of blinking significant, but so is the actual instant of the blink itself. Start a conversation with somebody and watch when they blink: Your listener will blink at the precise moment he or she 'gets' the idea of what you are saying, not an instant earlier or later. In editing terms, that blink will occur where a cut could have happened, had the conversation been being filmed."

"It's interesting about light and dark," he offers another time. "Because if you spend two hours watching a film at a movie theater, you are literally spending half of that time in the dark. For every frame of projected light—twenty-four of them per second—there's an equivalent frame, as it were, of pitch blackness: That's how the projector works. Which may be why we are able to experience films at all. In the earliest days of cinema, there was a great deal of concern that an audience would not be able to tolerate a tracking shot—that is when the camera itself pans laterally across a scene. A lot of people thought that such motion would provoke a sort of motion-sickness or seasickness in its viewers. And when it didn't, they couldn't figure out why. But that in turn may have something to do with the way our brains themselves process visual information, across a series of spurts or frames. Oliver Sacks has written about so-called kinematic vision, the way some of his patients experience a sort of stagger-vision, as if their internal projector had slowed way down, sometimes almost jamming, and sometimes even feeding individual frames out of order. Maybe all of us experience the visual world in such a manner, only so seamlessly that we don't notice it, unless we take ill—which in turn explains why humans were *neurologically* prepared, as it were, to process projected motion picture imagery from the very outset. Incidentally, it will be interesting, in this context, to watch how audiences respond to the coming of digital projection at movie theaters, which will no longer feature those intervening frames of darkness. And we're about to undertake that experiment, starting with Ireland, where by next year all movie theater projectors will be required to be digital."

From visual projection to the perception of sound. Unsurprisingly, Murch has developed elaborate theories regarding the perception of sound—some of which came into crucial play during his editing of that Valkyrie scene. Murch is convinced that we perceive sound along a spectrum from encoded to embodied—language existing on the extreme end of the encoded side of the spectrum, and music at the extreme end of the embodied—and that these types of sounds get processed on different sides of the brain. Having said that, a language we don't understand—say, Chinese—can be perceived as pure musical sound, whereas, at the other extreme, certain pure sounds (for example, a knock on the door) can get apprehended as virtual linguistic cues (in that instance, standing in for: "Somebody's here"). Through extended experience, Murch has come to understand that a film viewer can keep track of two and a half instances at a time to either side of the spectrum—thus, for example, by way of encoded information, two ongoing conversations around a dinner table in *The Godfather*, as well as a knock on the door—but no more. Any more than that and it all becomes auditory mush.

He actually discovered this law early on, when he was doing sound for the *THX-1138* film he cowrote with George Lucas. "There were several scenes with these supposed 600- pound robots traipsing about," he recalls, "and they'd been played by regular 175-pound actors, so the sound as recorded on the set just came off as all wrong on the screen. I solved the problem by going to the Museum of Natural History in San Francisco the middle of one night, this very reverberant space, and recording all sorts of footfalls very close up, and then returning to the editing studio—this was still in the days of tape and hand-splicing—and matching each footstep on the screen to one of my amplified footfalls, from left speaker to right speaker or vice versa, depending which way the robot was walking. And at one point I noticed how if there were just one robot on the screen, you had to be exactingly meticulous in matching footfall sound to footstep, the correct speaker and everything, and if there were two, the same thing—but if there were three or more robots, you could just serve up a chaotic welter of footfall sounds from any which speaker and nobody would be able to discern the difference." (Typically, with Murch, this discovery eventually led to all sorts of parallel insights—the fact, for example, that in many primitive languages, the counting system goes one/ two/many.)

All of this was to prove crucially important during the sound editing of the Valkyrie sequence. Coppola all along intended the sound-surround of *Apocalypse Now* to be a viscerally important aspect in experiencing the film. Indeed, early on he had been thinking about creating a unique theater, specially outfitted and located at the geographic center of the country, as the sole place where the film would ever be shown (though as Murch acknowledges, that scheme eventually proved, as he puts it, "economically impractical"). Still the two of them devised all sorts of cutting-edge technologies regarding the projection of sound that required an updating of the sound systems of each of the theaters at which the film was eventually shown and effectively ushered in a state-of-the-art upgrading of all such systems in theaters across the country over the next several years.

Anyway, in this context, the Valkyrie scene, with its overbrimming profusion of sounds (the steady thrum of the thwacking helicopters, shouted orders, explosions, small arms fire, footfall, and other sound effects, not to speak of the Wagnerian score itself), proved one of the most challenging passages in the film. Eventually—and again, this was still in the era of hand-spliced tape—over a hundred individual tracks had to be blended into six master tracks (one for the helicopter thwacks, another for the shouted orders, etc.), and after months of work, when each of those had been tweaked to perfection, the team went into the screening room and played them all at once, and the results were catastrophic: utterly undecipherable mush. At which point, Murch recalled the *THX* robots and their rule of two and a half, and further considering the way he'd come to see the brain as processing sound across an entire spectrum (encoded to embodied), expanded the *THX* rule into a law of five (as long as the five tracks were spread evenly across that entire spectrum). He went back into the sound studio and rejiggered the entire Valkyrie sequence, at every moment making sure that at least one of the six tracks had fallen away. And the result was pristine: "dense clarity," as he likes to say. (He eventually received an Academy Award for his sound design of the film—one of three he has garnered over the years.)

Murch's is a synesthetic sensibility—or at any rate, he continually frames his editing process in cross-sensory terms. (He speaks of the encoded/linguistic/left brain end of the spectrum as blue/green tending toward violet, and the embodied/musical/right brain side as orange tending toward red. In describing the various separate tracks of the Valkyrie scene, he is likely to characterize the explosions in orchestral terms as the percussion and the helicopter thwacking as the strings.) Many of his most powerful characterizations of his process get framed in terms of architectural metaphors: questions of spaciousness and constriction, with time playing the role of gravity. One afternoon he had to beg off on one of our dates: "It's been one of those days," he explained, "when the floor just suddenly gives out from under you and you fall two or three stories into the basement, which, in all fairness, turns out to afford its own interesting vantage." Another day he was describing to me how editing a film can get to be like building a boat, how the closer you get to finishing—which is to say the more you cut and cut and cut away at the thing—the more it begins to sound seaworthy: The cuts themselves just start sounding different. Other times the editing experience can itself take on aspects of the oceanic—the way, for example, he once told me how even after having gone over the same sequence in the current film literally hundreds of times, an individual passage could occasionally hit him in an entirely fresh way, cutting transverse of the expected rhythms of response, "like a sneaker wave."

"Film is such a curious medium," Murch commented another afternoon, leaning with his long legs spread out from his high chair, his back to the digital flatbed console. "The central dilemma of film compared to all other narrative media is that it's literal, in

that what you see is what was literally there, and yet we as film-makers in processing the narrative have to create a spaciousness, a sketchy ambiguity, that allows the audience themselves to piece it all together and make it powerfully their own." He paused for a moment. "The danger of a well-made bad movie, in this sense, is that it crushes the imagination of the audience."

He was tightening that scene of the Marines ecstatic before the Valkyries yet further (four and a half minutes of *Apocalypse Now* time would eventually get compressed to just over one and a half minutes in *Jarhead*), and he now recalled how "Ride of the Valkyries" had played a key role at the very outset of film history, that at the climax of one of the first feature films ever made—the execrably racist and phenomenally successful 1915 paean to the Reconstructionist South, *The Birth of a Nation*—D. W. Griffith had directed the orchestras accompanying his film to play Wagner's rousing anthem as backdrop to his depiction of the galloping Klan raids on those uppity Negroes and their carpetbagger allies (a precedent, Murch assured me, of which he and Coppola and Milius, all good film students out of UCLA and USC, would certainly have been aware as they contrived the Duvall scene, with its sly replacement of one set of Colored People by another). That in turn got him to talking about the sheer marvel of the development in a medium that is less than a hundred years old. "How did those guys do it back then, with their ridiculously limited resources—or even us, with our comparatively better developed array? At least now we have computers. I mean, right in the middle of it, you can lose sight of the marvel of it all, how a couple hundred people can peel off for a year and emerge on the far side with this miraculously involving and coherent thing, a two-hour movie. I imagine a hundred years from now, people will look back on these things and regard them the way we marvel at Gothic cathedrals, Chartres and the like, each more marvelous than the one before, and yet how could they have done it, in their case with nothing more than human muscle and, literally, horsepower?" (It occurred to me in this context, reversing the terms of Murch's analogy, that the cathedrals themselves had been built to awe-strike the masses, that they were in a sense the *Apocalypse Nows* of their day, and that even as they'd been designed to bring people closer to the God of love, they'd also, quite explicitly and effectively, served as recruitment devices for wars of inquisitional carnage. For that matter, cathedrals, with their hidden organist and total-work-of-God Weltanschauung, were Wagnerian projects in their own right—or else, maybe, Wagner was simply trying to tap back into their originary power in a subsequent, far less godly age.)

A few moments later, Murch descended (or should I say ascended?) an octave to his theory of the Three Fathers (for a richer elaboration of which, see the writer Michael Ondaatje's book-length interview with Murch, *The Conversations*), his own idiosyncratic genealogy of film, the notion that cinema rises at the intersection of Edison, Flaubert, and Beethoven. Edison, of course, standing in for all the innovations on the technical side; Flaubert, for the upsurge of realism (and specifically "closely observed realism," the way the French master could spend a whole page evoking how light and sound fell across an empty room, only in order to get at something far grander); and then Beethoven, with his expansion and exploitation of the idea of dynamics (the notion that "by aggressively expanding, contracting, and transforming the rhythmic and orchestral structure of music, you could create unprecedented emotional resonance and power"). All of it leading to film, a technology ideally suited to the dynamic representation of closely observed reality.

ANYWAY SO SOMEWHERE IN there I spent a weekend watching the original *Apocalypse Now* again and again, gnawing at this problem of whether it's even possible to imagine creating an antiwar film, or whether any depiction of war in film necessarily lends itself to military-pornographic exploitation.

I should perhaps note here that I'd been one of those who'd resisted the blandishments of the film when it first came out, in 1979—or rather, maybe the claims made on behalf of it and Michael Cimino's virtually simultaneous, equally ambitious, and similarly touted *Deer Hunter*. There was a lot of talk at the time about how these films were at last going to confront the moral depravity of the Vietnam War. "It was my thought," Coppola had said, "that if the American audience could look at the heart of what Vietnam was really like—what it looked like and felt like—then they would be only one small step away from putting it behind them." There was something strange in the air, this sense that we were somehow collectively going to be able to get Vietnam behind us by merely going to see *Apocalypse Now*, or even more tenuously, by belonging to a country in which such a film could be created (even,

or maybe especially, in the face of the government's opposition).
What exactly was it that we seemed to be hoping that Coppola
could do for us? There was moral hubris in Coppola's aspiration to
single-handedly confront the Vietnam experience with such ferocious lucidity that he might wrest penance for the entire country in
the process. And there was moral vacuousness in our secret yearn-
ing that he'd be able to do so.

In the event, furthermore, there always seemed to me a flaw
at the heart of both Cimino's and Coppola's efforts. I mean, it
seemed to me kind of important to note that, in the case of the
former, there were actually no recorded instances of Viet Cong or
any Vietnamese engaging in Russian roulette human cockfights—
or, in the case of the latter, of bands of Montagnard tribesmen,
dazed by suffering, lining up behind a demented Special Forces
officer, elevating him to godhood, and then following him over
the precipice into orgiastic violence and debauchery from which,
unable to rescue themselves, they had to be delivered by the
arrival of another, albeit differently conflicted, white man. If you
complained along these lines at the time, as I remember doing
to a friend of mine, you were likely to be told that no, no, you
didn't understand, Vietnam was merely the launching-off point,
that Cimino and Coppola were after something much bigger
than Vietnam—the taproots of masculinity, the abyss of existential dread, the lure of violence, etc., etc.—all the big themes—
and presently names like Nietzsche and Schopenhauer and of
course Conrad (or in the case of Cimino, Hemingway) would
start getting tossed around. And I just remember thinking, But
wait, there *is* nothing bigger than Vietnam. Vietnam, and what
we did there, is as big as we are ever going to get in our generation. Vietnam was all the theme a director could possibly hope to
encompass. And there was something fundamentally flawed in a
response that used it as a launching-off point for larger significa-
tions. (Wasn't that, after all, the origin of the Vietnam disaster in
the first place? For Johnson and Rostow and Nixon, Vietnam had

never been just about Vietnam either. It had always been about Something Much Bigger. God save those poor souls, I remember thinking, from Americans tracking Big Themes.)

Having said that, even then I could acknowledge the evident power, the fierce integrity, and even the ferocious lucidity of much of the filmmaking in *Apocalypse Now*, especially across the first half of the picture—in particular the Valkyrie scene and, even more so, the sequence detailing the catastrophically botched meeting (a mini My Lai) of the Navy speedboat with that peasant sampan on the river. (It turns out, incidentally, that the latter scene was never in the original script, and that it got conceived and inserted only as the film was being shot, and according to Coppola himself, at the specific urging of Walter Murch.)

And one's admiration for the film—over and beyond the Big Theme terms its admirers set for it when it first came out—only increases with time, or so I found myself feeling, watching it again and again that weekend.

And damn, but damn: that Valkyrie scene.

Kilgore's boy raises the bugle to his lips and lets rip with that cavalry charge, and I feel myself falling through a trapdoor of history, into, I suppose, an alternate genealogy . . .

The year being 1876, back in the days when cavalries still charged out on horseback . . .

July: Lieutenant Colonel George Armstrong Custer—preternaturally dapper, gung-ho, buff: oblivious—leads several mounted battalions of the Seventh Cavalry into wretched debacle at the Little Bighorn.

August: In Bayreuth, Richard Wagner inaugurates his stupendous Festspielhaus with the world premiere of his full Ring Cycle, the way he has always intended it be performed, with armor plated, horse-borne Valkyries striding powerfully onto the stage at the opening of the third act of the second play, a perfect manifestation of the Master's doctrine of Gesamtkunstwerk, the all-around, all-convergent happening, with all the arts (music, stagecraft, painting, literature) combined (none claiming precedence over the others—in fact, as he specifically stipulates, with the orchestra removed from its traditional position and hidden away down below, such that its sounds will seem to be rising from all over) in order to lavish the audience in a veritable debauch of sensory experience.

That same year, railroad tycoon Leland Stanford purchases an estate in Palo Alto and, having done perhaps more than anyone else to render horses obsolete as transportation, turns to raising them for sport, having enlisted the photographer Eadweard Muybridge in a novel effort to capture their stampeding gait in the fullness of its being. Within a couple of years, Muybridge will do just that through his innovation of animal motion studies, for all intents and purposes inventing cinema along the way.

Toward the end of that same year, the United States will see its most tightly contested presidential election to date. Samuel Tilden will actually win the popular tally and come within a single electoral vote of claiming the prize, only to see his mandate stolen by Rutherford B. Hayes, who triumphs by promising the Southern states that he will withdraw the federal army, thereby achieving the Klan dream of ending Reconstruction, an outcome immortalized not quite forty years later . . .

. . . as *The Birth of a Nation*, D. W. Griffith's own lavish Gesamtkunstwerk, featuring, as we have seen, at its climactic moment, the Klan riding on horseback to the rescue of embattled Southern white purity to the rousing strains of Wagner's "Ride of the Valkyrie" . . .

. . . a theme taken up once more twenty-five years after that, back again in Germany, in countless Nazi propaganda newsreels— the Luftwaffe in tight formation raining righteous terror down upon all the opponents of Aryan purity—thereby bearing out the insights of Theodor Adorno, who, as early as 1937, had been decrying how in "Wagner's case what predominates is already the totalitarian and seigneurial aspect of atomization; that devaluation of the individual vis-a-vis the totality, which excludes all authentic dialectical interaction"—the composer-conductor (as Andreas Huyssen recently characterized matters in his remarkable essay "Adorno in Reverse") beating the audience into submission through orchestration that has "the tendency to drown out the individual instrument in favor of . . . large-scale melodic complexes," all culminating in a phantasmagoria, which is to say, in Adorno's words, "the illusion of the absolute reality of the unreal," with (Huyssen again) "the drama of the future, as Wagner called his Gesamtkunstwerk," prefiguring "that nightmarish regression into an archaic past which completes its trajectory in fascism." Having thus nailed Wagner and Nazism, Adorno would go on to seek refuge, through the war years, in Southern California, where he would while away his days, sourly surveying what he came to see as Wagner's legacy in the machinations of the entire culture industry, and Hollywood movies in particular.

Which in turn brings us to the film schools of Southern California, a generation after that, steeped in some of the New Left critique of the Hollywood system that was Adorno's legacy, as well as in a whole set of soaringly Gesamtkunstwerk Sensurround ambitions of their own, from out of which would emerge the likes of Coppola and Milius and Murch, who, a few years after that—as a matter of fact in 1976, exactly one hundred years after Custer's debacle and Bayreuth's premiere and Stanford's purchase and Hayes's deal—would begin work on their own shattering masterpiece, complete with its ironically inverted homage to Griffith, that horrific Valkyrie raid of the choppers of the airborne cavalry, a scene that less than a generation later would be being deployed (pithed of all irony) to stiffen the resolve of an auditoriumful of jarheads at Twentynine Palms Marine base bound for a whole fresh war of their own, in a scene that, less than a generation after that, and in the midst of yet another whole new war, would itself be forming the fulcrum, the very hinge, of yet another effort to nail down the whole self-immolating, self-devouring, agonizedly churning monster of a perplex.

I TYPE OUT AN abbreviated version of the above and email it to Murch, and by way of reply he notes dryly how across his stay here in Manhattan, as he continues editing the picture, he has been a guest at the National Arts Club, off Gramercy Park, which is to say, the old Samuel Tilden mansion. So, go figure.

I took to trying to contact some of the other principals in the story. For example, Coppola himself, who proved to be traveling in Europe, raising money for a new project, and not terribly drawn, when I finally was able to track him down by email, to pursuing my various lines of inquiry. "Sorry," he explained. "I'm far away both geographically and every other way and not really interested anymore." Still, he did rouse himself from such disinterest long enough to note how he didn't "really accept that AN is prowar, though I can see that if you depict such violent acts in a stirring cinematic way, it's hard to avoid glorifying war. But that is only one thread in the total tapestry. I never really thought of the film as an antiwar film so much as a film about the dilemma of 'morality' in certain modern situations and more of an 'anti-lie' film. I guess," he concluded, "that to make a film that is truly antiwar, it would not be set anywhere near battlefields or theaters of war, but rather in human situations far from those."

John Milius, on the other hand, proved almost impossible to stopper, once I reached him by phone. Nor did I have any desire to do so. Famously voluble, with a legendary reputation for being borderline unhinged in the lavishness of his macho-patriotic self-presentations (in an early group shot of the team at Coppola's Zoetrope Studio, he cast himself as a Mexican bandito, with a big sombrero atop his beaming face and a belt of ammunition sashed round his ample belly; his subsequent credits included *Conan the Barbarian*, *Red Dawn*, and now the HBO series *Rome*; and he famously inspired John Goodman's character in *The Big Lebowski*), he also turns out to be immensely likable, though I kept being reminded of the similarly bearish and larger-than-life artist Ed Kienholz, of whom the dealer Irving Blum once confided to me,

"A quarter turn of the screw, just a quarter turn of the screw, and we could have had Adolf Hitler all over again."

"I'm always being portrayed as this extreme right-wing nutcase," Milius interrupted me at one point, perhaps sensing the way my associations were tending, "and though I happily admit to being a flagrant jingoist, I am just as much a seething Marxist as anything else—don't get me going on corporate greed or the so-called policies of the neocons."

I asked him about his inspiration for the Valkyrie scene. Was it true, as I had heard, that he had been banking off *The Birth of a Nation?*

"Nonsense," he insisted, "though it's true I had seen and studied and greatly admired that film in school, and was incidentally just about the only person in the room during the screening, Murch's and Lucas's and all their subsequent recollections notwithstanding. But, as it happens, it was a silent screening, there was no orchestral track, as I recall, so that wouldn't have been where I got it or what I was referencing."

(Murch stands by his version.)

"No," Milius continued, "it simply had to do with my being a surfer, surfing being my entire life in those days. Scratch the surface of any surfer and you'll find a marauding Viking at heart, if they'll only admit it. And that was the music streaming through my head out there on the waves during those years: Wagner and the Doors." Milius definitely doesn't strike one as a Beach Boys sort of guy.

"I was unusual in that crowd at film school, because I'd have given anything to be a Marine. As a surfer I'd spent a lot of time hanging out with the Marines off Pendleton, and I'd had every intention of joining up, in fact I tried, but I got rejected on health grounds, and I was devastated, I felt like I'd been rejected as a human being . . ."

What health grounds?

"On account of my asthma, just like my hero Teddy Roosevelt, who started an entire war, the Spanish American, as assistant secretary of the navy, then resigned so as to be able to fight in it, only to get rejected owing to his asthma, at which point he went and founded his own unit—'Good, go,' his wife said, 'maybe you'll get it out of your system'—headed down to Cuba, and ended up leading the most critical action in the most extraordinary way, the only man on horseback for the entire charge up San Juan Hill, getting shot at from all sides and surviving to tell the tale . . ."

(Now, there's a trapdoor for you: Teddy Roosevelt began serializing his best-selling account of those Rough Rider exploits in January 1899; the very next month, in February 1899, Joseph Conrad began publishing a novelistic rendering of an earlier set of adventures of *his* own, up the Congo River, albeit in an entirely different register: *Heart of Darkness*.)

"That's what I was dying to be able to do," Milius continued, "to go prove myself in battle—the same as all young men long to do, if they are honest with themselves, whether it's right or wrong or even sane, which is a debate that's been going on since we left the caves. Only there was no way I could found my own unit, so I did the second best, which was to write it. Every writer wishes he could actually be doing the thing he writes about. And that Valkyrie scene came from a vision I had of the exhilaration of war—right alongside the terror and the horror and the fear of being snuffed out. The glory of it! Nowadays—unlike during the Victorian era, when the glory was all that got discussed—nowadays it's the horror that always gets talked about. And either one by itself, of course, is a ridiculous half statement."

It turned out that Milius's specific vision (and its accompanying score) had a rather surprising origin. "By 1967, which is when we are talking about here, the Vietnam War had already turned frustrating: The soldiers being sent there had the same dedication as those who'd gone to fight in the Second World War, but it was becoming clear this was a botched job, they were being wasted, it was becoming a futile exercise. The myth of invincibility was crumbling: 'Just wait till the Marines get here!' people used to say, only they'd been there for several years already, and it clearly wasn't working.

"And then, in the midst of all that, came the Six-Day War—this small beleaguered nation, Israel, vastly outnumbered, completely surrounded by a host of enemies who were themselves being outfitted by the same Soviet Union that was outfitting our enemies in Vietnam, and their elite forces just sliced through them all. And I was beside myself, transfixed, I couldn't stop imagining the exhilaration of being in a tank racing through burning Arab villages, like a descendant of King David himself. And tracking that victory day by day, I was throbbing to the Doors—'Light My Fire' was the big hit that summer—and of course to Wagner . . ."

To Wagner?

"Sure, absolutely!"

Wagner: as the soundtrack for an Israeli army victory?

"Absolutely. The Israeli Army prided itself on its Teutonic tactics. Sharon—and those were the days when Ariel Sharon became one of my greatest heroes—had spent his time at Sandhurst"—the British West Point—"studying Rommel's desert tank fighting methods almost exclusively."

Are you, I asked Milius—I didn't quite know how to put this delicately—yourself Jewish?

"Absolutely," he replied. "My family came here in 1812! I had ancestors who rode with Quantrill." (William Clarke Quantrill: the fearsome Confederate guerrilla fighter who cut a swath through Bloody Kansas, sacking Lawrence at the height of the war, in 1863—within a year, as it happens, of the first concert performances, back in Europe, of the "Ride of the Valkyries"—a Klansman avant la lettre if ever there was one.) "My family always says I must be a product of regressive genes."

Presently we were talking about the actual filming of *Apocalypse Now*. "Francis and I would go round and round. I would say to him, 'Trying to make an antiwar film is like trying to make an anti-rain film.' Men seem to deserve war: Left alone, they always create it. I mean, just look at the news any morning, even today: The seed is there in Ken Lay or Bernie Ebbers, this urge to crush other men. Mankind isn't meant to work together: or rather, war turns out to be one of the few places where people can work together. Anyway, on a day-to-day basis, I'd go to the right, and Francis would go to the left, partly because we both knew how much it irritated the other, but in the end we'd usually come to an agreement."

I read him the passage from Swofford's book about the afterlife of films like *Apocalypse Now* and asked him about his own feelings about the film's legacy.

"I'm proud of it, are you kidding? Proud. I'm proud that we helped give the boys who came after a language. I love it how a few years afterwards, when the copters came barreling in on Grenada, they were playing the 'Ride of the Valkyries.' How, for that matter, you can't hold an air assault anywhere in the world today without playing that music. A commander in a tight spot in Kabul calls in air support, and a few minutes later—I saw this on TV—he turns to the camera and says how he loves the smell of napalm in the morning. I know that sometimes I come off sounding like a fiend, but I love it that we gave him that mantra.

"I'm proud to join the long line of military pornographers," he concluded with a dramatic flourish, "right up there with Homer and Shakespeare and Tolstoy and Hemingway."

I asked him how he would feel, though, if his mantras started being used to jazz up young recruits for a stupid war, one unworthy of . . .

"It would be great"—he didn't even let me finish my question—"completely fine with me. Those boys need mantras like that, they need to be juiced. They constitute the point of the spear, and the point needs to be juiced, to be oiled, to be kept ready, whether it's for a good war or a bad war. And we, the rest of us, in turn need people like that who will be willing and eager to constitute the point of that spear. Otherwise we will just end up like Rome, with the barbarians coming pouring in over the gates. That's always been the case. Always will be."

He subsided for a moment and then resumed, somewhat mysteriously at first. "Homer," he pronounced. "Homer. Can you believe what those assholes did to him with that film *Troy?*" He was clearly taking a fellow pornographer's umbrage. "Completely embarrassing. Me and my kid, we wanted to take a DVD of the thing, tie it by a cable to our car's bumper, and drag it up and down Hollywood Boulevard." He fell silent for another moment. "Hollywood," he resumed. "The only thing I can think of remotely as horrible as war: There are stories, things I have seen in that town that, believe me, I would never tell anyone."

HAVE YOU EVER ACTUALLY listened to the words the Valkyries are singing at one another as they ride out onto the stage amid all that surging music? Or, for that matter, thought about what they are actually doing? They are bearing all these battle-slaughtered soldiers up to Valhalla so that, revived to zombie-hood, they can be conscripted into guarding the fortress of the gods through all eternity (this is what anybody longs someday to be able to do?) . . . and, as such, the goddess sisters are calling out to one another:

> *Hoyotoho, hoyotoho! Heiaha, heiaha! Here Helmwige, bring your horse here—Put your stallion next to Ortlinde's mare, your bay will enjoy grazing with my gray—Who is hanging from your saddle?—Sintolt the Hegeling—Then take your bay away from my mare. Ortlinde's mare carries Wittig the Irming—I always saw them at enmity, Sintolt and Wittig—Heiaha! My mare is being jostled by the stallion—The warrior's quarrel even antagonizes the horses—Quiet, Bruno! Don't disturb*

*the peace—Into the woods with your horses for grazing and resting—Keep the mares far apart until our heroes' hatred has calmed—Hoyotoho, hoyoho!*

Really inspiring stuff.

(Though, actually, if you stop to think about it, maybe those jostled horses are a nice little touch of closely observed reality in terms of what actual wars are actually like, which is to say, as boring as all hell. Indeed, that such banality could be rendered so exciting may be the essence of Wagner, whether or not he understood his own mission as such.)

"IT'S TRUE," ANTHONY SWOFFORD was acknowledging one afternoon when I went to visit him in the Chelsea studio where he was putting the finishing touches on his next book, a novel. "When you watch that whole Valkyrie episode in the original movie, there is indeed, right in the middle of it, this incredibly bloody and terrifying scene of one of Kilgore's men, this black soldier, terribly wounded, stretched out screaming in agony as the medics try to tend to him—but later, you don't really remember him. It's Kilgore who you remember, at least if you're young and impressionable, with all his manly bravado. Him and those racing helicopters. Those are the images that have kids enlisting, that and the whole general sense of heightened clarity and vividness, which, incidentally, is true: At times life can be clearer and more vivid in the military. At another point in the film, Martin Sheen's character says something like, 'You'd never find out about yourself like this working in some fucking factory in Ohio'—and there's something to that, too.

"And yet, still, when you look at how the longer-term veterans razz the newbies—and there's a lot of that both in my book and in the film—partly it's just standard fraternity hazing, but part of it, too, I'm convinced, is that they can't believe these kids were so

stupid as to fall for all that crap and end up in this hellhole, and they're punishing them out of their own projected sense of ever having been such fools as to fall for it themselves."

I asked him if he worried about the long-term resonances and the afterlife of the film they were now making of his book.

"Well," he said, "while it's true that it was in part my hope, in writing *Jarhead*, that the horrors of war psychosis might permeate a bit deeper into the culture, I'm not sure that it should be the goal of a narrative film, for example, to turn people against war. And while art should expand rather than constrict people's moral range, as an artist you can't control the audience, only the art." He took a deep breath. "And frankly, I wouldn't be at all surprised if two years from now, when the DVD comes out, you were to find a roomful of Marines at the Twentynine Palms base screening the damn thing and working themselves into their own ecstatic rapture."

He paused. "That's just how it is."

"IT'S AN ENDLESS CYCLE," Bill Broyles Jr., *Jarhead*'s screenwriter, concurred, a few days later, when I reached him by phone at his Wyoming home. "Older men write about the truth of war as a cautionary tale, but young men hear the stories, they read the books and see the films, and they just can't grasp the warning; it's simply not the part that gets through. Those boys who went off to the Second World War, for example, had been raised on a steady stream of First World War movies, all through the twenties and thirties, films like *All Quiet on the Western Front*, with their shattering exposés of trench warfare, but all they remembered, when the time came, were the parades and the tossed flowers and the swooning girls at the outset. And we for our part were primed with *Sands of Iwo Jima* and all those other Second World War films."

Broyles served as a lieutenant with the Marines in Vietnam in 1969 and 1970, the first half of his term with a platoon west of Da Nang, the second half as a general's aide. "I spent most of my combat tour in Vietnam trudging through its jungles and rice paddies without incident," he wrote in a remarkably searching cover story on "Why Men Love War" in the November 1984 *Esquire*, "but I have seen enough of war to know that I never want to fight again and that I would do everything in my power to keep my son from fighting." The piece, which, notwithstanding that credo, then went on to anatomize the compelling lure of war—the sorts of things, he admitted, that veterans have a terrible time trying to explain to their friends and families when they come home, and that most don't even try—featured a haunting photo of Broyles and his then young child beneath a looming war monument. That boy is today on his third tour of duty in Iraq. "Yeah," Broyles admitted, when I pointed out the irony of the situation. "A lot of the time I spent working on this project, I kept thinking about me in Vietnam in 1970 and Swofford in the Gulf twenty years later and my own son there now, and there were days when I indeed got to feeling like some sort of medium."

He'd greatly admired *Apocalypse Now* at the time of its release and was likewise disturbed (if not entirely surprised) by the depiction of its reception years later by the Marines at Twentynine Palms in Swofford's book. I asked him whether he wasn't worried that a similar sort of reception might greet their current work years from now. "If kids at Pendleton get intoxicated by some of the things that they will be seeing in our film, it's not our fault." But wouldn't it bother him? "Absolutely, but we would still have to create scenes that are true. Otherwise you end up in a situation like those old literary tribunals in the Soviet Union, worrying whether something is socially constructive or not, and everything descends to the level of farce. And the truth is that while normal civilian life exists along a sort of spectrum, war pushes that spectrum out at both ends—it is both much more horrible and much much better than anything else. And if you are going to depict it honestly, that is how it is going to be."

Even so, Broyles chose to foreground the distinctly unsettling and problematic aspects of that Valkyrie screening at Twentynine Palms in his screenplay of Swofford's book. It comes at roughly the same moment in the film of *Jarhead*, structurally speaking, as does the Valkyrie scene in *Apocalypse Now*, and it carries much the same wallop (of course, in some senses, literally so). And it features all sorts of mirrorings beyond that obvious one. For one thing, the audience in the theater watching *Jarhead* is momentarily forced to identify, as an audience, with the audience on the screen, and as such to be roused right along with it (and then to be appalled at that arousal, and maybe even more so at its persistence). Then, as well, as Broyles points out, the scene really cleaves Swofford's story in two: "It constitutes the transition between their thinking they may yet be going to war and their knowing they are going to war, and the screen in this context is both preparing them and shielding them. The exuberance and the passion surging through the room masks a terrible fear: It's as if they can exult that Game Day is finally here, and yet this is no game, and they know it, and of all the emotions churning through that room, if fear is the least overtly expressed, it is nevertheless the dominant one."

"I WAS NEVER IN the army myself," the film's director, Sam Mendes, was telling me a few days later, when I paid a call on him at the sound studios where he and Murch and their team were laying in a temporary dub, prepping the film for previews. "Nor was I ever particularly drawn to war movies as distinct from movies per se." (His comment reminded me of that of a friend of mine, who, when I laid out some of the themes I was pursuing with this piece, noted how *Apocalypse Now* had never made him want to go out and make war, though it had made him want to go out and make movies.) "As it happens," Mendes continued, "in 2001, a psychic told me that my next project was going to be a war movie, and at the time I just said, 'No way.' But then I was sent the *Jarhead* book, and I was particularly drawn to the ways Swofford was laying blame for war culture on popular culture, or at least exploring their sources in each other, and then, too, the way he was so powerfully evoking the relationship between war and sex, for example, the rapture of the Marines during the screening of *Apocalypse Now*, all those boys together, how it really got to be like a good rough fuck for them."

Out of the corner of his eye, he'd been watching the screening of a few alternative versions of a later scene on the

sound studio's screen—a blasted desertscape with a surreal black-orange sky, oil rigs shooting up geysers of fire and smoke in the distance, and an oil-drenched white horse (!) staggering into the foreground—and he relayed a series of quick responses over to Murch before resuming. "I mean, my own sense of war, such as it is, and in particular of the Vietnam War, was shaped by Vietnam movies." Born in England in 1965, Mendes would have been ten as the Vietnam War ended, and not yet fifteen when Coppola's film came out. "I remember getting involved in a debate in college as to whether *Apocalypse Now* was pro- or antiwar, which was silly in a sense, since it is so obviously antiwar; but obviously part of its power came from the way it evoked the attractions of war, the virtually genetic pull, the way in which war may be the closest men get to something approaching the intensity of childbirth.

"Not that way, the other way, the way we had it before," he telegraphed over to Murch, who stabbed at a few buttons on his console. "Another thing that really appealed to me in Swofford's book," he went on, "was its evocation of that theme of waiting, of these highly trained, testosterone-buzzed Marines, prepositioned and then stranded out there in the desert for weeks and presently months on end, all hepped up with nothing to do but slowly go mad. As it happens, back in 1990, in the months leading up to the Gulf War itself, I had been rehearsing a production of *Troilus and Cressida* with the Royal Shakespeare Company, and there, too, in what is after all Shakespeare's major take on Homeric material, a considerable burden of the play falls around this theme of waiting—with everybody standing around waiting for Achilles to rouse himself from out of that epic funk of his—or so it came to seem to me at the time, and I shaded some of our readings in that direction. Of course, things eventually went so fast that by the time we finally got the thing onstage, the war was already fought and over."

I shaded our conversation over to Swofford's other theme of war films as necessarily military-pornographic. "I actually disagree with Tony there," Mendes indicated. "I can think of several war films where that wouldn't really apply. I mean, for instance, the first twenty minutes in *Saving Private Ryan*: Nobody witnessing that would have come out wishing that he could take a walk on that beach." But what about the rest of the picture? "Well, yeah," he concurred. "I suppose so. And there is the old problem of its being hard to make a picture about the downside of the porno industry, say, without slipping in a bit of titillation. There simply are people who find this kind of stuff a turn-on."

I asked him if he worried about the potential afterlife of his images.

"Not really," he replied, "in part because this was a different sort of war. You look at the Vietnam films, and it's as if they have LSD coursing through their veins, and the kids raised on those films were fully expecting a similar sort of rush when they got sent off to war. Instead, they got sent out to the desert, and all they really got was bottled water at room temperature, with room temperature often hovering around a hundred degrees."

He laughed mildly and then got up to return to his seat by Murch's side at the central console. On the screen, the oil-drenched horse stared dolefully out in momentary freeze frame, all four legs planted solidly on the ground, hooves sinking into the muck.


THE NEXT NIGHT I joined the team on the other side of the Hudson, at the Edgewater Multiplex, for a screening of the current version of the film before a preview audience of ordinary potential customers. When the press guy from Universal, with whom I'd spoken in advance, asked me about the general drift of my article and I proceeded to hint at some of its probable themes, he interrupted so as to make me understand, in no uncertain terms, that "the studio is definitely not positioning this as an antiwar film." When I now proceeded to mention that comment to Murch, he laughed indulgently. "Yeah," he said, "they're definitely getting a little antsy with this one." I asked Murch how close the team was to the final finished version of the film, and he pointed out that the current iteration featured filler music in spots, standing in for the final score Thomas Newman was still busy composing, and there were special effects, especially involving the oil well fires, that still needed to be laid in, that in fact they'd likely be tweaking it right up to the end, the editor famously being, as he quipped drolly, "like the sous-chef who's still sprinkling pepper onto the main course as they ferry it out into the dining room."

The lights darkened, and the Universal logo scrolled onto the screen in its full Wagnerian glory, after which the hall went black and the film proper began with Gyllenhaal/Swofford's uninflected voice-over welling up from out of the darkness. "A story. A man fires a rifle for many years . . ." And we were off.

And as the film continued to unfurl, I became increasingly convinced that, actually, Mendes and Broyles and Murch could well be pulling off the unlikely achievement of a war film that might in fact never be susceptible to military pornographic co-optation.

This was in part due to the fierceness with which that very issue had gotten laid out early on in the Valkyrie sequence, which in its latest iteration was implicating the theater audience all the more forcefully by starting out from behind the Marines, over their shoulders, our rows of seats in the movie theater blending right into theirs up there on the screen in an uncanny illusion, with that doubling somehow magically serving to inoculate the film against any similar form of eventual co-optation.

Furthermore, that scene itself began to ramify in all sorts of important ways through the rest of the film—specifically this question of war as sex, or to phrase it more directly, who gets to fuck and who gets fucked in war. As it happened, the First Gulf War did not include the usual retinue of brothels and prostitutes along the sidelines: Once posted in the remote desert, the grunts (and they were all men in that war, or at least in this film rendition) were simply stuck there, and stuck, specifically, to stew anxiously over the increasingly suspect fidelity of their loved ones back home: all sorts of fevered speculation continuously swirling around this theme (as if in grim, fuguelike counterpoint to the similarly repeated Marine motto of "semper fi"), culminating in particular in a devastating scene (conspicuously bookended, as it were, to the earlier *Apocalypse Now* homage) in which one of the grunts' wives sends him a video of *The Deer Hunter*, and everyone gathers round the VCR all excited for a reprise of their earlier pornographic rapture, which only increases in intensity when it turns out that the wife has in fact spliced some actual hard-core pornographic footage into the reel, which presently turns out to be of her herself ostentatiously fucking the slob next door as a way of getting even with her husband for all his imagined infidelities. From deer hunter to cuckold in one sickeningly fell swoop: horned revelations, indeed.

Beyond that, this particular war turned out to be unlike virtually any other in that the ground forces didn't even get to follow through with any triumphalist fucking-over of the enemy. After months of preparation, most of it with the grunts grimly languishing out there in the sweltering desert, the war, when it finally did come, proved an entirely one-sided affair, the side in question being the sky, from which the uncontested allied air forces rained down unutterable horror upon the vastly outgunned Iraqi conscript army, with the allied ground forces held in abeyance till the war was almost entirely over. In the film, one of Swofford's unit's only two actual engagements, and far and away the more terrifying one, turns out to be with friendly fire. Later, as they march in, a helicopter goes swooping by overhead, playing a song by the Doors over its loud-speakers, and one of the grunts shouts bitterly that they can't even have their own music! The Swofford character in particular, a sniper honed and trained within an inch of his life, literally never gets to fire a shot. "Yeah, there was just too little war to go around with that one," is how Milius parsed matters for me, empathetically, when we spoke about the First Gulf War. Broyles, for his part, noted how with that war, unlike Vietnam or most any other, both sides of the spectrum, the death-terror and the killing glory, got squeezed way in.

But not the horror. For it turns out the Marines in this instance, though they ended up doing hardly any fighting of their own, were nevertheless conscripted into the role of witnesses and forced, Buchenwald-like, to stumble in upon the appalling afteref-fects of some of those air raids (the famous turkey shoots, as they were referred to at the time). A miniversion of the notorious High-way of Death, a burnt-out traffic jam of twisted metal and charred human remains, stands in, in this film, for the mini-My Lai of the sampan massacre in *Apocalypse Now*, and there is nothing the slightest bit glorious about it. The footage left the Edgewater audi-ence as gut-punched as the soldiers up there on the screen. At one point, the Swofford character wanders off on his own over a berm, coming down upon a scene of yet more unspeakable carnage; when he returns and his staff sergeant asks him what he saw, he shakes his head blankly and mumbles, "Nothing."

And Nothing, too, is what you see in the pithed-out face of the homeless, washed-out Vietnam vet—haunted veteran him-self, one wonders, of something very like Kilgore's Valkyrie shock forces?—who toward the end of the film clamors onto the bus ferrying our returning heroes through their measly homecoming parade and slurringly thanks them for having done the country proud and restored the Marines to their former honor. Semper fi, semper fi, Hoyotoho!

Samuel Fuller once said that for a film to be truly true to the actual experience of war, bullets would need to be spraying out from the screen, taking out members of the audience at random, one by one, in scattershot carnage. This, of course, is not that film. But to the extent that Coppola was right in his insight that an antiwar film might of necessity need to exclude the depiction of war fighting itself (at the time I'd thought he had been referring to something like *Grand Illusion* or *King of Hearts*), the Gulf War of 1990 may turn out to have been almost unique in lending itself to that sort of treatment (at least from the American side).

Alas, its follow-on war, the one in which we are mired today, is nothing like that. And as the haunted veteran Swofford character himself clearly realizes at the end of this movie, standing ten years on and staring out from his middle-American suburban studio window into a scene that seems to transmogrify before his and our very eyes (to transmogrify and then to ramify with yet further bitter intensity with each passing month since Broyles and Mendes and Murch first composed the scene), we are still, yes, we are all still in that desert.

# DOUBLE VISION:
## The Perspectival Journey of the Oakes Twins
(2008)

TRY THIS: GAZING STRAIGHT AHEAD (as you will no doubt at some point be urged to do if you start hanging out with Trevor and Ryan Oakes for any length of time these days), extend your right arm straight out to your side, perpendicular to your gaze, your hand in a fist, your thumb pointing upward, starting out from behind your ear and now slowly arcing the arm forward. (The Oakes boys, that is: identical twins, just past twenty-five years old, both artists, now living in New York City but before that from out of West Virginia.) At first you won't see the upraised thumb, of course, but presently, there it will appear, at the periphery of vision ("at the corner of your eye," as they say). Keep moving your arm forward until presently the thumb's extended out there straight in front of your face at the center of your gaze; now with your left hand extended, thumb up, hand off the arcing transit, as it were, continuing along until eventually that thumb disappears behind your other ear. The thing is (as the Twins will explain with earnest enthusiasm and at quite considerable length), there was only a short part of that transit where you were seeing the thumbs with both eyes and hence with any sort of depth perception. Through most of the rest of the experiment, your nose was blocking the vision from out of one, and then the other eye. And yet your brain, your visual cortex, was weaving the scene into one continuous, undifferentiated experience. ("Pretty cool, no?" By now the Twins will have veritably lit up with boyish enthusiasm.)

Not getting it yet? Okay, try this: Closing your right eye, gaze to the right with your left. If you're wearing glasses you may want to take them off. Notice how your nose, looming huge, blocks a good part of the view in that direction. Now, shift eyes: closing your left eye and peering left with your right. Same thing. Pretty obvious. Only, now, with both eyes open, gaze right, and notice how your nose pretty much disappears from your visual field, even though your left eye is in fact clearly taking it in. (The Oakes Twins have been concocting little experiments like this and comparing their respective experiences pretty much since toddlerhood.) Once again, your brain, your visual cortex, suppresses the thing it doesn't need to see (the nose) and weaves together a continuous, undifferentiated vantage. (Other twins develop spooky secret languages; for their part, since early on, the Oakes boys have been engaged in a continuous tandem investigation into the very fundaments of visual perception.)

Or, all right. Try this: See that tree over there in the distance. Close one eye, and with your extended thumb block it out of your field of vision. Straightforward, easy. Now, close that eye, and open the other, and your thumb will seem to have shifted a few inches to the side; bring it back over, and you can block out the tree again. Okay, now leaving your thumb extended like that, open both eyes, and you will notice that you can see the entire expanse before you. Even though your thumb is manifestly blocking the scene, you can see the tree and everything to either side with perfect clarity. And in fact you're not seeing your thumb. Or rather, your thumb appears as a transparent double ghost of itself. (And it's by way of little experiments like these, rigorously plotted and pursued with redoubled single-mindedness, that the Twins have recently begun making some of the most original breakthroughs in the rendering of visual space, and in particular that of three-dimensional perspective, since . . . well, actually, since the Renaissance.)

WHAT IS ARGUABLY THEIR most remarkable invention to date, or at any rate the one that has so many people talking (experts ranging from artists like David Hockney and art historians like Jonathan

Crary to neurologists like Oliver Sacks), is based on two conceptual breakthroughs.

The first isn't so much a breakthrough as a recovery of long
lost knowledge. For through an extended process of investigation
(of which more presently), the Twins arrived at the insight that
contrary to virtually every representation in our daily lives, which
following the lead of Renaissance thinkers envisions us as fording into the world, gazing into the world, as if through a flat window (paintings, television, movies, computer monitors, the page
before you), in fact perceptually we each of us actually experience
the world as if we were inside, at the center of, a giant perceptual
sphere. Indeed, they came to realize, if you are going to represent
the world, something has to be curved—be it the line (as on a
Mercator projection), or else the lens (in photography), or else . . .
And here came their first insight: Why not the paper? Wouldn't it
be truer to the feel of vision as we actually experience it if one rendered the scene before one on a piece of paper shaped like a tranche
of the inner lining of a sphere? And as I say, in so thinking, they
were precisely upending a Renaissance way of visualizing the world
that has held sway ever since the breakthroughs of Brunelleschi
and van Eyck and the other giants of the early fifteenth century,
one that in turn had itself been grounded (as Erwin Panofsky
demonstrated so magisterially in the first part of his seminal 1924
monograph, *Perspective as Symbolic Form*) in the overthrow of the
prior antique/classical/medieval model of ourselves as living, precisely, at the center of a giant sphere.[1]

Their second breakthrough, the one that has artists in particular so astonished, is that the Twins have figured out a way of
rendering the world before them onto that curved sheet of paper,
in fact of tracing the world onto that page freehand, as if by way of
a camera obscura or a camera lucida projection, only without any
equipment whatsoever, other than their own binocular vision, or
more to the point, their visual cortex—deploying the same innate
capacities that allow any of us to see past our doubled ghost thumb

out onto the vantage before us. More on precisely how they got to this breakthrough and what exactly they are doing in a moment. In the meantime, though, just look at the results . . . (Figs. 1, 2 and 3)

IT'S A LONG STORY how I first got to know the Twins, one that I think I'll save for another time. But soon after having caught wind of their existence, I called on the two of them in the diminutive basement one-room apartment, just east of Union Square in New York City, that doubles these days as both their teeming workspace and their compact homepad (a set of narrow bunk beds tucked neatly into one corner). The boys are on the tallish side of average, thin, and somewhat more than conventionally handsome; indeed, with their high cheekbones and their intent, clean-cut, deferential, and yet at the same time eminently self-assured manner, they often put me in mind of a pair of variations on a younger, softer, somewhat plainer James Dean.

Actually, it's not exactly right to characterize them as hailing from West Virginia; rather they seem to have hailed from pretty much all over. Their mother, Elizabeth Poe (a distant relative, as it happens, of the brooding poet, who herself always gets referred to by the Twins, her only children, as "Poe"), proved something of an itinerant academic, an expert on children's and young adult literature (and occasional Caldecott judge) regularly in search of a better posting. Hence the family's moves from Boulder, Colorado, where the Twins were born in February 1982, to Wisconsin, then briefly to Scotland during their fifth grade year, then to Blacksburg, Virginia (for grades 6 through 11), and on to Morgantown, West Virginia, for their final year of high school. Their father Larry (referred to as "Lar" by the boys) is a clinical social worker (with an uncanny resemblance of his own to the actor James Cromwell), an easygoing professional who always seemed able to find suitable work wherever the family pitched up (he is currently a leading official overseeing the county's Head Start program in Morgantown).

1

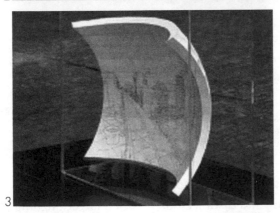

2

3

The Twins' aptitude for art didn't come from their parents. "Heck, we can't even draw stick figures," their father informed me when I went to visit them as well in the home they maintain on a lush hillside overlooking Morgantown and the banks of the Monongahela. On the other hand, the boys were also preternaturally verbal. Larry recalled for me a time he'd overheard them conversing. "Ryan was saying, 'Trevor, do you realize that we are hundreds of years old.' 'I know,' agreed Trevor, and I had to intervene, explaining to them that, well, actually, no, they were only three." And preternaturally independent. Poe remembered an incident even earlier than that, when they were still toddlers being cared for by a babysitter who'd been momentarily called away by a phone call. When she turned around, they were gone. "They'd made a break for it, crawling out the front door, down the driveway, and out onto the sidewalk. She was turning the house upside down looking for them, panic-stricken, when a few minutes later the phone rang and it was a neighbor all the way around the block wondering whether anyone might want to know that the twins were making a beeline down that street."

Ryan, for his part, told me about a time a few years later (though still in Colorado and hence before they were six) when the two of them had been sitting atop a bluff at the nub of a dead-end street near their house, gazing out across the plain stretching out down below, and trying to gauge exactly how far and how big a mound of dirt way off in the distance in fact might be. "So we decided to check it out. We clambered down the ridge, about two hundred feet, and then set off toward the clump, which involved crossing a busy highway and then hiking on for another mile or two. Turned out to be a construction site with a bunch of tractors and stuff, all very interesting from the kid point of view, and then we headed back home." What had their parents made of that little expedition? I asked. "They'll be hearing about it for the first time when they read your piece," Trevor replied, smiling.

The focus on size and distance was part of a larger ongoing

discourse. "On long drives," Trevor recalls, "we used to talk about the way a bug splattered on the windshield would appear to double if you looked out beyond it, and what then happened when you tilted your head from side to side." How old were they when they were doing this? "Oh," surmises Ryan, "three or four." They'd dissect the foreshortening of approaching rows of telephone poles, tapping out complicated rhythms with their fingers in syncopation with the passing poles.[2] Their mother had given them erasable markers, and they'd try to trace the outside world across the backseat passenger windows and then talk about why that was so hard to do. One time they were being driven somewhere at dawn, with the sun rising off to the side, and Trevor took to trying to figure out how far he could turn his head before the orange orb would disappear "into the black, as I thought of it" beyond his peripheral vision. They'd talk about that. They spent a lot of time analyzing their parents' potential sightlines as they hid in a pantry (playing with matchsticks) or up on the garage roof behind the basketball backboard. (What for other kids was just hide-and-seek for them proved but one more occasion for investigations into optical geometry.) Poe recalls how for a time Trevor used to go around saluting, "Aye, aye!" and then pointing to his eyeballs, gigglingly, "Eye, eye!" And how they were both able to freehand quite expressive versions of Garfield as early as three. And how the time they took them to see a children's theater production of The Wizard of Oz, a few years later, the thing that had the two of them most captivated wasn't anything transpiring onstage but rather the mechanics of the lighting. Some years after that, the boys would find themselves sitting on stumps about twenty feet apart, gazing off into the distance, and trying to imagine what the depth perception of a being with eyes twenty feet apart might be like. "Cool," they agreed.[3]

On the other hand (or perhaps as another aspect of the same general cognitive horizon), they were both profoundly dyslexic. In a house veritably teeming with children's books (to this day, Poe is the bane of the UPS guy in whatever town she alights, daily receiving boxes and boxes of sample volumes to add to her groaning shelves and piles), for the longest time, well into sixth grade, the Twins could hardly decipher a thing. "To our mother's chagrin," says Trevor. "Well, not chagrin," corrects Ryan, "more like dismay." "Yeah," agrees Trevor. "Dismay." Larry recalls how neither of them, though especially Ryan, "could manage to blend letters. Faced with the word 'Roger,' for example, they'd painstakingly sound out 'ruh-ah-geuh-euh-err'—completely clueless." (Quite remarkable, when one thinks about it, in a pair of twins who years later would find themselves veritably slicing and dicing the visual process, the better to comprehend its inner workings). At school in Wisconsin, they managed to score in the second percentile from the bottom in punctuation. "I was, like, 'Duh, they can't read a single word!'" says Larry. "For their part the boys were proud of it, went around laughing and bragging." (They had similar problems deciphering notes on a musical score, though they were both quite proficient at piano once they'd memorized a piece.) Meanwhile, they excelled in practically everything else: acing math, for example (except for word problems). "We had them on both handicapped and gifted tracks simultaneously," Poe recalls.

They displayed exceptional comprehension of anything read to them, and they loved being read to. Trevor would enjoy observing the shapes of the letters. And Ryan recalls how "When we were being read to, I'd look around the room and focus in on a little pleasing detail, like the way that the chair leg intersected with the carpet and the table met up with that intersection. I'd search out these little places to look at that had a resolution to them." As opposed to gazing on a text, which precisely was failing to provide any resolution whatsoever.

Through all those years, though, their true passion was for making things. "Let's go make stuff!" they'd exult, racing into the house the minute school was over, bounding down to their playroom. In fact this was the case even before they started going to school. They both recall fondly, and Larry confirms, how the last year of preschool they spent days beavering away out on their driveway, hammering together wood scraps into a claptrap boat that grew to over twelve feet in length. (Their preschool class put together a field trip to come witness the achievement.) "They had remarkable attention spans," observes Poe, adding, "That may in part have been—and this is one of the few things I think we can really take credit for as their parents—because we forbade them television." (It wasn't until years later that they first encountered Alf on a neighbor kid's TV, Trevor recalls, and the effect was quite unsettling.) They weren't allowed television; nor were they allowed coloring books ("I didn't want their imaginations squeezed between somebody else's lines," explains Poe). On the other hand, they were supplied with all the high quality art supplies—Elmer's Glue, colored papers, colored markers, Popsicle sticks, pipe cleaners, glitter powder, masking tape—they could desire. ("One time I came home and they had masking-taped the door shut from the bottom to as high up as they could reach," recalls Larry. "I kept trying to force it open, to no avail, and I could hear them laughing away inside at my hilarious predicament.") "The Popsicle sticks and glue and pipe cleaners," Trevor recalls dreamily, "—the whole arsenal of tools I learned to think with."

They were inseparable, and though profoundly ambitious hardly ever seemed to compete with one another. "They never cared which of them won the various art competitions," their mother recalls, "as long as one of them did." (For their part, the parents practiced a meticulous evenhandedness, so much so that to this day Poe will not tell them which was born first.) For the longest time neither would deploy the first person singular. It was always we-this and we-that. Indeed, Ryan insists that it wasn't until he was fourteen and for the first time found himself separated from Trevor for any length of time—for over a month, as it happens, when he received a scholarship to a governor's art camp, which Trevor didn't ("The thing is," Poe explains, "the competition only allowed for one winner from each school")—that he was forced to start thinking in terms of "I." The first several weeks there he mystified his teachers and fellow campers by continually referring to himself through a seemingly royal we, as in, "The way we see it is . . ." or "The way we always do it is . . ." And to a remarkable degree this pattern persists to this day. They are always referring individually to "our teacher," "our parents," or "our patron" in a way that actually becomes quite fetching.

Indeed, their twinship has seemed of the essence to both their method and their achievement all along. I was corresponding with the psychoanalyst and Hannah Arendt biographer Elisabeth Young-Bruehl the other day, and she observed how, "If you believe that thinking is an internal dialogue between you and yourself (which is how Hannah Arendt defined it in *The Life of the Mind*, following Socrates as Plato reported him), then you can understand how twins are rather uniquely positioned to have that conversation between themselves, externally, if they grow up sharing their thoughts. Friends and lovers can sometimes attain to this experience of the other as like another self, but twins uniquely get to have it over the course of an entire lifetime; they don't come into it as adolescents or adults finding each other. And if their minds work quite differently, or converse inwardly quite differently, as the Twins' minds seem to, you can get a remarkably rich, multivoiced complementarity." Which seems all the more telling and true when the conversation in question turns out to be about binocularity—two individuals completely in sync in an ongoing investigation into what it means to see with two eyes.

Seeing, and seeing with two eyes, was at any rate forming one of the principle motifs of the Twins' work by the time they got to high school. Thus, for instance, these paired drawings of Ryan's (Fig. 4) and, perhaps even more tellingly, these other paired drawings of Trevor's (Fig. 5), his response to an assignment to draw the same image twice, once "realistically" and the next time with more active marks (the striking thing here being that placed side by side

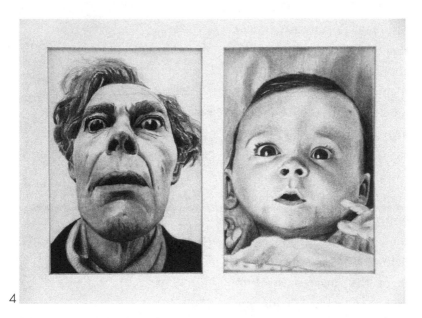

4

like this, they keep reading—and insist on being read—as the two eyes of a single face, even though they are both images of the same left eye). The walls of the Oakes parents' home today are bedecked with such high school marvels, hung about like so many instances of sloughed off skin, and it was fun being given the tour by the obviously proud if still somewhat bewildered parents ("I have yet to cease being amazed at how things keep developing for the two of them," admitted Larry). But in the end, two images really jumped out at me as harbingers of things to come. The one, Ryan's

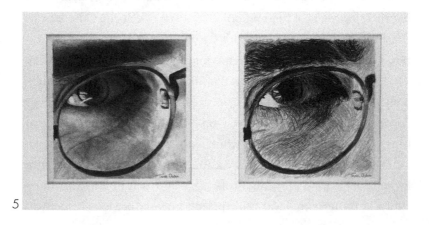

5

response to an assignment that he draw something in the stipple style—the view from high up a cliff with a close-up on a rock-climber's knuckles just then clambering up over the ledge (Fig. 6)—testified to an exceptional level of ambition and self-certainty (especially when you imagined the tandem duo down below whose coming achievement the image seemed to be announcing: "Climbing

6

Mount Perspective," it all but cries out). The other, from Trevor's junior year, arose as part of a yearlong series entirely given over to bagels—rhapsodic bagels, cubist bagels, close-up bagels, bagel sculptures, and bagel oils ("The award this year goes to Trevor for his bagel series," announced the principal at that semester's year-end ceremony, "though, Trevor, don't you think it's about time you learned to spell 'bagel'?"). The specific bagel image that stopped me cold though was this one (Fig. 7)—talk about premonitions.

Such at any rate were the sorts of things that Trevor and Ryan brought along to the various portfolio days art schools kept holding their last years of high school, including one at the Corcoran in Washington, D.C., for New York City's Cooper Union—an institution notoriously difficult to get into for any single applicant, let alone two, since only sixty students get admitted each year from throughout the country, all with full four-year scholarships. Uncowed, Trevor cornered senior faculty member Don Kunz and began explaining to him at earnest length, as is his wont, about the method behind a particular painting ("I used a palette knife. Do you know what a palette knife is? It's a kind of minispatula . . .") at which point Kunz interrupted ("Young man, I was using palette knives since long before you

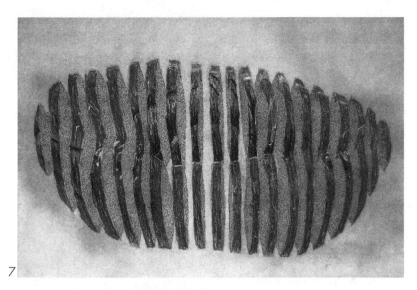

7

were born"). ("Oh," said Trevor, not the least bit fazed. "So then you know what a palette knife is. But anyway, what I did was . . ." and so forth.) Still, Kunz was quite taken with him, and in fact with both of them; he urged them both to apply on an early admissions basis, and presently, in an unprecedented development, both twins were admitted, on the basis of the separate excellences of their applications, and both decided to go.

THE FIRST YEAR AT Cooper Union was given over to classes in the so-called fundamentals, with the student body divided into sectional groupings of fifteen students each, and the Twins were assigned to separate sections (the better to foster individual development, as far as the authorities were concerned), which was fine by them. Indeed, all the way through school, they'd make a point of signing up for different sorts of classes (Ryan taking more painting and drawing, Trevor more sculpture). "We looked at it as a way of surveying a wider range of what Cooper Union had to offer," says Ryan, "because we could always share information and techniques. And we didn't need to be being exposed to the same things for our thought process to keep moving along on a similar keel."

And indeed, they shared dorm rooms and studio space throughout. Not infrequently, depending on their relative immediate workloads any given week, they would do each other's homework (the academic equivalent of dating the same girl, unbeknownst to her). "Perfectly acceptable to us," says Ryan (referring to the homework, while declining to comment on the question of the girls).

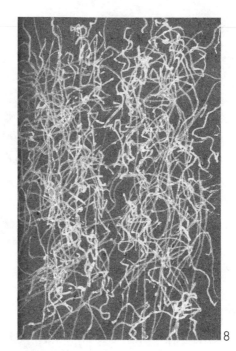

8

For his part, from early on, Ryan focused on ways of "justifying my marks," as he puts it, accounting as rigorously as possible for why and how his energy was getting expressed on any given surface before him, and on how to keep such expression from turning merely arbitrary. Thus, for example, that first winter, he spent a lot of time staring out his dorm window recording onto the page before him the way individual flakes of snow fell, one transit layered atop the next—letting wind and gravity dictate the work's outcome. (Fig. 8) Presently, in similar fashion, he'd start spending hour upon hour fashioning his own brushes, as a way of tending to (and indeed intending) another aspect of the process he otherwise found overly arbitrary.

Trevor, for his part, began taking corrugated cardboard panels and cutting them into three-inch squares, piling those squares one atop the next (the corrugations all running parallel) so as to form three-inch cubes, which he then laminated and started placing one beside the next, though with thin little shim-wedges at the back between each cube, thereby presently enforcing a gentle curve in the ever lengthening row (a curve he would come to recognize

9

as the inner arc of a wide circle). The extended nine-foot-long cardboard-cube row eventually read as completely opaque, a solid brown wall, unless, that is, you happened to drift over to one particular spot, roughly fifteen feet away (the center, as it were, of the circle in question), at which point all the corrugations lined up and (magic!) the row seemed to disappear entirely. Around the same time (in response to an assignment that he fashion something that would take a long time to make), Trevor returned to the thought tools of his youth, gluing one wooden match lengthwise to the next, the rounded bulbs all abutting at the top, the square bases all meshing at the bottom, presently emerging with another curving object both beautiful in itself and peculiarly fraught with as yet not quite realized implications. (Fig. 9)

Meanwhile, their more general perceptual inquiries continued unabated. They grew ever more fascinated by peripheral vision, and in particular the way it was experienced corporeally from out of the contours of the human face—the way for instance the field of vision seemed wider horizontally than vertically (understandable when you realized that your eyes were placed horizontally one beside rather than atop the next in your face, and that furthermore your jutting browridge tended to interfere with the view looking up—but also suggestive of an evolutionary prehistory in which our ancestors were more likely to have faced threats welling up from the ground than raining down from the sky). Testing the limits of their perceptual field, come nightfall, they would climb to the roofdeck of their seven-story apartment building and then lie horizontally, their heads tilted back slightly (to compensate for that annoying browridge), and realize, to their astonishment, that in that manner they were able to take in not only the full hemisphere of stars above but also virtually the entire 360 degrees of the surrounding girdle of city lights. Human perception!

There were the conversations as well in which they began to take note of the curious way in which their noses severely narrowed the extent of their depth of field. They became convinced that a person's nose, even though usually occluded by the operations of the visual cortex such that it tended to disappear from view, served to anchor the scene, though not in the way one might expect, as a beacon pointing the way ahead, as it were, right down the middle of the visual field. Rather, it might be more accurate, in considering bifocal vision, to think of the nose as appearing doubled to either side of the visual field, as it were bracketing or bookending the scene before us. And this was a phenomenon, they came to feel, with implications not only for vision generally but for art-making in particular. One day Ryan was studying a recent suite of abstract paintings by Trevor (Fig. 10), and never one to accept the arbitrary nature of anyone's mark, he took to focusing in particular on a seemingly recurrent triangular motif off in the lower corner of several of the paintings. "Wait a second, Trevor," he announced exultantly. "That's your nose!" Such shapes appeared not only in Trevor's paintings but in those of other students as well. And indeed, come to think of it, in those of all sorts of other far more accomplished artists.[4]

10

Presently the two of them would extend these nose-investigations with more analytic rigor, literally mapping the contours of their own depth perception by each of them, with one eye closed and then the other, having the other twin record the precise place where a laser dot first appeared beyond their nose as it slowly made its way across a screen opposite. (Figs. 11 and 12) The result in both cases, variations on a shieldlike shape (denoting the shape of the respective visual fields in which they were able to see the laser dot with both eyes, as opposed to with just one eye or the other, and hence with any degree of depth perception) gave rise to further considerations. For example, they took to wondering whether it might not be the case that actual shields (the antique or medieval armor kind) served not only to protect their owners from their opponent's attack but also to prevent anticipation of

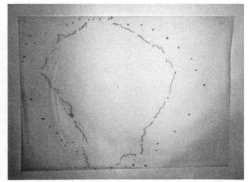

1, 12

the direction from which their own next attack would be coming, precisely by blocking out their opponent's entire zone of depth perception. When they raised this possibility with neurologist Oliver Sacks recently, he in turn observed how it has long been noted in the literature that lepers (whose noses have fallen off) display preternaturally good depth perception; he also surmised that in much the way basketball selects for tall people, this might explain why boxing seems to select for flat-nosed individuals (which is to say that boxers don't come by their flat noses from getting hit while boxing; instead, all things being equal, having flat noses going into competition would make them less likely to get hit in the face in the first place). David Hockney, for his part, with whom the Twins subsequently spent an entire afternoon in concentrated discussion, recalled Piero della Francesca's celebrated portrait of the Duke of Urbino, a nobleman whose profile was conspicuously out of whack on account of the fact that, having been blinded in one eye as a result of a fencing accident, he'd had the bridge of his nose surgically carved away to give his remaining eye a wider field of vision, quite a necessity in those murderously conspiratorial days.

Much of sophomore year Trevor spent elaborating on the match-tranche he had created at the end of the prior year, which is to say, lavishing months and months on the creation of an entire match mound, or dome, a truly gorgeous matchstick hemisphere. (Fig. 13) And the longer he labored over the thing, the more the boys began to realize that the object was evincing a remarkable property: If you turned it over (Fig. 14), every single one of the nine thousand individual matchsticks was (of course, now that you stopped to think about it) aimed at the same focal point in the hollow center of the hemisphere.[5] Thus inspired, Trevor returned to his corrugated cardboard sculpture and decided to extend it as well, laying six rows vertically atop the original arcing length of wall, except not straight up vertically, rather curling inward (through the regular deployment of further shims), such that the resulting wall now read as a tranche of the inside of a sphere, with

13

14

all its corrugated hollows pointed at the same vanishing point, from which locus the seemingly opaque piece once again (only even more startlingly) suddenly disappeared (Figs. 15 & 16).

These material investigations (Trevor thinking, as ever, with his originary tools) presently set the stage for a series of conceptual breakthroughs by the Twins working in tandem (at one point I asked whether anyone else among their fellow students or teachers tended to get caught up in their conversations, but Ryan explained that usually their growing enthusiasms—related as I can well imagine at exhaustive length—met with blank if benign stares, and that they were exceptionally lucky to have had each other as inexhaustibly attentive sounding boards). For starters, they quickly recognized that the match dome mimicked, or anyway modeled, both the way light rays sped out from a single light source, say the sun or a lightbulb, and the way they sped into the eye itself. Then one really bright spring day, as they sat in a Central Park grove out behind the Metropolitan Museum, "under a pink blossoming tree, looking at a dark brown tree branch," as Ryan recalls, they suddenly realized how they were surrounded by, or immersed in, a "hyper-saturated foam" of such light-splays. The sun sent out its infinity of light beams; any single one of those beams might hit, say, a spot on a pink blossoming branch, provoking another spherical explosion of light beams, only one of which would enter any given eye, along with the infinity of other converging discrete beams ricocheting off the infinity of other surfaces. The eye in turn would be gathering in its own infinity of beams, from all of those surfaces, some farther off than others.[6] Indeed, as the Twins now began to characterize the process, binocular depth focus was "like eating with chopsticks," the sight lines from each eye intersecting, like chopstick tips grasping food, on whatever detail of the visual field one happened to be focusing on at the moment. This in turn helped to account for the double-ghosting of objects intervening in front of that distant point of focus (farther up the separate chopstick stalks, as it were), which they were also beginning to notice.

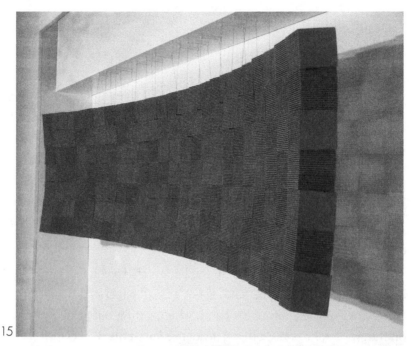

15

16

In the old days, Poe had told me, her dyslexic sons had taken notes in class by way of a flowing series of drawings and ideograms. Now they took to elaborating their bourgeoning theories through diagrams and figures strewn across any piece of paper they could find: notebooks, napkins, Post-it notes. (One day their classmate Oscar dropped by their pad and happened upon a savagely scrawled-over Post-it note with the legend "The whole reason perspective happens," which set him to laughing hysterically. To this day, whenever they get together the three of them crack up at the memory.)

By this time (junior year), they had moved into the basement digs that have served as their homebase to this day. Trevor decided he was going to try to contrive a silkscreen roomscape that would be true to the act of looking as he was fast coming to understand it. That is, with one distant point in focus, the rest of the intervening scene progressively fracturing into double ghosts. In preparation for doing so, he would spend hours on end trying to get one eye to focus on a distant spot, the other, simultaneously, on the intervening obstruction. The complexities involved were proving incredibly daunting.

But then, another Sunday in the Park with Trevor, this time by himself, he happened to be holding out a small paper pad parallel to the ground in the palm of his hand, when, gazing out at the leaves on the ground, he noticed that if he focused with his right eye on the leaves and his left eye on the right side of the paper pad, a doubled ghost image of the pad would seem to land, as it were, atop the leaves on the ground (or vice versa)—an image so distinct and so vivid that he could trace it out exactly with his pen. Not the whole scene before

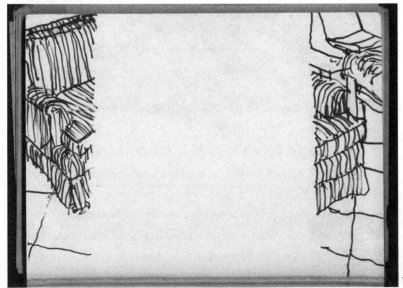

17

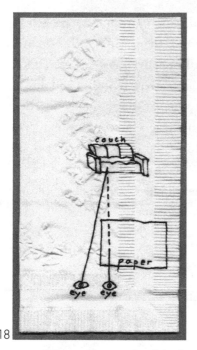

18

him: just a sliver, "a bookmark's worth," as he characterized it: a vertical slice. (As wide, he presently came to understand, as the chopstick wedge emanating from out of his two eyes, the right eye converging on the leaf, the left eye's vantage interrupted by the notepad.) Coming home that evening, Trevor demonstrated the method for Ryan, drawing a vertical slice of the sofa before him. (Fig. 17) "Pretty cool, huh?" he remarked, to which Ryan, ecstatic, responded, "Are you kidding! It's spectacular!" (Talk about justifying one's lines!)

Using this method (a diagram of which Ryan now sketched out for me on a nearby napkin—Fig. 18), Trevor began working up a series of drawings, detailing one bookmark slice of the scene before him on the left side of his paperpad, another slice on the right side, leaving the intervening space empty. At week's end, during a classroom critique of the resultant drawings, Trevor's teacher completely ignored the drawing's method, so entranced was he by the conceit of the intervening emptiness, upon which he rhapsodized at some length. When Trevor tried to explain that he hadn't been the least bit interested in the empty part of the page, the teacher responded, "Well, then it's just a gift! Isn't it wonderful how sometimes we get gifts like that?"

Back home, both Trevor and Ryan were now perfecting the technique: drawing a bookmark slice and then folding that part of the page back and drawing the next slice over, and then folding that next part of the page, until they'd been able to draw, or actually rather trace, an entire scene with uncanny precision.

But there was a problem: The bookmark analogy wasn't quite

exact. For in fact the image projected, as it were, onto the page, was wider at both the top and the bottom of the page. Which stood to reason if you thought about it: Given the relative angles of vision both up and down, wider swaths of the world were arriving up and down there than onto the middle of the page. This was simply another instance of the kind of distortions that plague all conventional perspective systems, the reason Greenland looms so much bigger than it actually is on a Mercator projection (Newtonian physics sufficing, as it were, for most operations at the middle of our experience but breaking up into curved Einsteinian vistas at the extremes).

They couldn't simply bend back the page along the curved expanse, since the next slice would prove even more curved. Momentarily flummoxed, they looked over at Trevor's matchstick dome, and a lightbulb went off, shedding insights in every direction.

WHAT WOULD IT BE like, they wondered, if they could find a way of drawing on the inside of a sphere? Or rather, if they could, as it were, press a traditional gridded rectangle into the form of spheroidal segment and then use the interior surface of the thus smeared-out grid as a drawing platform? Each square would naturally pinch into a sort of lozenge, with the tiles toward the center pretty much square and those toward the corners and edges growing progressively more diamond-shaped (the lengths of the sides of each tile would of course remain equal and unchanged). One would have as well to custom-shape each pinched parallelogram of paper accordingly (sort of like the tiles on the space shuttle). But were one able to contrive such a concave grid, one might then imagine securing it atop a tripod easel, with a headrest at the center to hold one's eyes steady. Or rather one's left eye, since with one's right one would need to be seeing past the edge of any given tile out onto the world beyond. (The process could be either additiv—starting with an empty grid and adding one tile at a time—or subtractive, starting with a grid entirely filled over with blank tiles and working from the right edge inward, removing

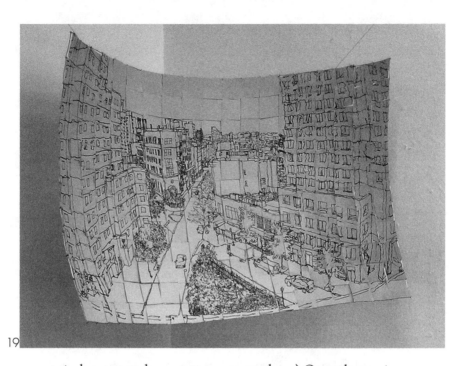

19

vertical rows one by one as one went along.) Once the tracing was finished, it would be a relatively simple matter to go back and tape the now drawn-over tiles together into that full concave scene, which would in turn read as much truer to the lived experience of perspective than any traditional Renaissance windowlike approximation. All of which presupposed one was going to be willing to spend the hours and hours and hours to make it happen—which, however, given the history of these two particular boys wasn't likely to present that big of a problem.

That, at any rate, being how the Twins did indeed spend most of their last year at Cooper Union (Ryan for his part meanwhile contriving ever more astonishingly supple brushes as well). Their first grid did in fact take just about forever to fashion, what with having to calculate and recalculate the dimensions of each square, and then to contrive the pieces of paper to fit. And since they had fashioned the grid out of soft wire, it only lasted two drawings (Fig. 19). A second grid, made out of slightly stronger wire, lasted hardly any longer, though it occasioned somewhat more assured images.[7]

GRADUATING FROM COOPER UNION in 2004, the boys started cobbling together a livelihood by working as studio assistants to artists further along in their careers, landing occasional jobs in interior design and construction, and increasingly, by custom-crafting ever more exacting paintbrushes for artists ranging from Cecily Brown (one of their former teachers at Cooper Union) to Alex Katz. Meanwhile, though, they continued to ponder the challenge of fashioning a more durable concave grid, perhaps this time out of sheet metal: one problem, however, being that they no longer had access to the metalworking facilities at Cooper Union.

Some years earlier, though, as it happens, after the family had moved to West Virginia, they'd established contact with a distant cousin of Poe's, a seasoned master machinist named Willis Bowman ("in his eighties," says Trevor; "no: seventies," counters Ryan; "okay, seventy-five or so," offers Trevor, and Ryan demurs) (actually he was in his midsixties) who was living on a small farmstead in Southern Ohio: and their grandfather now fronted them enough travel and motel funds to enable them to go consult with him. "Willis is extra-smart about metalworking and materials science and technology," Ryan insists, "more knowledgeable we're sure than any college professor; and throughout his life, as factories all around the area have been modernizing, he's been buying up all this magnificent old machinery and installing it in his barn." Willis gave the boys full run of his barn shop and answered any questions they had, though he was the kind of mentor who liked to give his wards plenty of room to learn from their own mistakes.

They decided to fashion a large domed solid over the outer surface of which they could then contrive a cardboard template model of their eventual sheet metal grid, and somehow they got it into their heads that the best way to do so would be to fashion it out of wood. So Willis went along with them as they located a four-foot-tall tree stump on a nearby hill and chain-sawed it down; he helped them maneuver the felled stump into the scoop of a tractor (the thing weighed about a ton, and all of this was happening in

20

the dead of winter), conveying it over to the barn, where from one precarious crane to the next they managed to pivot-winch the thing over to a huge metal-lathing machine on the far side of the barn. As Willis watched on bemused ("He told us he was pretty sure we were 'going around the barn to get to the house,' is the way he put it"), the boys set up a radial jig carousel and across the next several hours, working the bore in and out and back and forth, spewing veritable dunes of sawdust in every direction, they managed to carve out a big wooden dome, which, once they'd sanded the thing smooth, they then somehow managed to haul back to their motel room, where they spent the next several days improvising the intersecting cardboard templates (both curving along their bases and perpendicular at their joints), from which they would then be able to fashion their eventual sheet metal grid (ants boiling out of the insides of the dome the entire while). (Fig. 20) It turned out that, just as Willis had surmised, each of the resultant curved template strips was identical, most of the complexity the boys had conceived of beforehand canceling itself out, and there would have been a whole lot easier way of doing this. Still, back at the farm, Willis now let the boys excavate strips of scrap sheet metal out of two abandoned school buses he keeps around for the purpose, which they then fashioned into the flat, inch-wide curving bands dictated by their cardboard templates, laying in the variously angled intersection notches wherever indicated. Presently they slid the intersecting metal bands into place, with Willis himself performing the exceedingly delicate welds at each crosshair intersection. (It was, as I say, a very cold winter, and though Willis had improvised a way of heating the barn burning used motor oil he'd col-

21

lected for free from surrounding gas stations, giant barrels of the stuff double-stacked all about the barn, this presented challenges of its own, challenges rendered all the more disconcerting—and the boys crack up laughing as they recount this part—when Willis blithely proceeded to perform those flame-spewing welds with the concave grid lying atop a thin plywood platform stretched across one of the barrels. And what did their parents think of that? I ask. "They'll be hearing about it for the first time," they tell me, "when they read about it in your piece.") Still and all—slow-motion presto: a good week's worth of work later—they had a concave metal grid, which they now affixed atop a sturdy tripod (Fig. 21).

WITHIN A COUPLE WEEKS of their return to New York, they received their first commission: the view from the roof of the Union Square Cinema (Fig. 3 above). Their patron had a friend who was selling his apartment next door (with a virtually identical view) so as to be able to move back to London, and the guy wanted to offer that friend this extravagant souvenir. The thing is, once the boys had completed the drawing, the patron liked it so much that he wanted to keep it for himself. (I, too, am especially fond of this one: in particular the exceptionally realistic way the foreshorten-

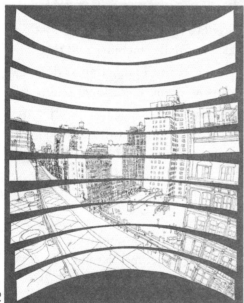

22

ing ledge seems to fall away to the left—exactly the sort of effect that tends to get distorted in more conventional perspective renderings.) He asked if they could make him a copy for his London friend so that he could keep the original, which now afforded them the opportunity to develop a system for the meticulous reproduction of these concave drawings. Indeed, once they fanned the curved strips out flat once again across a level board (though this time horizontally, for some reason: a butterfly spread) and photographed that, the resultant high res tiff file (Fig. 22) could be blown back up to identical size as the basis for an exact copy, or else either bigger or smaller (the latter forming the basis for a series of jewel box—or rather, actually, Lucite baseball collectors' box—editions of subsequent drawings).

Shortly after that—another long story—they learned that the top floor of the Chrysler Building with its tall tight triangular windows was momentarily vacant, and somehow (the boys can be

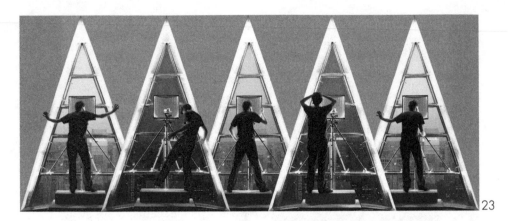

23

exceptionally winning) they managed to procure permission to set up shop up there for several weeks, eventually emerging with their most ambitious cityscape to date, the entire Manhattan skyline gazing north vividly splayed out below them. Occasional photographs documenting the process—Trevor clambering into position at the optical cockpit behind the concave easel (whose tripod, incidentally, so as to allow for a better vantage, had been secured to a board spread atop a grouping of tall filing cabinets)—formed the basis for another striking series of modular works (as in, for example, Fig. 23).

And so they continued on, one such concave drawing after the next, each one taking several days, sometimes several weeks to draw. Generally speaking, it was Trevor in the drawing cockpit (for one thing, he had developed an astonishing capacity to decouple the focus of his two eyes for hours at a time—not an easy thing to do even for a few minutes: Just try). Indeed, with this particular body of work, Trevor had taken the conceptual lead, though Ryan was every bit as involved in realizing the cumulative vision. "Ryan is the more down to earth of the two," Lawrence Cacciatore, a Cooper Union administrator and longtime fan and observer of the Twins' work, surmises. "Trevor gets it all spatially configured and conceptualized, but there's something missing, and Ryan fills that gap: He helps bring the project in." Something like one of those fraternal Hollywood director-producer relationships,

I hazard. "Yeah," Cacciatore agrees, adding, "As it happens, I'm an identical twin myself, and I can understand what it means to want to complete your brother's thought or enterprise, not as a matter of competition or dominance, not for you to be the one completing it, but rather such that it will be complete." Meanwhile, as the months passed, Trevor's hand was becoming more and more assured, the sheer draftsmanship evidenced in the tracings becoming ever more authoritative.[8]

Curiously, as the years now began to pass, the Twins seemed indifferent to pursuing any conventional gallery representation. Or rather, perhaps more precisely, they didn't seem to need to be working themselves into a desperate lather, seeking after same. Rather, in a throwback to their early Renaissance counterparts, they just naturally seemed to attract a network of well-heeled patron-enthusiasts (largely artworld outsiders: environmental lawyers, currency traders, and the like) willing and in fact eager to help bankroll their ongoing travels and investigations (for example, by paying for a trip out to California so they could show their concave vision machine and its resultant drawings to artist David Hockney, who, as I say, ended up spending the better part of a day thoroughly engrossed by the project).

Most recently, the Twins have been in Chicago, lugging their concave easel tripod from site to site, recording a variety of iconic cityscapes in anticipation of their first museum show this coming fall, at the Spertus Institute on Michigan Avenue. (Full disclosure: It was I, in my sometime role as artistic director of the Chicago Humanities Festival, which likewise convenes every November, who initiated that match.) A few months back I visited them out on the AT&T Plaza in the city's Millennium Park, where they had pitched camp in order to capture a vantage of that other formidable optical device, British sculptor's Anish Kapoor's splendidly gleaming, silvery mirroring Cloud Gate (affectionately known to all Chicagoans as "the Bean"). Trevor was hunkered into his contraption: In a fresh innovation, he was no longer steadying his head by leaning his chin into a foam-cushioned rest but rather had slotted his entire skull into a sort of plaster of Paris helmet (which he assured me was much easier on his neck muscles, though it did give him the general look of a mad scientist freshly escaped from a nearby lunatic asylum). (Fig. 24) They'd been at work on the image for several days already and were still only halfway through. At that particular moment, Trevor was tracing in the horizontal lines of the plaza's paving stones off in the distance, and surveyorlike, he'd sent Ryan out to walk each consecutive crack back and forth, the better for him to be able to plot the exact place where Ryan's foot hit each line. Completely oblivious, just over to Ryan's side, a young Japanese couple, in full bridal regalia, had picked that precise moment and that precise vantage (with the Bean, of course, as backdrop) to photographically immortalize their union, and completely oblivious, their photographer was continuing to snap away as, equally oblivious, Ryan, intent on Trevor's hand signals, inched resolutely forward, deeper and deeper into the Japanese couple's splendid wedding shots. Trevor had just begun to reach that point in his process where the Michigan Avenue skyline, smeared in a

24

25

vast swooping reflection atop the Bean's convex pate, was in turn beginning to show up in his own concave rendering. The sun was gleaming bright and needlelike at the top of the Bean at the peak of its midday transit, and I now asked Ryan, who had wandered back over, where, given the length of time it was taking them to draw the vista, they were going to place the sun in their drawing. "Oh," he replied, "we never include anything that moves in these drawings, so in fact we won't be including the sun at all."

The Twins presently completed the drawing of the Bean (Fig. 25) and set off down the street[9] to start work on another vantage, this time of the Spertus Institute's startlingly fractured postmodernist glass facade jutting out into the rest of Michigan Avenue's urban cliffscape. Meanwhile, they also set to work on a fresh project. Working with the world renowned Pollich Tallix artists' foundry in Upstate New York (veteran of projects with the likes of Jasper Johns, Roy Lichtenstein, and Claes Oldenburg), and with the backing of their patrons, they were going to be taking the Bean drawing and blowing it up onto a six-by-six-foot stainless steel concave shell, for eventual display, right there in Millennium Park to the side of the Bean itself—the better to allow passing visitors to gauge the full effect of their method, and the full marvel of their own capacities for depth perception.[10] (Fig. 26)

Looking further into the future, the Twins talk about how they'd someday like to contrive a similar blow-up of one of their images as big as the entire far wall of a long gallery space. First, though, Trevor wants to improve the concave grid easel, for one thing fashioning it out of a stainless steel one-third as thick as the current version (and hence that much more transparent). Meanwhile, it turns out that they got the scrap-metal, tree-bore molded model slightly wrong: The perpendicular slats are all pointing (matchsticklike) to a focal point at the center, where Trevor's left eye, the one gazing out onto the paper tiles, is frozen in place; whereas if you think about it, or anyway might yourself realize if you ever tried to use the thing, the slats should be pointing just slightly off center to where the right eye is, the one gazing out beyond into the world. As a result, the current grid easel features a smattering of subtle but nonetheless annoying blind spots. To tackle this problem, it turns out that their solid wooden dome would be of no use, but the straight mathematics involved—that is, in getting all the slats, both vertical and horizontal, to line up with a point those couple inches off center—are unbelievably forbidding. Though not, of course, to Trevor: In classic fashion, he has been doggedly reinventing spatial trigonometry for himself, pouring forth literally thousands of separate calculations, a separate series for every single one of the 149 crosshair intersections of the grid.[11] He's pretty sure he's got the problem licked now, and as soon as they get a chance, the boys hope to actually fashion their new concave easel.

26

Beyond that, Trevor and Ryan are entertaining other schemes as well. Trevor has taken to watercoloring his concave vistas—getting past mere line, that is, and into atmospheric color. One day recently back at their homepad, Trevor pulled out for me a blank concave armature, just like the kind he'd otherwise be drawing over, only they'd painted the entire surface of this one a bright even yellow. Up ahead, he explained, when they got a little more time, they were going to try to fashion a set of red fins, jutting up inward from the concave skin of the armature, sort of perpendicular but not quite, in such a way that when the viewer placed his chin against the headrest and lined up his two eyes just right, one eye would take in the yellow backdrop, and the other would see only the red fins (each of which would be so fashioned as to block out that eye's vantage of the individual yellow tile immediately beyond it and nothing else). If they can get the scheme to work, they are expecting that the viewer's visual cortex will meld the two colors together, and what the viewer will

27, 28

then see will be an even orange expanse, which in fact won't be there at all. (Either that, or else maybe, with the two eyes fighting for dominance, the view will strobe or swirl back and forth between the yellow, red, and orange—the swirls in turn being evidence of electrical activity in the visual cortex, where the two eye images are being merged.) If that experiment works, they then propose to lay in one full image against the concave backboard, and then spread a sliced up version of the same vantage, only slightly shifted over, across the protruding fins—thereby provoking much the same sort of three-dimensional illusion that would otherwise require special glasses or else an old-fashioned bifocal stereoscope to attain. Only, this time, once again, the effect would require no other special equipment than one's own two eyes and visual cortex.

Of all their future projects, however, arguably the most intriguing may involve a revisioning of some of mankind's earliest visual manifestations. Because remember that double ghosting thumb—the way nearby objects double up at the forefront of the visual field when one is focusing off in the distance (even though we have grown so inured to this phenomenon across the dailiness of our lives that we no longer notice it)? Lately, in their spare time, Trevor and Ryan have been surveying imagery from Neolithic cave art all over the world, and they keep coming upon this sort of thing (Fig. 27), and this other (Fig. 28). Could it be, they've recently taken to wondering, that such doublings of silhouettes were meant to betoken the relative closeness of the animal in question—or, even more beguilingly, that in the olden times, before our distant ancestors had grown inured the way we have, that that was just the way they actually went around experiencing the world?

Just wondering, as one always seems to be doing when one finds oneself hanging out with the Oakes Twins these days. Just wondering.[12]

# BLOCKAGE AND GRACE:
## Mark Salzman Lying Awake
(2000)

LAST WEEK, MARK SALZMAN, the forty-year-old author of four often luminous volumes (a pair of memoirs and a pair of novels), released his most accomplished work to date, a fictional narrative entitled *Lying Awake*. The book, a lean (its typescript came in at under a hundred pages), seemingly effortless tour de force, was, according to its author, the product of nearly six years of agonized blockage, doubt, and misgiving.

"Sister John of the Cross pushed her blanket aside, dropped to her knees on the floor of her cell, and offered the day to God." Thus begins Salzman's improbably absorbing tale of a cloistered Carmelite nun in the midst of a spiritual crisis. Every moment a beginning, she thinks, every moment an end. Presently, she gets up, dons her robe and wimple, and goes over to her desk to review a sheaf of poems, the writing of which had kept her up till well past midnight the night before. They are the latest evidence of an out-pouring of grace that mysteriously began three years earlier, slaking what had degenerated into a dry and cramped midlife vocation.

She rises, tidies her room, and silently carries her washbasin down the hall to the dormitory bathroom. She empties its contents into the sink: "The motion of the water as it spiraled toward the drain triggered a spell of vertigo. It was a welcome sensation." Instead of going to the choir to wait for the others, she returns to her cell, kneels down once again, and unfocuses her eyes:

> *Pure awareness stripped her of everything. She became an ember carried upward by the heat of an invisible flame. Higher and higher she rose, away from all she knew. Powerless to save*

*herself, she drifted up toward infinity until the vacuum sucked the feeble light out of her. A darkness so pure it glistened, then out of that darkness, nova.*

In the radiance, Salzman records, Sister John "could see forever, and everywhere she looked, she saw God's love." At length, thoroughly ravished, she returns to herself and, as soon as she can move again, opens her notebook, and begins once more to write.

End of the first brief chapter. During the next few chapters, it becomes evident that Sister John's visitations have been arriving at an increasingly harrowing physical price, that they are preceded by ever more debilitating headaches, and that in fact something is decidedly wrong. Eventually, she breaches the walls of the convent community to go to an appointment with a neurologist, who gives her a battery of tests, including a CT scan.

These tests uncover a small tumor in the temporal lobe, just above Sister John's right ear. Such tumors elsewhere in the brain have been known to occasion convulsions and seizures. Although they manifest themselves epileptically in the temporal lobe, too, as the neurologist now tries to explain, here the seizures tend to be more psychological, or even spiritual, in character—fever spikes of transcendent well-being. Dostoyevsky was said to have suffered from such visitations, and so, apparently, did St. Teresa of Avila, the founder of the Carmelite Order.

Sister John is devastated by the diagnosis ("Please, God, take anything, take my life . . . but don't take Yourself away from me, don't tell me I haven't known You at all"), and unconsoled by assurances that the tumor is eminently operable. Returning to the convent, she is racked with misgiving: Had this entire passion merely been some kind of vast illusion, or rather, was it God's manner of making himself felt in her life? What is she to make of her ongoing (and more and more wrenching) transports? Then again, perhaps she is expected to think of the operation itself as a test of her faith.

But the prospect of returning to the aridity of her prior monastic existence is almost more than she can bear. After such knowledge, what forgiveness—and what grace?

This, then, is the vocational crisis, the existential crux, to which Salzman's narrative brings his protagonist, the shadings of which he only now starts to draw out at length—heartrendingly—like a master cellist.

A MASTER CELLIST, AS it happens, being what Salzman himself once seemed on the way to becoming. We were talking about that alternative life one morning recently as we sat out on the yucca-shaded back porch of the wood-and-stucco bungalow he shares with his wife, the documentary filmmaker Jessica Yu, in the chaparral foothills of the San Gabriel Mountains, on the outskirts of Los Angeles. Salzman is unlike anything you would have expected if *Lying Awake* was the only one of his books you ever read. (On the other hand, he's exactly like what you would have expected had you encountered only his two books of memoir, *Iron & Silk* and *Lost in Place*.) He's neither Catholic nor particularly religious in any conventional sense—and he isn't the slightest bit dour. He's spry and mischievous: a human gleam. He's powerfully built (if somewhat on the slight side), with a mime's bearing. He shambles about with a sort of lope and is subject to explosions of glee. Yet, at heart, he's a mournful fatalist, which is to say that he is truly the son of the father to whom he dedicated his second book, *Lost in Place*, a memoir of "Growing Up Absurd in Suburbia," in the following terms:

> *For Joseph Arthur Salzman,*
> *artist, astronomer, social worker, beloved father*
> *and good natured pessimist,*
> *whose reaction to this book was to say that*
> *he enjoyed it, but felt that my portrayal of him was inaccurate.*
> *I put him, he complained, in an excessively positive light.*

Salzman's mother, Martha, on the other hand, has a sunny disposition. Formerly both a concert pianist and a concert oboist, she later became a harpsichordist and teacher. It was from her side that Mark's love of music flowed, though not, as it happens, immediately. "I started with the violin, and then piano, but neither of them really took," he now recalled. "Then, one evening, my parents dragged me to a cello recital—I was about seven at the time—and from the moment the young player walked onto the stage with that instrument I was captivated; I was enthralled. I mean, the shape of it, the color, the varnish like the glaze on a caramel custard. And for a second, as the guy was setting up, I got a peek at the far side of the instrument, and it was like a tiger's back, all gloriously striated, and the way he then held the thing, as if he were riding a tiger, holding it by the neck and drawing the music out of it—and the sound! My God, I was completely hooked."

For the next ten years, Salzman devoted himself to the cello— well, not entirely. It turned out that he, too, was torn between two passions. Only, in his case, as readers of *Lost in Place* know, the other consuming enthusiasm of his adolescence was kung fu: He established an incense-reeking shrine in his parents' basement, in Ridgefield, Connecticut, and swathed in tie-dyed pajamas and a Surprise Bald Head Wig (his parents wouldn't permit the thirteen-year-old to shave his head), he practiced kicks and lunges for hours at a time. After which, he practiced his cello.

And he wasn't half bad at it; at sixteen, he was accepted at Yale, having applied as a potential music major. Two weeks before starting Yale, however, Salzman ventured up to Tanglewood, in Lenox, Massachusetts, to attend a recital by Yo-Yo Ma. "And that was absolutely one of the transformative experiences of my life," he said. "I'll never forget how Yo-Yo walked out onto the stage. I mean, most performers walk out completely stiff, like this, and you can sense the sobriety; the utter focus, the intense concentration—the barely concealed terror. And I don't even mean that as a criticism: The technical level expected of performers nowadays is so insanely high that you'd be crazy if you weren't terrified. Yo-Yo, by contrast, came out like this—totally relaxed, guffawing, almost slap-happy, casually waving to friends in the audience, you know, 'Oh wow, great, what are you doing here?' Completely, but completely, unfazed.

"And then he started to play. Bach—the Fifth Suite for Unaccompanied Cello. And his playing was so beautiful, so original, so intelligent, so effortless that by the end of the first movement I knew my cello career was over. I kid you not. People talk about Yo-Yo Ma's superhuman technique. Let me tell you: Superhuman technique is only the tip of the Yo-Yo iceberg. What really sank my ship was how much he was obviously enjoying himself: He was lost in the music, freed by it, speaking through it, in love with it. He was enjoying himself as much playing as most of the rest of us do when we're listening, and as I myself never did when playing, not to speak of practicing.

"When I heard Yo-Yo play, I suddenly realized that I wasn't just inadequate—I wasn't even making music. I was training to be a showoff, that's all. My playing was to true music what a résumé is to a piece of real writing. My true calling, I realized, was not the cello, never had been. My true calling was to teach kung fu. So I put the cello into deep storage, and reporting to Yale, I majored in Chinese."

Salzman excelled at Chinese. In 1982, just out of college, he traveled to Changsha, the remote capital of Hunan Province—an unusual undertaking for an American in those early days of the Communist thaw—to teach English at a medical college and, more to the point, to study Chinese martial arts at their very headwaters. Returning to New Haven two years later, he set about composing a memoir of the experience, the narrative that became *Iron & Silk*, his first book. (During this period, he met Jessica Yu, a beautiful and self-assured Yale sophomore, who was the daughter of a Shanghai-born oncologist. Somehow, their early relationship survived both her relative obliviousness regarding her own Chinese origins and his disconcerting habit of smashing his bare fist into a steel plate a thousand times a day as part of a conditioning ritual.) *Iron & Silk*, which was published in 1986, proved to be a considerable success and, indeed, had something of a Holden Caulfieldesque popularity on college campuses. It was later the basis for an ill-conceived movie, starring Salzman himself, filmed in mainland China. (The shoot ended on June 3, 1989, the eve of the Tiananmen Square massacre.) One would have no conceivable reason to look for that film nowadays except that it allows one to witness Salzman in full martial ecstasy: a startling vision.

Once Jessica had graduated from Yale, the couple moved to her home haunts, in the San Francisco Bay Area, where Salzman wrote a novel, *The Laughing Sutra*, a magic-realist picaresque that traces the adventures of a Chinese orphan and his sidekick, a mysterious two-thousand-year-old knightly warrior. The couple presently transplanted themselves to Los Angeles, and Jessica started making independent documentary films. A few years later, she won an Academy Award for a short-subject documentary, *Breathing Lessons*, about a writer who spent most of his life in an iron lung. (At that year's televised ceremonies, Jessica, sheathed in a borrowed strapless black gold-embroidered Mary McFadden dress and draped in similarly borrowed Harry Winston jewels, began her acceptance speech with the observation "You know you've entered new territory when your outfit costs more than your film.") Mark, meanwhile, had begun work on his second novel, *The Soloist*.

"So here I was," Salzman resumed. "This was maybe fifteen years since I'd more or less abandoned the cello, and I was finding myself writing this novel about an embittered failed wunderkind, a cello prodigy whose career had suddenly and mysteriously come undone at the age of seventeen." Salzman interrupted himself, laughing. "I love it when people come up and ask, 'Where do you get your ideas for your novels?' Anyway, suddenly it was as if this character had become hypersensitive to pitch, or his sense of tonal confidence had broken up, and he was unable to continue concertizing. He'd fallen away into an empty, deracinated life of teaching, and now he was middle-aged, and what with one plot turn and another, he finds himself given charge of this little Korean boy, a phenomenal cello prodigy, and all these feelings start welling up in him.

"As I was coming to the end of the book, I realized how badly I wanted this cellist to be able to enjoy playing once again—not as a concert soloist but just as someone who loves playing for the sake of the music, who strives for the ideal that music represents but isn't destroyed by failure to reach that ideal. And as I was writing that scene I had the stereo playing in the background, and on came Bach's Fifth Suite, the one that Yo-Yo Ma had been playing the day he tore through the hull of my ship and sent me to the bottom of the ocean. I was describing this moment when the cellist, alone, drags the bow across the strings, just to hear the music come alive, and how it does come alive for him, and how now when he makes mistakes he no longer cares, he doesn't think of them as a crime against music but, rather, as an act of nature, like the random cracks that show up in those Oriental teacups everybody's always raving about.

"After I'd completed that scene, I remember thinking, If I can do that for him, why not for me? So I rented a cello—my own was still back in Connecticut in deep storage—and I tried acting out the scene I'd just written, and it was wonderful. That was ten years ago, and I've been playing every day since, and I can honestly say that nowadays, playing, I feel the way Yo-Yo looked.

"How I sound is an entirely different matter."

I'D COME OUT TO L.A. because I'd heard that Salzman had recently started offering a performance piece—cello and narrative—that relayed the saga of the composition of his new novel, set to a score by Bach. There was to be a performance that very afternoon in the Mark Taper Auditorium of the L.A. Central Library.

I hurried downtown and was comfortably in place when Salzman came onto the stage, cello in tow, wearing a gray T-shirt and casual black pants, relaxed, guffawing at the audience's friendly reception, waving to longtime pals scattered in the seats. Laying the cello on its side, for the moment, but declining as yet to take his seat beside it, he launched into his talk.

"Bach wrote six suites for unaccompanied cello," he began. "They were nearly lost—in fact, the autograph manuscript was never found, and only a few copies, handwritten by his wife, managed to make it though. Once rediscovered, for the longest time they were simply ignored, mistaken for exercise études. The story goes that at the age of thirteen the prodigy Pablo Casals was rummaging around in a secondhand shop in Barcelona, and he found a dusty copy of these pieces he'd never heard of; he bought them, took them home, studied them, and was later to describe the experience as the greatest revelation of his life. He worked at them every day for twelve years until he had the courage to play them publicly, and then he seemed to never stop performing them, with absolutely intimidating authority. These pieces have become to cellists what Shakespeare's plays are to actors, or Rembrandt's painting to painters: the foundation of the repertoire, the music we can forever return to and never exhaust." (In *The Soloist*, the boyhood mentor of Salzman's protagonist asserts "that Bach's musical inspiration was divine in origin, and that to play Bach properly was an act of religious devotion.")

Salzman went on to suggest that he had developed a theory as to why these pieces become so meaningful to cellists. "Because, you see," he said, "I believe these pieces function as stories—not specific stories. I don't mean, for instance, that the Second Suite is about the birth of Bach's twenty-third son, or anything like that. No, I think that when we play them our emotions take a journey that so closely resembles a narrative journey that I believe there's got to be a relationship between the two. And I want to illustrate this point by taking you on two parallel journeys—the musical one, of course, but then another as well, the narrative of the genesis of my most recent novel, from its original conception to the final version." He'd be performing Bach's Third Suite, he explained, which, like the others, consisted of six movements; similarly, the story of his novel's evolution could be broken into six segments.

Before proceeding, Salzman assured his audience that he wasn't going to be making any great claims for his musical competence. He went through some of the same points he'd gone over with me about the history of his vocation as a cellist, invoking George Bernard Shaw's observation that "Hell is full of musical amateurs: music is the brandy of the damned." He then recounted how he'd been reading a tale by the neurologist Oliver Sacks about an Italian immigrant whose temporal lobe epilepsy had resulted in visions of his boyhood village so vivid that he'd felt compelled to render them as paintings. Sacks had pointed out that such epilepsies are sometimes characterized by an intensification of emotional life and a general sense of illumination and faith. "And I found myself thinking, Imagine if someone already committed to religious life were to develop such a disorder. Wouldn't she interpret its symptoms as a confirmation of her vocation? And let's up the stakes: Let's say that under the spell of such seizures she starts writing poems, and they start getting published, and they start selling, so much so that the royalties save her convent from bankruptcy. A lot of these convents are hanging by their fingernails. Only there are problems, of course, not the least of which is the jealousy of her fellow nuns. Furthermore, if the condition goes untreated, it could get worse. On the other hand, if these are valid mystical experiences and she gets an operation to have the disorder treated, she might be giving up the graces of God just in order to improve her health. How would she experience this news? And what would she do?"

Salzman picked up his cello and sat down. Taking the bow, he smiled broadly and announced, "The Prelude!" He momentarily pulled the bow aside, and added, exultantly, "Isn't that a great idea for a novel?" before launching into the piece with robust self-confidence. (As he played, I was reminded of a scene in *The Soloist* in which the protagonist recalls hearing of a scuba diver who grabs a passing whale by its fin and finds being pulled along by such a creature to be the most incredible experience of his life. Salzman's protagonist adds that it can't have been that different from playing onstage.)

After the Prelude, Salzman said that the next movement was called an Allemande and was more tentative, reflective, and searching in tone. "Questions stumbling toward answers" was how he put it—"not unlike what I myself was going through in the months after my first inspiration. For example, what sort of person was this nun? How old was she? What had made her first decide to join the order? And how early had her disorder kicked in? And then, as well, other sorts of questions, like: Why had my last three books sold so few copies? Why was I so conspicuously absent from the *New Yorker*'s 'Twenty Best Young Fiction Writers in America' issue last year? What was that all about? I mean, really, was I just a 'nichey' writer, as mediocre a writer as I was a cellist? And, more to the point, my last protagonist had been impotent and this one was celibate: Why didn't my characters ever have sex? But seriously, I took to wondering, how could I make this book more interesting, more . . . you know . . . more commercial?" He gazed out at the audience for two beats, longingly, searchingly, before picking up his bow once again and announcing, "The Allemande."

When that movement ended, Salzman declared, "Now comes the Courante, which is confident, pleased with itself, reckless even, but you get the sense that it's headed for danger, like those bubbly teenagers in all those horror movies. Because the thing is, then I had an idea: What if my nun falls in love with her neurologist? Let's say he's one of those cold doctors who don't relate well to patients. Maybe he's mourning the loss of the identical twin brother with whom he'd shared such a close identity; she is mourning the imminent loss of her sense of the presence of God. They have something in common. Sparks fly. This attraction develops, and they have to decide what to do. In the end, they decide to go their separate ways, but both are changed for the better by the experience.

"What a great idea! It'll be like a cross between the movie *Witness* and the movie *Awakenings*; my people will get in touch with Robin Williams's people; we'll package it all with Winona Ryder as the nun; I'll make so much money that I'll have medical benefits, a pension plan, an investment portfolio. I'll throw a party for the twenty best young writers in America, and it'll be like the prom scene in *Carrie!*" He was beside himself. He marshaled his bow once again: "The Courante."

Setting aside his bow at the end of that movement, which he had indeed raced through with almost reckless gusto, Salzman said gravely, "And now comes the slow movement, the Sarabande, the center of emotional gravity of the entire piece. If I had to give it a title, I'd call it 'Facing the Consequences of Hubris.' But still in C major, and C major is an optimistic key, so it's not about complete defeat, at least not yet." He took a deep breath. "I spent the next five years writing my surefire best seller. Five years, and it was the most terrible experience of my life. I could not get my characters to act like real people. I couldn't get them to talk like real people. Hell, I couldn't even get them through doors: 'Her hand reached toward the handle of the door' . . . 'Her hand extended toward the oaken knob of her' . . . No no. No. Jeesh. By the third year, my concentration was so shot that any sound distracted me and just drove me crazy, so I took to wearing a huge towel wrapped around my head and stereo earphones on top of the towel, and that worked except that I have two cats, and they liked to sit on my lap when I worked, which distracted me. And so I made a tinfoil skirt, because cats don't like tinfoil. I wore that outfit every day, until one day I saw the gas-meter reader hiding behind a tree outside, staring in at me, and that distracted me even more. So I finally moved to the one place where I felt so trapped that the only way I could get out was through writing, and that was the passenger seat of my car, out in the driveway, in which I proceeded to pretty much ensconce myself for a whole year. Now, I drive an old station wagon with a moon roof, and one of the cats was still so angry about the tinfoil skirt—and now, on top of that, the move outside—that every day she would walk out, clamber up the hood and up the windshield, and plant herself squat squarely in the middle of the moon roof. And I tell you that the view from where I sat was the perfect metaphor for what I was going through: Writing that novel, I was just staring up a cat's ass.

"Anyway, finally I finished, and all I felt was exhaustion; there was no joy. But I thought that maybe others, reading my manuscript and not knowing what had happened, would say, 'It's beautiful; it was worth it.' So I sent it out, and the response came back, well, mixed. My friends said they liked it, but they more or less knew that was a requirement of the job. My editor back in New York sent me thirty pages of notes, and they were severe criticisms. I remember one sentence in particular: 'Mark, we need to talk about main characters.' My agent said, 'I think this belonged in the oven a little longer.' People looked at me with pity.

"I was like the literary equivalent of a beached whale. I couldn't even look at a sentence without my eyes crossing. I thought about abandoning the project. But what was I going to do if I just scuttled it? Who was to say that I wouldn't just hit the same wall with my next effort? And what if it was that close to working and I just needed to push myself a little further? Hell, the Unabomber had published more than I had over the past five years. At least he was getting something out there. I decided I had to go on somehow, and all I could think of was throwing it all out and starting from scratch." Salzman seemed to tremble palpably at the memory of the experience as he reached once more for his bow: "The Sarabande."

The music was indeed lugubrious, almost excruciating. "So," he resumed, when it was over. "On to the fifth movement, the Bourrée, which is in effect two short pieces, the first in C major, the second a dark shift into C minor, and then the first played all over again, C major, but transformed by the experience of having passed through the other.

"The problem was obvious: The love story never belonged there. I had to return to my first impulse and focus entirely on the nun's question: Had hers been an authentic relationship with God, or was it, rather, solely with her own longing to be holy? And the next year was a good year: no tinfoil skirt, no car. And, when it was done, I felt vindicated. I had passed my own test; I myself had stuck it out; I was an artist after all. I completed a manuscript, and last summer, when I performed a first version of this talk at a writers' conference in Sun Valley, I was able to report that I'd learned what writing's all about. The book was done, and it was good. Meanwhile, I'd sent the manuscript off to my editor, and a few weeks later I called her up and I asked her, all expectant, how she liked it, and she said, 'I missed the doctor.' But then I reread the book myself, and I fell completely apart: because the thing was, it did suck. I had written a bad book. And I was destroyed.

"Anyway, that October I'd been scheduled to spend five weeks at one of those New England artists' retreats where you get your own cabin and everything is geared toward fertile solitude—you know, you don't even report for lunch, they tiptoe up and leave a picnic basket on your porch so you don't have a second of distraction. I'd been imagining that, finished with my nun book, I'd be starting a new project: I had no idea what I was going to do. But now I was afraid I'd become like Jack Nicholson in *The Shining*. There'd be all those happy artists prancing through the forests with their picnic baskets, and they were all going to have to die, one by one.

"But my wife, my wise, wise wife—and can you imagine what I'd been putting her through all those years?—she told me that a change of scenery would be good. And so I went, though without any particular intention of writing: That book had hurt me enough. I just wanted to exist as if in a kind of Zen retreat.

"And you know what? It was like waking from a bad dream. All of a sudden, everything was like a gift: the fall colors, the sounds, the little homemade cookies in the picnic baskets. But mainly the removal of all the reminders of art as a profession, as a way of making money or gaining a reputation and the like. Rather, here I was in a community of people who seemed dedicated to art almost like a sacred pursuit. And the irony was not lost on me that I was now living essentially like a Carmelite nun."

He smiled and reached for his bow. "The Bourrée." After he completed that passage, he hardly paused before declaring, "Which brings us to the last movement, the Gigue, which in effect proclaims, 'Eureka! We're done!' I had my cello with me there in the cabin, which was a perfect place to be playing Bach: those reverberant wood walls. And I took to playing it every day, and it was while playing that suddenly I had this truly astonishing insight.

"The thing is, I'm agnostic. I was raised in a nonreligious family. Before I started the book, pretty much all I knew about Christianity was what I'd learned from Linus on A Charlie Brown Christmas. My character had dedicated her life to living by faith, not reason. Whereas, of course, I live by reason. I'd assumed that such a character would be quite a stretch for me, but that was all right: A good writer welcomes that kind of gulf.

"But it turned out that it wasn't that much of a stretch after all," he went on. "The artistic wager—the commitment to devote ever lengthening years of one's life, say, to the production of a novel, the conviction that such a commitment will make any sort of difference to anyone else—is manifestly unreasonable.

"I take it on faith that art is worthwhile. I go on because I believe it's the right thing to do, not because I know it is.

"Suddenly, sitting there in my cabin, I realized that all along I'd been living my nun's life myself. And, once I saw that, the book wrote itself in five weeks, with me in a state that I can only describe as euphoric. I was the one the other artists wanted to kill.

"The words were coming to me with labels attached: 'Put me next to him.' And, when it was done, the way I felt about that book made everything that had come before worthwhile: They were no longer six years of sorry-ass bungling but, rather, now I could see them all as a purposeful journey toward . . . toward . . . well, I don't know, I suppose toward a new level of obscurity and financial crisis, but toward a new level of understanding as well.

"For me, art and music are alike in that they are about creating dissonance and then feeling compelled from within to resolve it. Bach literally could not stand leaving a dissonant harmony unresolved. In ordinary life, we face dissonances every day which we can't resolve—there's not enough time, we don't have the authority or the influence or the knowledge. But when we write or listen or read or play we relive the experience of making the journey from chaos to order, and that feeds us, reminds us, heartens us, gives us courage to face all the journeys where there is no such promise. And that's why Bach's suites are stories." Salzman smiled. "And so, to the Gigue!"

IN THE DAYS AFTER Salzman's performance at the L.A. library, I reread *The Soloist*, and I was struck by its first lines:

> This morning I read an article suggesting that Saint Theresa of Avila, a sixteenth-century Spanish mystic noted for her ecstatic visions, suffered from a neurological disorder known to cause hallucinations.

It turns out that Salzman was being haunted by the idea behind *Lying Awake* long before he started that book. And, more confounding, the insights that Salzman's cellist protagonist manages to struggle his way toward—the saving epiphanies that rain down like grace upon him at the novel's end—were the very sort that Salzman himself could have benefited from, if only he'd been able to recall and marshal them:

> On that day I began to have a different idea about why I couldn't play onstage anymore. I'd always assumed it had to

*do with my sense of pitch, because that was certainly what I'd noticed had changed. I couldn't hold onto the dead center of notes anymore because my pitch had become too sensitive; my fingers couldn't keep the notes pure enough. It felt like trying to split hairs with a butter knife.*

But now the aging wunderkind starts to think that maybe the problem never had anything to do with his ear; that, rather, it had to do with his very ambition toward perfection.

*For all practical purposes [I] forgot that absolute intonation does not exist. As my mind focused on the impossible goal of achieving pure intonation, I became unable to feel the music.*

He starts to understand that "You cannot make great music happen; you can only prepare yourself for it to happen." And that, in a sense, is the saving insight that finally descended like grace upon Salzman at that writer's colony—and descends in the end on the protagonist of the book he created there, although it descends on the two of them in opposite ways. The paradox is that succeeding to write is the grace that falls on Salzman, even as what he writes about is the seeming evaporation of that capacity in Sister John:

*A group had formed at the Blessed Virgin's shrine to pay respects. Mother Emmanuel left to join them, but Sister John stayed behind to finish clearing the fountain. When she got the water flowing properly, she stepped back, took her bell out of her pocket, and rang it. The sound cheered her, then vanished into the deep blue air, which seemed to go on forever.*

The key word in that passage, which concludes the book, is "seemed." The deep-blue air seems to go on forever, in contrast to the blinding certainty that consumed Sister John in the midst of those fever spikes of transcendence with which the book began: She could see forever, and everywhere she looked she saw God's love.

It may just be that seeming is the human portion—the transcendent grace, a knowledge that is damnably difficult to attain and even more difficult to sustain. It is something that artists—and not only artists—seem to learn and forget all over again as they struggle to return to where they started. The irony here is that the moment Salzman (and his protagonist Sister John) realized the futility and the vanity of seeking perfection was the moment that Salzman was at last able to achieve something approaching a perfect little novel.

# Afterword: On Grace and Narrative and the Current State of the Uncanny Valley

**WHICH BRINGS US, AS** per Joyce, by a commodious vicus of recirculation back to our old medieval friend Nicolas of Cusa and his n-sided polygon embedded inside a circle. For isn't that what Salzman's tale of blockage and release is all about?

You keep adding sides (facts, details, premises, and surmises)—triangle, square, pentagon, hexagon, and so forth—all the way out toward infinity, and the more sides you add the closer you might seem to be getting to the circle that is God, or anyway true knowledge of God, or shall we say Truth, or just Being? But the further away you in fact are getting, for of course, as we saw all the way back there at the beginning of this book (when we were considering the digital animation of the face), the whole point about a ten-thousand-sided polygon is that it has ten thousand sides and ten thousand angles, whereas a circle has merely one side and no angles. ("You may feel separated from grace right now," Sister John's father confessor tries to reassure her at her moment of greatest doubt, "but in reality you are probably closer to it now than you ever were before.") At some point, Nicolas argues, you have to make the leap—the leap of faith, as he called it—from the chord to the arc, a leap no less forbidding and transformative whether you do it at the beginning or the end. And one that can be accomplished only through the descent, as it were, of grace.

You work and you work and you work at something that then happens all by itself. It would not have happened without all that work, which, as Salzman's cellist notes, is preparation, preparation toward receptivity. But the work cannot be said to account for the final product, the way an effect can be accounted for in terms of its causes, because there is all that work and then there is something else that is gratis, for free. And it's an endless mystery.

Writers know that moment and pine for that moment—the moment when the accumulation of detail mysteriously and almost of its own accord seems to blossom forth into a seamless whole (a whole that announces itself through the fact that when you tap it, as it were, it no longer rings false: it rings true), but they also know the moment cannot be hurried.

It is in this sense that the central story in Mark Salzman's *Lying Awake* can be read as an allegory for the labor and grace of the literary endeavor, but only in the sense that literary creation is itself metaphorical of, and partakes of, everything else: which is to say, of all Creation.

Which in turn takes us back to Salzman's China, though this time to Lao-tzu (604-531 BC) and the eleventh entry of his *Tao Te Ching* (as translated by Stephen Mitchell, with a slight tweak of my own there at the very end),[1] where we read

> *We join spokes together in a wheel*
> *but it is the center hole*
> *that makes the wagon move.*

> *We shape clay into a pot*
> *but it is the emptiness inside*
> *that holds whatever we want*

*We hammer wood for a house*
*but it is the inner space*
*that makes it livable*

*We work with being*
*but nonbeing is where we live*

FINALLY, A FEW THOUGHTS on the current state of the Uncanny Valley, at least as it pertains to the digital animation of the face, with which this whole walkabout began.

It's coming on a decade since I first undertook that investigation for the good folks at *Wired*, and in the meantime there've been a slew of breathless claims, especially recently, that the Uncanny Valley has at last been forded. Such at any rate was the frequently expressed contention of James Cameron in the lead-up of the release of his umpteen-gazillion-dollar blockbuster *Avatar*: "No matter how much art and technology we threw at this thing, if it wasn't in the eyes of the characters—if you didn't see a soul there—it would just be a big clanking machine," he told one weblog. "We've all seen movies that never quite get out of the Uncanny Valley—the negative effect that is created when something approaches human (in appearance) but isn't quite there; it creates this creepiness. And our goal right from the get-go was that we were going to have to get over that Uncanny Valley. These characters were going to have to be real, to be alive. And what the actors did was going to have to come through 100 percent."[2] For their ascent up the steep far side of the Valley, Cameron and his crew deployed an exponentially souped-up version of motion-capture, adding to the number of dots splayed across the actor's face and, more importantly, jamming the camera in tight through a miniaturized helmet device. Advances in computer technology furthermore allowed them to convert the captured image, virtually in real time, into its feline Navi counterpart. And the effects were indeed startlingly lifelike.

Though I myself have had my doubts about the wider contention. For one thing, the *Avatar* team cheated, at least in terms
of their Uncanny Valley–fording claims, by rendering the Navi
skin a thickly made-up blue: a simple Newtonian challenge, evad-
ing the quantum complications inherent in rendering standard
human (and as we have seen, especially Caucasian) flesh tones.
Beyond that, the very foreignness of the Navi conceit (the fact
that these were necessarily otherworldly beings with whom we
as humans were not familiar) meant that we would discount any
uncanny misgivings, chalking them up to the very otherness
of the beings represented. Which is to say, the animators still
weren't quite there: They still couldn't digitally render a believable ordinary human face.

Still, who knows? With the relentlessly compounding speed
of technical innovation, they may yet arrive. And meanwhile, if
anything, over the past ten years, the uncanniness seems to be
going in the other direction. The more mere humans gear themselves up with digital devices, the more machinelike in their affect
and mannerisms they themselves seem to be becoming. The man
coming at you walking down the street, fiercely engaged in an argument, seemingly with no one there. Google cofounder Sergey Brin

declaring, "We want to make Google the third half of your brain."[3] The rows of operators, hooped to their monitors in those Bangalore digital sweatshops. Pavlovian poll-driven television-lashed political pseudo-movements. Talk about Creepy!

On the other hand, there remains the intimate marvel of narrative, the swell and pull and thrall of stories—and that everyday miracle, thank God, appears as timeless and unchanging as ever. Just the other day there was an entirely goofy, completely winning short little photo-animated video zapping all about the web: "Marcel the Shell with Shoes On." Directed by Dean Fleischer-Camp and sublimely voiced by a divinely high-pitched Jenny Slate, the just over three-minute-long stop-motion short focused all its attention on a tiny little hermit crab shell perched atop those eponymous plastic pink miniature doll shoes, a single googly eye wedged into the shell's opening, as he dispenses his observations on life through a tiny animated mouthhole at the base of his shell belly. What does he use for a hat? A lentil. What does he use for a beanbag chair? A raisin. What does he use for a pen? A pen. But it takes the whole family. At one point, Marcel lets slip that his one big regret in life is that he will never have a dog. So great is his longing, he goes on, that every once in a while he ties a leash fashioned from a single strand of human hair around a clump of lint and drags that lint clump around as his pet. He's even given it a name: Alan. And sure enough, a few frames later, there they are, that nutty little shell trailing his frisky little tuft of lint, the lint getting caught behind a chair leg, the leash pulling taut, Marcel sighing, "Come on, come on, I loooove you," the lintball bounding free. And it is a completely amazing little moment: because you can't help but believe in the fervent love that shell has for that stupid dustball—a projection no less real and heartfelt than the one you yourself are experiencing at that very moment for that same damned little shell. (An effect considerably more tidally powerful than anything in *Avatar*, achieved at one-gazillionth of the cost.)[4]

Years ago—and this will date me (I was maybe about twenty-five at the time, a cub freelancer on one of my first stories)—I had the idea to go back to my kindergarten playground and see what was passing for humor there among the newbie set. I just loped onto the field and hung out for a couple days at recess (one could never get away with such behavior nowadays). Anyway, the kids were perfectly happy to regale me with the latest in kid wit, and the point is the jokes were exactly the same as they'd been in my day, and told with the very same oblivious cluelessness. Mommy, guess what? What, Sally? I made a dollar! How'd you do that, dear? The boys bet me that I wouldn't be able to climb the pole but I did. Oh, silly, they just wanted to see your underpants. Well, I fooled them: I wasn't wearing any! Belly laughs and guffaws all around. And so forth. And it got me to thinking. Because maybe it was the jokes that are the true living entities on this third planet from the sun, and we, the humans, maybe merely the endlessly flowing medium in which they abide.

The same with stories. God invented Man, the wise man says, because he loved stories. And maybe the other way around: Man invented God for the same reason. Or maybe Narrative invented both of us: couldn't do without us. Hallelujah.

Amen.

# Notes

(Pages 1–26)

## UNCANNY VALLEY:
On the Digital Animation of the Face

1. Nicholas of Cusa, *On Learned Ignorance*, trans. with a commentary by Jasper Hopkins (Minneapolis: The Arthur J. Banning Press, 1985), 52 ff.
2. Jean-Paul Sartre, "Faces, preceded by Official Portraits," trans. Anne P. Jones, in *Essays in Phenomenology*, ed. Maurice Natanson (The Hague: Martinus Nijhoff, 1966), 157–63.
3. Ludwig Wittgenstein, *Zettel*, ed. and trans. G. E. M. Anscombe (Berkeley: University of California Press, 1967), #452.
4. Jorge Luis Borges, "On Exactitude in Science" (The Land of the Cartographers), trans. Alastair Reid (unpublished typescript).
5. Kurt Godel's first incompleteness theorem (both date from 1931) posits that any adequate axiomatizable theory would of necessity be incomplete. (Thus for example, the sentence "This sentence is not provable" is true, but not provable in theory.) Godel's second incompleteness theorem took things further, positing (and here I am of course simplifying things) that in any consistent axiomatizable theory, the consistency of the system is not provable within the system. One of the finest elaborations on the intellectual, philosophical, and cultural ramifications of Godel's work can be found in Douglas Hofstadter's *Godel, Escher, Bach: An Eternal Golden Braid* (New York: Basic Books, 1979).
6. Masahiro Mori, "Bukimi no tani" ("The Uncanny Valley," trans. K. F. MacDorman and T. Minato), Energy 7 (4), 33–5. Also, *The Buddha in the Robot: A Robot Engineer's Thoughts on Science and Religion*, trans. C. Terry (Tokyo: Kosei Publishing, 1981).

## FOUR EASY PIECES
Motes in the Light
1. For more on Bill Morrison's film, see "Splendors of Decaying Celluloid," pp. 147-162.


## THREE IMPROBABLE YARNS
Mr. Wilson in Belgrade
1. The documentary can still be heard at:
   http://soundportraits.org/on-air/museum_of _jurassic_technology.


The Poem on the Train:
A Letter to the Editor of *The Threepenny Review*
1. And then it happened all over again. Around the time I was compiling
   this book into its final form, I was once again on the train into town—
   same train, passing just about the same junction, doing just about the
   same thing, this time as it happens riffling through that week's just
   arrived issue of the *New Yorker* (October 11, 2010), when my eye snagged
   on some phrases in somebody else's poem—Zeno, St. Sebastian—which
   in turn got me to thinking about that old saw about how, if you stopped
   to consider the implications of Zeno's paradox (remember, the one I
   discussed earlier at the end of my "Uncanny Valley" piece at the outset
   of this volume, how if a speeding arrow first has to get half way to its
   target, and then halfway across the remainder of the distance, and then
   halfway across the remaining remainder, and so forth, then it can never
   actually reach its goal), well, then you'd realize that St. Sebastian must
   have died not from his wounds but from fright. My gaze drifted down
   to the bottom of the poem to catch the name of its author, Billy Collins, then up to the title—"Table Talk"—then on to its first lines:

> Not long after we had sat down to dinner
> at a long table in a restaurant in Chicago
> and were deeply engrossed in the heavy menus,
> one of us—a bearded man with a colorful tie—
> asked if any one of us had ever considered
> applying the paradoxes of Zeno to the martyrdom of St. Sebastian.

And I veritably sputtered. Because, wait! That was me, that was I, that was the author of this footnote that evening at the long table in the Chicago restaurant. I was the bearded man in the colorful tie (in fact I was wearing that very same tie on the train that day), I'm the one who told Billy Collins that joke.

Uncanny, too, the way that, just like Pinsky, Collins couched the joke in what became a meditation on death, and an exceptionally moving one at that (you can now find it in his latest collection, *Horoscopes for the Dead*).

But I guess the lesson of this whole story for me is that I really have to stop telling jokes to poets.

## Popocatepel (My Grandfather's Geographical and My Medical Fugue)

1. For more on my composer grandfather Ernst Toch's life, see my own biographical essay on him, "My Grandfather's Last Tale," at the website of *The Atlantic Monthly*, reprinted in my *Vermeer in Bosnia* collection (Vintage, 2005).

# SOME PROBES INTO THE TERRAIN OF HUMAN RIGHTS

## Gazing Back: The Disappeared

1. Marjorie Agosín, "Buenos Aires," trans. by Celeste Kostopulos-Cooperman, in *Circles of Madness: Mothers of the Plaza de Mayo* (Fredonia, New York: White Pine Press, 1992).
2. Zbigniew Herbert, "Mr. Cogito on the Need for Precision," *Report from the Besieged City and Other Poems*, trans. John and Bogdana Carpenter (New York: Ecco Press, 1985), 64–68.
3. See the illustrated catalog, which includes an essay by Reuter: *Los Desaparecidos / The Disappeared*, North Dakota Museum of Art, 2006, Charta Publications. Also the show's ongoing website: www.ndmoa.com/pastex/disappeared/index.html.

   Following the show's opening there in Grand Fork, North Dakota, Reuter received a grant from the Lannan Foundation that allowed her to tour the exhibition throughout Latin America—including to Buenos Aires, Montevideo, Santiago, Antigua/Guatamala, and Bogotá—(where it was almost always rapturously received, and with the same critical trope: Why hadn't anyone there in Latin America had the idea to mount such a show?), and variously around the United States as well (New York; Washington, D.C.; Santa Fe; Laramie; and El Paso).

During its stop at the Museo del Barrio in New York City, the *Times's* critic Holland Cotter concluded his rave review (4/7/2007) by echoing his Latin American counterparts: "Why is it that an on-the-road exhibition from a small museum in the Midwest is the most potent show of contemporary art, political or otherwise, in town? All I can say is that curators in our local museums should pay a visit, and ask themselves that question."

4. See pp. 5-6 in the "Uncanny Valley" piece above. Jean-Paul Sartre, "Faces, preceded by Official Portraits," trans. Anne P. Jones, in *Essays in Phenomenology*, ed. Maurice Natanson (The Hague: Martinus Nijhoff, 1966), 157–63.

5. Maurice Merleau-Ponty, "The War Has Taken Place" (June 1945), in *Sense and Nonsense,* trans. Hubert and Patricia Dreyfus (Evanston: Northwestern University Press, 1964), 150–51.

6. W. S. Merwin, *The Miner's Pale Children* (New York: Atheneum, 1970), 85–8.

7. Of the three instances illustrated in this volume, the first, on page 109, was a group effort, thirteen Argentinian artists working under the name *Identitad* who in 1998 responded to a very specific, albeit quite wrenching plea from the *Abuelos de Plaza de Mayo,* the Grandmothers of the Disappeared, who noted how approximately twenty years earlier over two hundred of their daughters had been kidnapped when pregnant. Their husbands, the unborn children's fathers, likewise kidnapped, had been summarily killed, but the girls were kept alive until they could deliver, at which point they too were murdered, and the infants given over to otherwise infertile military families for adoption. What the grandmothers realized is that their grandchildren (all the while unknowing as to the circumstances of their births) were now coming to be roughly the same age that their parents had been at the time of their deaths. Was there any way, the Grandmothers wondered, that the artists could help them find the children in question? In response, the *Identitad* group created a labyrinth of photos and mirrors: a picture of a young mother at the time of her death ranged at eye level, then one of her young husband, then a mirror, at once symbolizing the further disappearance of their child, implicating the visitor to the installation in that family's fate, and maybe, just maybe, allowing one specific passing visitor to recognize him or herself in the visages of this young disappeared couple. The effect of the piece was quite overwhelming, the faces doubling and redoubling in the echoing forest

of mirrors, the wending path going on and on: surely there couldn't be more around the bend, and yet there were. And indeed, from the start the piece began to work its magic: at the opening three grandchildren, now in their twenties, discovered their true identities, and since then so have another five. And the most magical aspect of the piece is that once such discoveries occur, the pictures in question are removed: the piece is designed, over time, to disappear!

The second image from the show in this volume, on p. 111, is part of a vaster installation, "Between Roots and Air," in which the Guatamalan artist Luis Gonzalez Palma floats haunting photographic portraits of an unsmiling, classically beautiful Mayan woman, her shawl-covered head held high, her eyes looking straight into the camera. In a country where Mayan people characteristically look away when approaching someone of European descent, or step off the sidewalk to allow the European to pass, Palma has said "everyone will be forced to look into the eyes of the Mayan people in my photographs." Tens of thousands of whom were liquidated in that country's dirty war.

Finally, the third, on p. 112, is part of a sequence of photographs of various sizes, ranged one beside the next in the corner of a room by the Columbian master Juan Manuel Echavarría. He has titled the resulting piece "NN (No Name)" and explains: "I found this mannequin abandoned in a courtyard of an old textile factory in Bogota. It was a mannequin of a child. Made of burlap and plaster, it caught my attention. I took it to my home and kept it for nine years until I decided to bring it out again. I photographed this mannequin as if I was doing an emotional autopsy, looking closely at the different parts of the body and its different wounds. It was a body that I immediately associated with the mass graves and the massacres, which keep occurring in Colombia. Here was a corpse that presented cuts that could have been done by machete and other cutting instruments. This child's body became a metaphor of mutilation."

## A Berlin Epiphany

1. Czeslaw Milosz, "Campo dei Fiori," trans. Louis Iribarne and David Brooks, in The Collected Poems (New York: Ecco Press, 1988), 33-5.
2. Wislawa Szymborska, "Reality Demands," in Poems New and Collected 1957-1997, trans. Stanislaw Baranczak and Clare Cavanagh (New York: Harcourt, 1998), 232-3.

Around the same time (which is to say the time of the seemingly interminable Bosnian war), Szymborska actually composed another poem around the same theme, "The End and the Beginning," (pp. 228–9, in the same book), which begins

> *After every war*
> *someone has to tidy up.*
> *Things won't pick*
> *themselves up, after all.*
>
> *Someone has to shove*
> *the rubble to the roadsides*
> *so the carts loaded with corpses*
> *can get by*

and then goes on like that for several stanzas, before arriving at these lines, so resonant with our purposes here:

> *Someone, broom in hand,*
> *still remembers how it was.*
> *Someone else listens, nodding*
> *his unshattered head.*
> *But others are bound to be bustling nearby*
> *who'll find all that*
> *a little boring.*

And similarly, a few lines further on:

> *Those who knew*
> *what this was all about*
> *must make way for those*
> *who know little.*
> *And less than that.*
> *And at last nothing, less than nothing.*

That marvelous Szymborskian Nothing again . . . Till finally:

> *Someone has to lie there*
> *in the grass that covers up*
> *the causes and effects*
> *with a cornstalk in his teeth,*
> *gawking at clouds.*

Gawking, that is, at the clouds over Berlin that clean cerulean springtime afternoon, and with that cornstalk in his teeth no less, as in Eisenman's wheatfield, but also—and here trapdoors open onto trapdoors—it seems certain to me, in allusion to that earlier miniature masterpiece of Szymborska's (in this instance, as with the Milosz, clearly welling out more directly from Poland's own wartime experience of the forties), "Could Have" (same book, p. 111):

It could have happened.
It had to happen.
It happened earlier. Later.
Nearer. Farther off.
It happened, but not to you.

You were saved because you were the first.
You were saved because you were the last.
Alone. With others.
On the right. On the left.
Because it was raining. Because of the shade.
Because the day was sunny.

You were in luck—there was a forest.
You were in luck—there were no trees.
You were in luck—a rake, a hook, a beam, a brake,
A jamb, a turn, a quarter-inch, an instant . . .
You were in luck: just then a straw went floating by.

So you're here? Still dizzy from
another dodge, close shave, reprieve?
One hole in the net and you slipped through?
I couldn't be more shocked or
speechless.
Listen,
how your heart pounds inside me.

My own emphasis there: "just then a straw went floating by." Which is to say you were hiding underwater, the Nazis in hot pursuit, such that coming up for air would likely have proved fatal, you were running out of air, desperate, gasping, gagging, and just then a straw went floating by. (Every single one of those clipped phrases opens out onto a short story like that, or even a novel.)

At any rate a straw goes floating by . . . or so might a boy bring himself to imagine years later, lounging lazily in an open field, staring dreamily up at the clouds, a cornstalk in his teeth.


# FOUR WALKABOUTS
## Waking Up to How We Sleepwalk

1. For my profile of Knud Jensen and his museum, see another of my books, *A Wanderer in the Perfect City: Selected Passion Pieces* (Chicago: University of Chicago Press, 1996).
2. Jonathan Schell, The Fate of the Earth (New York: Knopf, 1982), 231. It's interesting to note how powerfully Schell's lines—and for that matter the entire performance I describe in this piece—originally composed to draw attention to the nuclear peril, today likewise rhyme up against the specter of global warming and ecological devastation more generally.


## Dario Fo on Broadway

1. In the years after that marvelous walk, I sometimes took to fantasizing a documentary film project, a fantasy that became all the more vividly plausible in the wake of the release of Alexander Sokurov's 2002 tour-de-force impressionist survey of the history of his homeland, *Russian Ark* (2000 extras, dozens of costumers and choreographers, eight months of rehearsals, the camera meandering through 33 rooms of the Hermitage Museum in St. Petersburg in a single astonishing extended 96-minute take). My idea would consist in a similarly extended single take one evening, the steady-cam weaving in and out of the back alleys running between Broadway theaters along 44th and 45th and 46th streets, slipping in and out the back doors of one theater after the next, floating through the wings backstage, coming to gaze upon the various actors in midperformance and then beyond them at the hushed suspended audiences, then back out again through the dim alleys (the stagehands out for a smoke, the rats scurrying among the trash bins) into the next theater, the next show, the next audience, and then out again, and so forth . . . a dreamy ramble through that monadology of reverie. Will never happen, of course: you could never get the producers to agree, and even if you could, the unions could never be prevailed

upon to bend their precious rules, and even if they did, the lawyers would require permissions release from every single member of every audience (god forbid somebody should be captured unknowing in the midst of their rapt absorbtion). But sometimes still I sit by my window when evening falls and conjur it all clean to myself.

## FIVE FURTHER ADVENTURES IN THE NARRATIVE
Still Not Finished: On Vincent Desiderio's *Sleep*

1. I was hardly the first to be struck by this tendency of Desiderio's. In a marvelously supple piece of reporting in the January 29, 1995, *New York Times Magazine*, growing out of Desiderio's first show at Marlborough, the novelist Ellen Pall had described how the artist's mind "hopped furiously from idea to idea. Socialism, Cubism, Barthes, Zola, Habermas— names and theories flew like the spray of sawdust thrown up under a whirring blade." A tendency that seemed all the more remarkable in the context of that show, which had featured several devastatingly immediate images of a small child perilously ensnared in all manner of high-tech life-support equipment, the very fate, as it then happened, of the Desiderios' own small son, but images that Desiderio kept insisting on discussing with Pall, albeit quite eloquently, in terms of the crisis of abstract expressionism, the fate of figuration, and so forth. "How could Desiderio speak so cerebrally of paintings that all but punched the viewer in the chest?" Pall wondered. "Between his words and his images—between his intellect and his imagination—yawned a curious gap." A gap that her piece then went on to anatomize and to bridge with a novelist's keen penetration.

2. Tomas Tranströmer, "Sentry Duty," in *Selected Poems 1954-1986*, ed. Robert Hass (New York: Ecco Press, 1987), 111-2.

  Or, in the words of Paul Blackburn's "Matchbook Poem," in *The Collected Poems of Paul Blackburn* (New York: Persea Lamplighters Series, 1985):

> BUT WHY do you always go to the wall?
> Why does he go to the wall?
>
> You go to the wall
> because that's where
> the door is
>
> maybe.

3. Or phrased another way, while you may occasionally find yourself objecting, with considerable validity, Come on, it's *only* painting—there are moments, or anyway, extended occasions, when for Desiderio, painting can seem to be *everything*, or at any rate can be made to stand in for everything.

4. In one of the stories in her marvelously (and in this context portentously) titled collection *Enormous Changes at the Last Minute*, Grace Paley insists that "Every character, real or invented, deserves the open destiny of life."

## Double Vision: The Perspectival Journey of the Oakes Twins

1. Thus Panofsky (*Perspective as Symbolic Form*, translated from the 1924 German original by Christopher Wood, Zone Books, New York, 1991) (italics mine):

> Exact perspectival construction [i.e., Renaissance perspective] is a systematic abstraction from the structure of this psychophysiological space. For it is not only the effect of perspectival construction, but indeed its intended purpose, to realize in the representation of space precisely that homogeneity and boundlessness foreign to the direct experience of that space. In a sense, perspective transforms psychophysiological space into mathematical space. It negates the differences between front and back, between right and left, between bodies and intervening space ("empty space"), so that the sum of all the parts of space and all its contents are absorbed into a single "quantum continuum." *It forgets that we see not with a single fixed eye but with two constantly moving eyes, resulting in a spheroidal field of vision.* It takes no account of the enormous difference between the psychologically conditioned "visual image" through which the visible world is brought to our consciousness, and the mechanically conditioned "retinal image" which paints itself on our physical eye. For a peculiar stabilizing tendency within our consciousness—promoted by the cooperation of vision with the tactile sense—ascribes to perceived objects a definite and proper size and form, and thus tends not to take notice, at least not full notice, of the distortions which these sizes and forms suffer on the retina. *Finally, perspectival construction ignores the crucial circumstance that this retinal image—entirely apart from its*

*subsequent psychological "interpretation," and even apart from the fact that the eyes move—is a projection not on a flat but on a concave surface.* Thus already on this lowest, still prepsychological level of facts there is a fundamental discrepancy between "reality" and its construction. This is also true, of course, for the entirely analogous operation of the camera. (pp. 30-1)

This curvature of the optical image has been observed twice in modern (post-fifteenth-century) times: by the great psychologists and physicists of the last century, but also (and this has apparently not been remarked upon until now) by the great astronomers and mathematicians at the beginning of the seventeenth century. We should recall above all the words of the remarkable Wilhelm Shickhard (1592-1635), a cousin of the Württemberg architect and Italian traveler Heinrich Schickhardt: "I say that all lines, even the straightest, which do not stand *directe contra pupillam* [directly in front of the eye] . . . necessarily appear somewhat bent. Nevertheless, no painter believes this; this is why they paint the straight sides of a building with straight lines, even though according to the true art of perspective this is incorrect . . . Crack that nut, you artists!" This was endorsed by none other than Kepler, at least insofar as he admitted the possibility that the objectively straight tail of a comet or the objectively straight trajectory of a meteor is subjectively perceived as a curve. What is most interesting is that Kepler fully recognized that he had originally overlooked or even denied these illusory curves only because he had been schooled in linear perspective. He had been led by the rules of painterly perspective to believe that straight is always seen as straight, without stopping to consider that the eye in fact projects not onto a *plana tabella* but onto the inner surface of a sphere. And indeed, if even today only a very few of us have perceived these curvatures, that too is surely in part due to our habituation—further reinforced by looking at photographs—to linear perspectival construction: a construction that is itself comprehensible only for a quite specific, indeed specifically modern, sense of space, or if you will, sense of the world.

Thus in an epoch whose perception was governed by a conception of space expressed by strict linear perspective, the curvatures of our, so to speak, spheroidal optical world had to be rediscovered. However, in a time that was accustomed to seeing perspectively—but not in linear perspective—these curvatures were simply taken for granted: that is, in antiquity. In antique optics and art theory (as well as in philosophy, although here only in the form of analogies) we constantly encounter the observations that straight lines are seen as curved and curved lines as straight; that columns must be subjected to entasis (usually relatively weak, of course, in classical times) in order not to appear bent; that epistyle and stylobate must be built curved in order to avoid the impression of sagging. And, indeed, the familiar curvatures of the Doric temple attest to the practical consequences of such findings. Antique optics, which brought all these insights to fruition, was thus in its first principles quite antithetical to linear perspective. (pp. 33–5)

2. Ryan: "Granted, I would think maybe everybody doesn't practice this type of behavior (tapping fingers in syncopation with the passing telephone poles) but I think it's just an acknowledgment that your vision is almost like a physical appendage that extends from your body, and that effectively you reach out and touch with your vision what you see with it. Such that when you're driving down the road and seeing the lines pass and the guard rail undulate, in a sense you are experiencing this with your entire physical body and translating that into movements with your hand—all that is just another way of acknowledging that."

See Hubert Damisch in his book *The Origin of Perspective* (1987, translated by John Goodman for the MIT Press, 1994, p. 46): "In this respect the visible resembles the tangible: my hand can touch something only because it can itself be touched, and if vision, as Merleau-Ponty put it, following Descartes, is 'a palpitation of the gaze,' it follows that the person who gazes must not be unfamiliar with the world upon which he looks: From the moment I see, my vision must be complemented by a complementary vision, or another vision, myself seen from without as another would see me, installed in the midst of the visible, in the process of considering it from a certain spot."

Granted, Damisch and Merleau-Ponty take this insight about the tangibility of vision somewhere other than where Ryan was taking it, though as we will see in the upcoming discussion of their twinship, this parallel question of the gazer as simultaneously constituting himself reciprocally, as gazed-upon, is not without its pertinence to the situation of the Twins.

3. Incidentally, they were also quite synesthetic, and remain so, as evidenced by the following exchange I recorded one day:

> T: Well, we used to do a game with each other where you'd go through the whole alphabet and say what color letters were.
>
> R: Numbers and letters have a color association, for some reason.
>
> W: The same?
>
> R: No. Different. We used to compare that a lot.
>
> T: Like A is yellow.
>
> R: No, A is green.
>
> W: Is that still the case?
>
> T: I'm not sure.
>
> R: I remember when we first started college, we wrote down what it was so we could see if it shifted. But I think it's pretty consistent. For me A is green and four is also green, because they have the same shape. We can go through it. I say A is green.
>
> T: A is yellow.
>
> Both together: B is blue.
>
> R: C is yellow.
>
> T: Yeah, C is maybe some sort of orange.
>
> R: D is . . .
>
> T: Green.
>
> R: Brown.
>
> T: E is orange.
>
> R: Yeah, E is orange. F is purple.
>
> T: Yeah, yeah. G is bluish.
>
> R: G is sort of black.
>
> T: G is like a royal blue.
>
> W: And numbers?
>
> R: One is white. Zero is clear.
>
> T: (laughs)
>
> R: It is.
>
> T: All right.
>
> W: What about for you?
>
> T: One would probably be white.
>
> R: Two is light blue.

4. Consider, for example, this Cezanne; Or this Matisse, keeping in mind here, as the Twins like to point out, the way that not only is the nose protruding from the side but the master's famous circular eyeglasses (with the eyes beyond them) seem to find an echo in the table and the fishbowl as well.

Or this Morris Louis; or this Roy Lichtenstein; or (maybe my favorite) this Rembrandt (with its distinctively doughy nose intact):

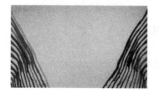  

5. Actually, as Trevor is the first to admit, the matches didn't actually want to form themselves into that perfectly even hemisphere. After he'd laid down the bottom circle and proceeded to lay in the next row, something strange began to happen; the shape started torquing mysteriously, seemingly wanting to express a much more irregular configuration. (He figures that this tendency had something to do with the difference between the spheroid nub at the one end of the match and the squared off bottom—and he will be more than happy to elaborate at considerable length on this hypothesis if you ever have the time.) So he cheated that first time around, laying in the necessary shim-corrections so as to achieve the perfect hemisphere. But later on, during senior year, curiosity got the better of him and he went back and created a more

naturally extruding ziggurat, and to his astonishment, the seemingly random results echoed the sort of consistent-rule-generated chaos one might find in Stephen Wolfram's *New Kind of Science*.

6. Without any philosophical or academic training, the Twins here seemed to be merrily straying into the territory of Leibniz's *Monadology*. Too bad he wasn't around to talk to them.

For that matter, the Twins seemed to have likewise recapitulated a set of notions deep ingrained in some of the earliest of Greek thought. In the chapter on the senses in his seminal (and exhaustively titled) *The Origins of European Thought about the Body, the Mind, the Soul, the World, Time and Fate* (Cambridge University Press, 1951), the venerable classicist Richard Broxton Onians, late of the University of London, mined the ancient Greek language itself to reveal that the pre-Socratics and their heirs seemed to believe that the seat of thinking was not so much in the head as in *the lungs*, and that each of the senses partook of a sort of breathing in and breathing out. Thus, for example, "Empedocles taught that from objects there came emanations or effluences which enter the eye by tiny passages and that from the eye there goes forth a ray toward the object. To Timaeus, who also apparently was connected with the Pythagoreans, Plato assigns a belief that from the object 'flows flame' and that 'the fire in the eyes flows forth.' According to the Placita, Plato taught that sight was the result of a 'fusion of rays, the light of the eyes flowing out to some distance into the kindred air and the light from the objects meeting it,' with which we may compare another account (from Plutarch): 'raylike breath of the eyes coming forth mingles with the light around objects and blends with it.'" (Onians, p. 77) And so forth.

7. The first grid they fashioned by taking thin wire strips and creating a flat perpendicular grid, rows of vertical wires intersect by rows of horizontal wires, resulting in an even matrix of two-inch squares with every single intersection hammered and then, using a thinner wire, lashed with hemostats into a secure meld. They then manually pulled and pinched the corners of the resultant rectangle into a vaguely bulging shape, hanging the resultant concave segment upside down from the ceiling, with its four corners pointing toward the floor, and spinning the thing to locate and repair any unevennesses. With compass and calipers they then measured the angles of every single now-pinched diamond (the sides remained the same two inches throughout but every parallelogram was differently squeezed), and individually cut each paper tile accordingly. ("That," says Ryan, "took a long, long time.") The first time out in the field, they

followed an additive process: starting with an empty grid and inserting one tile at a time, tracing it over through the binocular technique, and then adding on the adjacent square. Once finished, and before taping all the tiles into their final concave form, they tacked the 361 completed tiles onto a flat blank wall in vertical arcing strips (pinched tight at the center waist, as it were, and spreading away toward the top and bottom). And it was while studying that version of the drawing that Ryan realized that they didn't in fact have to be rendering each blank paper tile individually, that they could save a whole lot of time rendering long vertical strips. He left a note to that effect for Trevor, who concurred, though for reasons too complicated to explain here (though Trevor will be happy to go over them for you, at great and entirely thoroughgoing length, if you ask), he suggested that instead they make horizontal strips, completely covering over the concave grid before they started drawing, and then, moving from right to left, proceed to draw through a series of vertical swaths, cutting each completed vertical row away (through the sequence of horizontal strips), thereby generating the same number of completed individual tiles though in a much more efficient manner. Which is what they did with their second stronger wire concave grid, and is in fact how they operate to this day.

8. To any who would dismiss the excellence of Trevor's achievement in this regard, along the lines of, "Well, no wonder, he's just tracing," I am reminded of a comment of David Hockney's, when, even after he had become convinced that Ingres had been having recourse to a camera lucida across his many pencil portraits of English gentry on their grand tours through Rome, he still insisted: "But look at that line! No one else using a camera lucida was able to wrest forth such an expressive line." Indeed, as he subsequently commented, in a slightly different context, "It's not that easy. The truth is that if you need a device [like a camera lucida] to be able to draw, it won't be of much use at all. On the other hand, if you don't, it can be immensely useful." (See the fifth chapter in my own *True to Life: Twenty Five Years of Conversations with David Hockney*, University of California Press, November 2008).

9. In the meantime I'd returned to New York, but they sent me a jpeg of the processional.

The next morning, the front page of the Arts and Leisure section of the *New York Times* featured the following

image, flanking a piece on a recent resurgence of interest in the children's books illustrations of the masterful Tomi Ungerer.

10. That incised stainless steel megaversion, when it was indeed completed and mounted to the side of the Bean itself several months later, proved quite a sensation among passersby. Indeed, in much the same way that people in the park tend to prefer the view of the surrounding urban skyline as reflected in the Bean to the view of the skyline itself, so now, many of them preferred to spend long swaths of time gazing at the image of the Bean as captured in the Twins' steel rendering to standing before the Bean itself. "People can't help themselves," as Hockney likes to point out. "We seem almost primordially drawn to representations." (After its several months' residence beside the Bean, the Oakes's aluminum piece, for its part, was eventually moved to a semipermanent place of honor, in the corridor connecting Terminals 2 and 3, at O'Hare International Airport.)

11. In typical Trevor fashion, the graphs and columns of calculations working through the process are themselves quite beautiful.

    As was one trial cardboard model, where it turned out he'd gotten one tiny factorial consistently wrong all across the process. A botched job, but itself a thing of splendor.

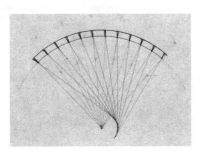 

12. One last thing I've recently taken to wondering about is whether the Twins' method might in turn shed some light on what's going on with some of those celebrated autistic visual prodigies—for example, Stephen Wiltshire, the boy (now man) so powerfully profiled in Oliver Sacks's *An Anthropologist on Mars* (pp. 195-243). I wonder in part because of the striking similarity of the imagery Wiltshire produces (the quality and the density of the lines, etc.), as for example this instance of a Chicago view, as it happens portraying a vista just up the street from where the Twins were working.

Even more intriguing in this regard is the way Wiltshire goes about producing these images, since he almost invariably works from memory, snapping, as it were, a single frame from the swirl of life and then reproducing it back home, working for hours—and often from one side of the page to the other, as if spooling out a xerox of the image, much as the Twins do in their own laborious procedure. Some of Wiltshire's most amazing feats in recent years have been the panoramas of cityscapes seen from the air, based on a single helicopter transit, and then poured forth, over a period of days, with astonishing self-assurance and without the slightest hesitation, onto a single, meters-long, *concave-curved* sheet of paper. See Wiltshire's webpage for literally dozens of these marvels: www.stephenwiltshire.co.uk.

The thing I end up wondering though is whether Wiltshire is in some sense tracing these images onto the page. Whether his visual cortex has an added time capacity, as it were, such that he is able to glimpse a passing scene in the real world, retain an exact copy of the scene in his memory, and then somehow "project" the ghost of that scene onto the page (much as the Twins do in real time), thereafter simply dragging his pen over the projected image.

## AFTERWORD:
### On Grace and Narrative and the
### Current State of the Uncanny Valley

1. Lao-tzu, *Tao Te Ching*, trans. Stephen Mitchell (New York: Harper & Row, 1988).
2. See www.reelzchannel.com/movie-news/4184/james-cameron-discusses-avatars-uncanny-valley.
3. See www.businessinsider.com/sergey-brin-we-want-google-to-be-the-third-half-of-your-brain-2010-9.
4. See www.youtube.com/watch?v=VF9-sEbqDvU.

# Sources and Image Credits

Here follows an inventory of the venues for the original publication of all the pieces in this volume, along with a comprehensive checklist of the book's imagery. The author and publisher extend their gratitude for their cooperation to all the instutions involved, and note that the copyright on all the visuals in this book remains securely lodged with their respective copyright holders, irrespective of the fair use appearance of those visuals in these pages.

## COVER ART:

© Mike Tansey, detail from *Derrida Queries de Man*, 1990. Courtesy of the artist and Gagosian Gallery.

## UNCANNY VALLEY:
### On the Digital Animation of the Face

Originally published in *Wired*, June 2002

> **Fig. 1:** Neil Fleming, digitally rendered character from *Final Fantasy: The Spirits Within*, directed by Hironobu Sakuguchi for Square Studios, distributed by Columbia Pictures, 2001.
>
> **Fig. 2:** Shrek. Designed by Dream Works Animation. Distributed by Paramount Pictures.
>
> **Figs. 3 & 4:** Hugo. Synthetic character designed by Industrial Light and Magic.

## FOUR EASY PIECES
The first three originally published in *Brick* magazine #75, Summer 2005

On Coming Face-to-Face with Myself
> **Fig. 1:** David Hockney, "Lawrence Weschler, July 14, 2002."
> **Fig. 2:** Breyten Breytenbach, "February 1, 1983."

Torqued Brueghel
> **Fig. 1:** Richard Serra, *The Matter of Time*, 2005. The Guggenheim Museum, Bilbao {note this is not the installation of the same sorts of works at LA-MOCA discussed in the piece}

Motes in the Light

The Judd Ant
First published in *The Chinati Foundation Newsletter* #15, October 2010
> **Fig. 1:** Donald Judd, 15 Untitled Works, 1980-1984. Chinati Foundation, Marfa,Texas.


## THREE IMPROBABLE YARNS

Mr. Wilson in Belgrade
*LA Times Book Review*, February 4, 2001

The Poem on the Train: A Letter to the Editor of *The Threepenny Review*
*Threepenny Review*, Summer 1995

Popocatepetl (My Grandfather's Geographical and My Medical Fugue)
*Threepenny Review*, Winter 2003


## SOME PROBES INTO THE TERRAIN OF HUMAN RIGHTS

Sentries (with Richard Avedon)
*The New Yorker*, January 10, 1994
  Photos of ten human rights monitors by Richard Avedon

Swallowed Up in Rwanda
*The New Yorker*, April 25, 1995
  Photo of Monique Mujawamariya by Richard Avedon

Exceptional Cases in Rome:
The United States and the International Criminal Court
*The United States and the International Criminal Court*, Ed. Sewall & Kaysen,
    American Academy of Arts & Sciences, 2000

Gazing Back: The Disappeared
Essay for the North Dakota Museum of Art catalog, 2005/6
    All images courtesy of the museum
        **Fig. 1:** *Identitad (Identity)*, by a co-operative of fifteen Argentinian
        artists (Carlos Alonso, Nora Aslán, Mireya Baglietto, Remo
        Bianchedi, Diana Dowek, León Ferrari, Rosana Fuertes, Car-
        los Gorriarena, Adolfo Nigro, Luis Felipe Noé, Daniel Ontive-
        ros, Juan Carlos Romero and Marcia Schvartz) in collaboration
        with the Grandmothers of the Plaza de Mayo, Argentina, 1998
        **Fig. 2:** Luís Gonzales Palma, detail from "Between Roots and Air,"
        Guatamala, 1996-7
        **Fig. 3:** Juan Manuel Echavarría, detail from "NN (No Name),"
        Columbia, 2005

A Berlin Epiphany
*Virginia Quarterly Review*, Fall 2006
        **Fig. 1:** Peter Eisenman, *Memorial to the Murdered Jews of Europe*,
        2005. Berlin.


# FOUR WALKABOUTS

Waking Up to How We Sleepwalk
*Artforum*, Summer 1982
    Photos of Billedstofteater performance piece at "Krig og mennaske"
    (War and Man) peace day at Louisiana Museum, Humlebaek, Den-
    mark, August 1981, courtesy of the Museum

Dario Fo on Broadway
*The New Yorker*, December 3, 1984

Tomislav Gotovac: Naked in Zagreb
*The New Yorker*, January 14, 1991

Sharon Lockhart: The Nō Film
*Threepenny Review*, Winter 2005

## FIVE FURTHER ADVENTURES IN THE NARRATIVE

Splendors of Decaying Celluloid: on Bill Morrison's *Decasia*
*New York Times magazine*, September 22, 2002
> Stills from the motion picture *Decasia: The State of Decay*, by Bill Morrison. Hypnotic Pictures, 2002, courtesy of Mr. Morrison.

Still Not Finished: On Vincent Desiderio's *Sleep*
*Vincent Desiderio, Paintings 1975-2005*, Distributed Art Publishers (DAP)/ Marlborough, 2005, also *Virginia Quarterly Review*, Fall 2005
> **Fig. 1:** Vicent Desiderio, *Sleep*, 2005.
> Seven Bridges Foundation, Connecticut.
> **Fig. 2:** Gilles Peres, *Grave near Pilice Collection Farm near Srebrenica*, 1996.
> **Fig. 3:** Henry Moore, "Tube Shelter Perspective,
> The Liverpool Street Extension," 1941. Tate, London.
> **Fig. 4:** Vincent Desiderio, *Cockaigne*, 2003.
> The Hirshhorn, Washington, DC.
> **Fig. 5:** Pieter Brueghel the Elder, *The Land of Cockaigne*,
> 1567. Alte Pinakothek, Munich.
> **Fig. 6:** Jan van Eyck, *The Last Judgment*, ca. 1430. Detail.
> Metropolitan Museum of Art, New York.
> **Fig. 7:** Willem de Kooning, *Excavation*, 1950.
> Art Institute of Chicago.
> **Fig. 8:** Jackson Pollock, *Mural*, 1943.
> University of Iowa Museum of Art.
> **Fig. 9:** Vincent Desiderio, photo collage study for *Sleep*, 2005.
> **Fig. 10:** Leonardo da Vinci, *The Last Supper*, 1495-1498. Detail
> Santa Maria delle Grazie, Milan.
> **Fig. 11:** Michelangelo, *The Last Judgment*, Detail of Christ and the
> Virgin, 1535-1541. Sistine Chapel, Vatican City.
> **Fig. 12:.** Slave Ship. From *The History of the Rise, Progress and
> Accomplishment of the Abolition of the African Slave Trade by the
> British Parliament* (1808), Vol. I. Thomas Clarkson.
> **Fig. 13:** Michelangelo, *Battle of the Centarus and Lapiths*, ca 1492.
> Casa Buonarroti, Florence.
> **Fig. 14:** Jan Vermeer, *The Lacemaker*, ca 1665.
> Louvre, Paris.
> **Fig. 15:** Rembrandt, *The Anatomy Lesson of Dr. Nicolaes Tulp*, 1632.
> Mauritshius, The Hague.

Valkyries Over Iraq:
Walter Murch, *Apocalypse Now, Jarhead*,
and the Trouble with War Movies
*Harper's*, November 2005
> Stills from the motion pictures *Apocalypse Now*, directed by Francis
> Ford Coppola, 1979. Paramount Pictures; and *Jarhead*, directed by
> Sam Mendes, 2005. Universal Pictures.

Double Vision: The Perspectival Journey of the Oakes Twins
*Virginia Quarterly Review*, Spring 2009
> All images courtesy of Ryan and Trevor Oakes, with exception of final
> two images of Paleolithic art from the Chauvet Pont-d'Arc Cave in the
> Ardeche region of France

Blockage and Grace: Mark Salzman Lying Awake
> *The New Yorker*, October 2, 2000

# AFTERWORD:
On Grace and Narrative and the
Current State of the Uncanny Valley
> **Fig. 1:** Nicolas of Cusa by the Master of the Life of the Virgin (c. 1460)
> **Fig. 2:** Still from *Avatar*, directed by James Cameron,
>    20th Century Fox, 2009
> **Fig. 3:** Marcel and his pet lint Alan, still from the film short "Marcel
>    the Shell with Shoes On" directed by Dean Fleisher-Camp, 2010

# NOTES
Images in Notes to "Double Vision"
4. Paul Cezanne, *View of the Domaine Saint-Joseph*, late 1880s
>    Metropolitan Museum of Art, New York
>  Henri Matisse, *The Goldfish*, 1910, The Hermitage, St. Petersburg
>  Morris Louis, *Theta*, 1961, Museum of Fine Arts, Boston
>  Roy Lichtenstein, *Little Aloha*, 1962, Gagosian Gallery, New York
>  Rembrandt van Rijn, *Self-Portrait in a Soft Hat and Embroidered Cloak*,
>    Etching, Museum of Fine Arts, Boston

5. Trevor Oakes match piece; Evolution of cellular automaton, Stephen Wolfram, *A New Kind of Science*, Wolfram Media, 2002, p. 29

9. Painting by Tomi Ungerer, 1979, featured in a show in Strasbourg which was in turn discussed in an article about Mr. Ungerer in the *New York Times*, July 27, 2008

11. Refinements on the grid, Trevor and Ryan Oakes

12. Stephen Wiltshire, "Chicago Street Scene, August 14, 2009"
    Photo of Mr. Wiltshire drawing a panoramic view
    Both images from his website, www.stephenwiltshire.co.uk

# Acknowledgments

THE PIECES IN THIS volume, as can be seen in the preceding list-ings, are gathered from several decades of work with several dif-ferent publications, which is to say with entire teams of editors, fact-checkers, grammarians, fellow writers, and indispensible back-stoppers of all sorts, the warp and woof of an entire career. By this stage, cataloging all of them would take a whole other volume—one that I personally would cherish (it has been one of the particular delights of putting together this collection that it has allowed me to bring so many of those friends back to mind)—though I suspect such an exercise would try my readers' (and cur-rent publisher's) patience.

Having said that, I do still want to highlight my lasting appre-ciation for the support and forebearance of (originally) William Shawn and (latterly) Tina Brown at the *New Yorker*, and of my per-sonal editors there (successively) John Bennet, Pat Crow, and Jef-frey Frank; Richard Avedon, and since his passing, James Martin, and Michelle Franco of the Richard Avedon Foundation; Chris Anderson and Steve Silberman at *Wired*; Wendy Lesser of the *Threepenny Review*; Michael Redhill of *Brick*; Ted Genoways and the late Kevin Morrissey of the *Virginia Quarterly Review*; Ingrid Sischy of (in those days) *Artforum*; Luke Mitchell at *Harper's*; James Lovell of the *New York Times Sunday Magazine*; Steve Wasserman of (in those days) *The Los Angeles Times Book Review*; Laurel Reuter of the North Dakota Museum of Art; and Todd Bradway at Distrib-uted Art Publishers.

And then too, of course, especially speaking of forebearance, I want to extend deep writerly thanks to all the subjects of these pieces: it has been one of the particular joys of my career that early on I reached a stage where I was able to write primarily about people I admired, and a further blessing that across the writing so many of them evolved into dear personal friends as well.

Speaking of deep and abiding friendship, I am so pleased that the publication of this volume affords me the opportunity to acknowledge, by way of dedication, two of my most treasured companions, fellow journeymen on the marvelously wending byways of Life's Narrative, Oliver Sacks and the late Tom Eisner: master storytellers both and profoundly inspiring role models: capacious, funny, and wise.

I want to extend particular thanks to the remarkable artist Mark Tansey, whose deliciously vertiginous painting, *Derrida Queries DeMan* (1990), with its sly allusion to Sherlock's death-embrace of Moriarty at Reichenbach Falls, has for years been the image I kept hoping we might be able to have gracing the cover of this collection; and thanks to Maestro Tansey's generosity, there it is. Uncanny Valley, indeed.

And what a pleasure, as well, to be back in the good firm hands of Jack Shoemaker, one of my first publishers back at North Point Press, now at the helm of that original firm's newest incarnation as Counterpoint: he and his staff there, especially including managing editor Laura Mazer and designer Domini Dragoone, have made it all seem effortless, and I know it wasn't.

My career has been immeasurably assisted over the years by the ministrations of my successive agents Flip Brophy, Deborah Karl, and now, for the past decade, the wry and enthusiastic Chris Calhoon.

Finally, of course, as ever and may it ever be so, I want to thank my endlessly put-upon bride Joasia, and our endlessly surprising, inspiring, and confounding daughter Sara: their prints are all over this thing. As is my love for them.

# About the Author

LAWRENCE WESCHLER, A GRADUATE of Cowell College at the University of California at Santa Cruz (1974) was for twenty years (1981-2001) a staff writer at *The New Yorker* magazine, where his work shuttled between political tragedies and cultural comedies. Since 2001 he has been the director of the New York Institute for the Humanities at NYU, and for part of that time (2005-10) he was concurrently the Artistic Director of the Chicago Humanities Festival. A frequent contributor to *Harper's*, the *Atlantic* monthly, *The Believer*, the *New York Times* and the *LA Times*, and several programs over NPR, he is also a contributing editor to *McSweeney's*, *Threepenny Review*, and the *Virginia Quarterly Review*, and a curator at *Wholphin*, the DVD Quarterly.

He has been a Lannan Literary Fellow, honored with a Guggenheim Fellowship, and is a two-time winner of the George Polk Award. His book *Mr. Wilson's Cabinet of Wonder* was shortlisted for both the Pulitzer Prize and the National Book Critics' Circle Award. In 2008, his book *Everything That Rises* was granted the NBCC Award for Criticism.

He has taught variously at Princeton, Columbia, Bard, UCSC, and Sarah Lawrence, and is currently Distinguished Writer in Residence at the Arthur Carter Journalism Institute at NYU.

The author of well over a dozen books, he thinks of many of them as paired commentaries on each other. Thus, for example, his recent counterpunctal biographies of Robert Irwin (*Seeing is Forgetting the Name of the Thing One Sees*) and David Hockney (*True to Life*); or the way his *Boggs* book consciously sets out to do for money what his earlier *Mr. Wilson's Cabinet of Wonders* did for museums. In that context, he thinks of this current volume, *Uncanny Valley*, as existing in a distinct dialog with its predecessor collection, *Vermeer in Bosnia*.